THE BIG
BOOK OF
FLIGHT

ROWLAND WHITE

BANTAM PRESS

LONDON · TORONTO · SYDNEY · AUCKLAND · JOHANNESBURG

For Mum and Dad

TRANSWORLD PUBLISHERS
61–63 Uxbridge Road, London W5 5SA
A Random House Group Company
www.transworldbooks.co.uk

First published in Great Britain
in 2013 by Bantam Press
an imprint of Transworld Publishers
Trade paperback edition published in 2014

Copyright © Project Cancelled Ltd 2013

Rowland White has asserted his right under the Copyright,
Designs and Patents Act 1988 to be identified as the author of this work.

A CIP catalogue record for this book
is available from the British Library.

ISBN 9780593073056

Addresses for Random House Group Ltd companies outside the UK
can be found at www.randomhouse.co.uk
The Random House Group Ltd Reg. No. 954009

Typeset in Century Schoolbook.
Designed by Bobby Birchall, Bobby & Co.
Additional design by Richard Shailer and Nick Avery.
Illustrations by Patrick Mulrey.
Printed and bound in China.

2 4 6 8 10 9 7 5 3 1

Prophecy
(From 'Locksley Hall', 1835)

For I dipt into the future, far as human eye could see,
Saw the Vision of the world, and all the wonder that would be;
Saw the heavens fill with commerce, argosies of magic sails,
Pilots of the purple twilight dropping down with costly bales;
Heard the heavens fill with shouting, and there rain'd a ghastly dew
From the nations' airy navies grappling in the central blue;
Far along the world-wide whisper of the south-wind rushing warm,
With the standards of the peoples plunging thro' the thunder-storm;
Till the war-drum throbb'd no longer, and the battle-flags were furl'd
In the Parliament of man, the Federation of the world.
There the common sense of most shall hold a fretful realm in awe,
And the kindly earth shall slumber, lapt in universal law.

ALFRED, LORD TENNYSON
(1809–92)

Contents

Introduction

One way or another, we all want to fly. Whether it's floating above the ground through the power of dreams, or a yearning to strap into the cockpit and zoom skywards on a pillar of jet thrust, we're all in there somewhere. From leaning into a corner on a Honda Fireblade motorbike to the three-dimensional sub-aqua ballet of scuba diving, it all, I think, boils down to a desire to fly. Freedom and sensation ... it's an irresistible combination, and it grabbed me early.

Born a little too late for the glory days of *Eagle* comic and *Look and Learn*, I had the *Ladybird Book of Flight*, *The How and Why Wonder Book of Flight* and, perhaps most treasured of all, the *St Michael Pictorial History of Aircraft*. I thrived on a wholly un-PC diet of *Warlord* and *The Victor* comics, and had an enduring fascination with Airfix models (the catalogues of which I pored over, returning to the same dramatic images of aircraft time and again). I begged to stay up late to watch TV programmes such as the Royal Flying Corps drama *Wings*, or the BBC's *Squadron*, in retrospect, an unlikely ten-part series about the fictional adventures of 370 Rapid Deployment Squadron. Although unreal, and with sets even more rickety than those on *Crossroads*, it had aeroplanes in it, and that was enough for me. Alongside this required viewing, aviation authors Paul Brickhill, Ralph Barker and the brilliant Bill Gunston (at one point, I believe, the most borrowed author in British libraries) wrote the books I wanted to read.

Keen as I was on 'Roy of the Rovers', Judge Dredd, *Star Wars* and Adam and the Ants, I could also hold forth about Douglas Bader, the Dam Busters and the maximum thrust – with full afterburner – of a J-79 turbojet engine.

Adolescence curbed my enthusiasm a little. Even I realized that there was nothing the slightest bit cool about staying in to watch anything featuring Raymond Baxter. But the lull was only temporary. Ultimately flight and flying offered things that were much more valuable than cool: namely, inspiration, wonder and visceral excitement.

On holiday with my family a few years ago, we visited a bird sanctuary in the hills. With our two children – my wife Lucy was heavily pregnant with number three – we sat down on rows of tiered wooden benches for a falconry display. As the handlers prepared for the show, a single large raptor was released and climbed high into the clear skies until it had all but vanished. While the demonstration continued, the bird was forgotten. But at the end of the show, we were invited to look up and soon we were all tracking it. Suddenly, it tucked in its wings and began to dive towards the ground. At first it was impossible to gain any appreciation of the falcon's speed, but it quickly became clear that she seemed to be moving unnaturally fast. Her dive was carefully controlled with small, instinctive movements of her tail and neatly folded wings, but it was unnerving to see her plummet straight towards the ground with a terminal velocity way beyond 100 mph. Just when she seemed too close to avoid smashing into the midst of her slack-jawed audience, she swooped a couple of feet over our heads – so low that we could feel the disturbance in the still air as she streaked past. She then followed the descending contours of the stadium-style seating towards her handler where, with perfect precision, she flared and dropped gently on to the waiting leather gauntlet.

It was majestic – a sight so thrilling that I found myself blinking back tears of joy, grateful for a pair of sunglasses to hide such an emotional response to the awe-inspiring display I'd just experienced. No wonder the lure of flying has such a hold.

As long as human beings have lived alongside birds, we've wanted to join them. Our efforts to do so have rarely been as elegant or as smooth, but they have been dangerous, exciting, intriguing, clever, unexpected, loud, spectacular, courageous, ambitious, unsuccessful and brilliant. And sometimes, on rare occasions, like that extraordinary diving falcon, they've moved us.

The Big Book of Flight is a celebration of all those efforts. For me, the only real criterion for including something was whether or not it was interesting, so as a reference book, this volume is neither comprehensive nor necessarily useful. In fact, it's probably not useful at all because the choices I've made are determinedly personal ones. But usefulness was never the point.

I still can't help but look out of the window (at work) or run out of the house (at home) if I hear the sound of an unfamiliar aero-engine. And the urgent, growing realization that this time it's unusually close and low gets my heart beating even faster. If what follows prompts a few people to experience the same joy and excitement, then this book's been better than useful. I hope it will surprise, entertain and fire people's imagination in the same way the books I grew up with captured mine.

RW
Cambridgeshire
December 2012

Dreams of the Birdmen

Icarus and His Successors

As a lame old man, Oliver of Malmesbury, an eleventh-century English monk, was the first person to see a comet that was later said to have been a warning of the Norman invasion. That, though, was not the reason why centuries later a pub in Malmesbury was named in his honour. His limp had more to do with it. In fact, he was lucky to reach a grand old age at all.

The pub was called the Flying Monk in honour of Oliver's leap from an abbey watchtower 150 feet high while clad in a pair of homemade cloth wings. He was reported to have been in the air for nearly 15 seconds before crashing to the ground and breaking both legs – a failure he put down to forgetting to use a tail. But in breaking his legs, Oliver was one of the luckier birdmen.

For most of mankind's time on Earth, attempts to fly like a bird were likely to end in death. That was what happened to Icarus. Legend has it that he escaped from Crete with his father, Daedalus, on feather and wax wings, but he flew too close to the sun, the wax melted and he fell to his death. Then there was Bladud, a ninth-century BC king of the Britons, reputedly the father of King Lear. Although no documentary evidence exists, Bladud supposedly founded the city of Bath, using magic to create the hot springs. And all this after curing himself of leprosy, contracted in Athens, by covering himself in mud after observing that pigs didn't suffer from the affliction. Wearing wings built with help from the spirits of the dead, Bladud leapt from a London tower and killed himself.

Human beings have, it seems, never been content simply to let flight remain the preserve of the birds. Throughout antiquity beasts such as lions and lizards – and, in the case of Pegasus, a horse – have been given wings and the power of flight and turned into griffins, dragons and the like (although it wasn't until the twentieth century that Walt Disney managed to get an elephant aloft, in the animated film *Dumbo*). But when it came to powered human flight, man's first recorded attempts fared no better than those of their mythical predecessors.

OPPOSITE: *This man's expression was typical of a look found on the faces of most early aviators.*

Just after the turn of the first millennium AD, a Turkish scholar by the name of Ismail ibn Hammad al-Jawhari, climbed to the top of a mosque in Nishabur with a pair of wooden wings strapped to his arms. From the roof, he revved up the large crowd that had gathered to witness his achievement. 'Oh, people!' he shouted. 'No one has made this discovery before. Now I will fly before your very eyes. The most important thing on earth is to fly to the skies. That I will do now!' He jumped, and then, just a few seconds later, he slammed into the ground and died.

Unlike Oliver of Malmesbury, fifteenth-century polymath and genius Leonardo da Vinci remembered to include a tail on his ornithopter design. Yet despite Leonardo's ground-breaking work in other areas, such as human anatomy, his elegant design still depended on the assumption that the human body was sufficiently strong to keep itself in the air. It would be another 200 years before it became apparent that it was not.

This leads one to wonder quite what Robert Hooke, the respected curator for scientific experiments at London's Royal Society, was getting at when in 1674 he noted in his diary that he'd told a fellow member 'that I could fly, [but] not how'. His claim remained unsubstantiated and also highly unlikely because, around the same time, the Italian scientist Giovanni Borelli, taking a break from inventing submarines and underwater breathing apparatus, concluded that men's muscles were too weak for them 'to be able to fly craftily by their own strength'. He was right.

But still the birdmen kept jumping, and limbs kept snapping. A little over twenty years after Leonardo's death in 1519, a Portuguese man, João Torto, launched himself from a cathedral equipped with calico-covered wings and an eagle-shaped helmet. He was fatally wounded on 'landing'. A century after Leonardo designed his ornithopter, his compatriot Paolo Guidotti crashed through a roof wearing wings of whalebone and feathers and broke his thigh. Then, in 1742, a 62-year-old French aristocrat called the Marquis de Bacqueville tried to fly across the Seine from a terrace at the top of his riverside mansion. He smashed into a barge and broke his leg. In 1770 French clergyman Pierre Desforges broke his arm after failing to persuade anyone to test-fly his contraption from a church lookout tower on his behalf.

Real progress towards controlled manned flight only really came about once the idea took hold that flapping like a bird was not the best way to stay airborne. The first person to grasp this was the British engineer Sir George Cayley, 6th Baronet and owner of Brompton Hall near Scarborough

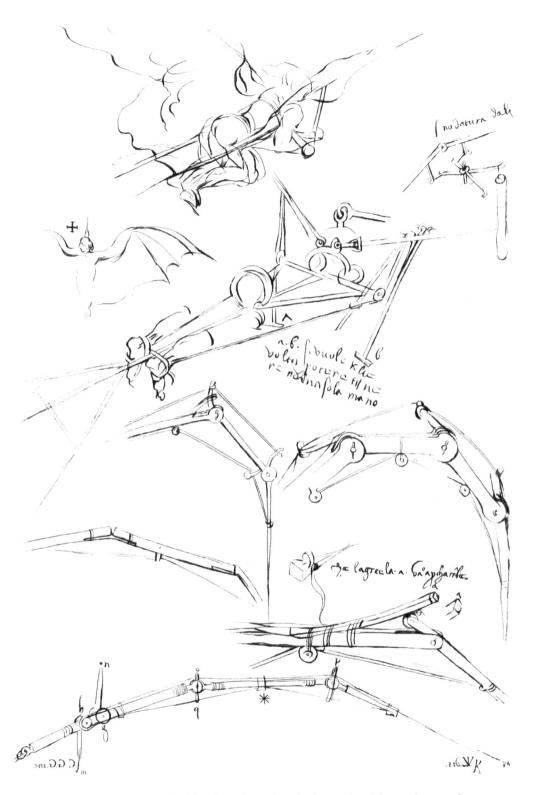

Leonardo da Vinci called his flapping wing device an 'ornithopter', a word derived from the Greek for 'bird' (ornithos) and 'wing' (pteron). Neither the word nor the device caught on.

'Glider King' Otto Lilienthal takes to the air near Berlin in the early 1890s.

in Yorkshire. Inspired as a boy in 1783 by the Montgolfier brothers' hot-air balloon flight over Paris, Cayley made it his life's work to understand the principles of flight.

Realizing that the steam engines of the day were too heavy for his purposes, Cayley designed his own internal combustion engine using an alternative fuel he called 'oil of tar' (petrol). This fuel, however, was prohibitively expensive, and it would take nearly another century to create a practical fossil fuel-powered aero-engine. Nonetheless, Cayley became part of the birdman business. After observing the flight of birds, he designed an unmanned glider that first took to the air in 1804. He was soon claiming that his work was contributing to a goal that 'will in time be found of great importance to mankind'. By 1853, four years before he died, he had persuaded his coachman to fly across a shallow Yorkshire valley in a larger glider. There were no broken limbs this time, yet Cayley's pilot was reported to have said to his boss, 'I wish to give notice. I was hired to drive, not to fly.'

He was wise not to want to push his luck. Cayley's 'noble art of aerial navigation' was still in its infancy, as the next birdman to advance manned flight found to his cost. German engineer Otto Lilienthal published his seminal work *Birdflight as the Basis of Aviation* in 1889 at the age of 41. He flew his first glider two years later. Over the next five years he made some 2000 flights, accumulating just five flying hours. Still, the 'Glider King', as he was dubbed, had flown longer and further than anyone else in history. But on 9 August 1896, during his second flight of the day, his glider stalled. He crashed to the ground and broke his back. Two days later, like so many previous birdmen, he died from his injuries.

The Glider King's influence, however, was immense, directly inspiring aviation pioneers Wilbur and Orville Wright. And unlike the birdmen who had preceded him, Lilienthal had understood exactly what he was doing and why it mattered. Just before slipping into unconsciousness for the last time, 36 hours after his crash, Lilienthal whispered to his brother, 'Sacrifices have to be made.' With those prescient last words, which sum up the story of aviation, he laid claim to being the first person with the 'Right Stuff'.

But it's not what Lilienthal said on his deathbed that really captures what this book is about – although there's plenty of the Right Stuff to come – so much as something he said when he was very much alive: 'To invent an aeroplane is nothing. To build one is something. But to fly is everything.' That's what this book is about.

In the pages that follow there are some what-ifs, a few designs that never made it, and there's a romance about them certainly – but only because we can glimpse their potential and attach to them the feelings they'd provoke if they were real. An aeroplane that makes it off the drawing board makes the heart beat a little faster. But that moment when an aircraft's nose rises from the runway ... that's when it really starts to matter.

What Goes Up

How an Aeroplane Flies

There are four forces at work on any aeroplane: lift, thrust, gravity and drag. Whether or not any aircraft will fly boils down to making sure you've got the right balance between them.

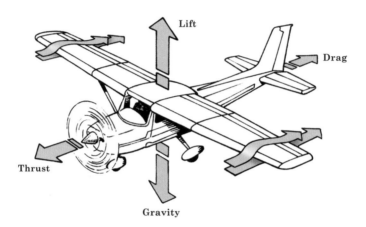

Lift

Lift is generated by the effect of air moving over the wing when the aircraft is travelling forwards. (If you've any doubts about the force that can exert, just consider a strong wind, which is nothing more than moving air.) The reason that force lifts the aircraft rather than, say, slamming it into the ground is the shape of the wing: flat on the underside and curved from front (the leading edge) to back (the trailing edge) on top. As the wing travels forward, it cuts the air in its path, separating what flows over the wing from what passes beneath it. But because of the curve of the wing, the air passing over the top is made to travel further. This makes it less dense than the air travelling straight along the flat surface beneath. As a result, the air pressure above the wing is reduced, while that below the wing stays the same. High pressure beneath and low pressure above generates lift. The faster the wing travels through the air, the more lift it generates.

Thrust

Forward thrust is a prerequisite for flight, even for a glider, which, towed to altitude, then uses gravity to generate forward speed in the same way as a cyclist freewheeling down a hill. But to climb to height without help, an aircraft needs to provide its own forward thrust, and that requires an engine. More than aerodynamics, it was the lack of engine that held back early attempts at powered flight. How wings generated lift was understood before the technology to build a sufficiently light, powerful engine was mastered.

Gravity

If an aircraft loses power, gravity is both a friend and an enemy. Pointing the nose down and going downwards will ensure that drag doesn't slow you so much that your wings are no longer able to generate lift. But at the same time it is also bringing you inexorably towards the ground. Without more power, you *will* come down.

Drag

Like a housefly, drag would appear to serve no useful purpose. It's the force caused by the airframe itself as it tries to move forward through dense, fluid air, so is something that power and streamlining need to overcome – until you need to land, that is. At that point, drag or resistance to the air is essential to help the aircraft slow down. When the airbrakes pop up from the wings on your flight to the sun, just remember that.

Changing direction

When the Wright brothers filed their first patent, they didn't claim to have invented the aeroplane, but rather a way of controlling it. An aircraft moves through three dimensions, and the brothers invented a system to control all three. The principle, and the effect of the controls, remains the same.

In the cockpit, there are two directional controls: the control column or 'stick' controls the ailerons (by moving it to the left, you lower the left wing and raise the right; move the stick to the right and you achieve the opposite); it also controls the elevators which affect pitch (push forward to lower the nose, pull back to raise it). The rudder pedals control yaw (right foot to swing the nose to the right, left foot to swing it left).

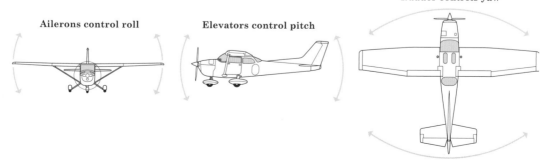

Ailerons control roll   Elevators control pitch   Rudder controls yaw

Aeroplane

The Anatomy of an Aircraft

The illustration below shows a Cessna 172 Skyhawk. In choosing a typical aircraft to illustrate all the bits and pieces, the little Cessna is a good bet because more Skyhawks have been built than any other aircraft in history. And they're still making them today. But I could have chosen a Boeing 747, or an F-4 jet fighter, or the Red Baron's First World War Fokker triplane. While all four aircraft certainly look very different, they all share the same basic set-up.

Lift is provided by the wings. Forward thrust comes from the engine, whether propeller, jet or even rocket. And control in three axes – roll, pitch and yaw – comes from the elevators, ailerons and rudder, which are marked in blue.

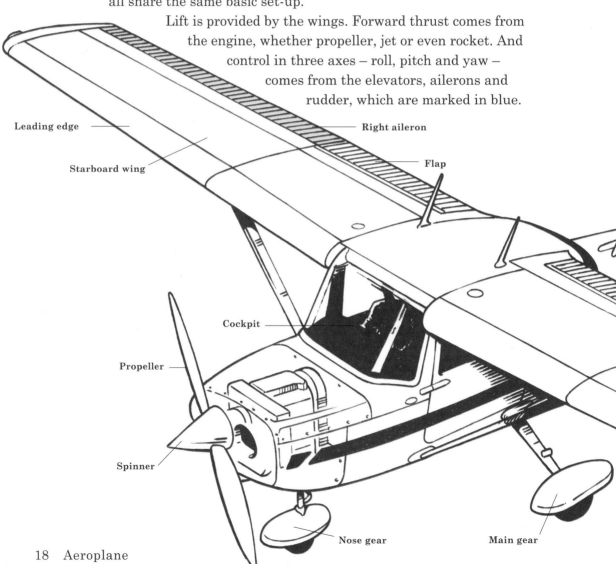

Leading edge

Right aileron

Starboard wing

Flap

Cockpit

Propeller

Spinner

Nose gear

Main gear

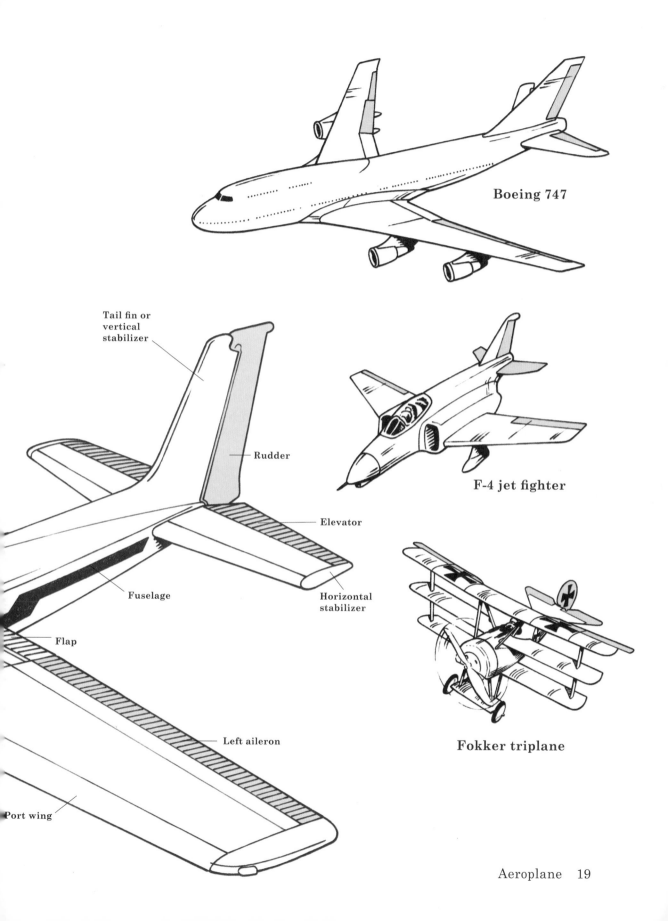

Boeing 747

Tail fin or
vertical
stabilizer

Rudder

F-4 jet fighter

Elevator

Fuselage

Horizontal
stabilizer

Flap

Fokker triplane

Left aileron

Port wing

It's All Hot Air (part one)
The Story of Ballooning

It was early morning on 21 March 1999 when Bertrand Piccard and Brian Jones touched down in the Egyptian desert. They had been airborne for 19 days, 21 hours and 55 minutes, during which time they'd covered 25,361 miles. They had also become the first men to circumnavigate the globe by balloon, powered by nothing more than high-altitude winds.

During the epic journey, *Breitling Orbiter 3*, their giant 180-foot-high silver helium and hot-air balloon, had reached heights of 37,000 feet and speeds of over 160 knots. Piccard and Jones were suspended underneath in a gondola constructed from Kevlar and carbon fibre, which provided good protection, but was far from comfortable. The red gondola was about the size of a camper van and they were cooped up in this for nearly three weeks. The two men, cold and cramped, slept in shifts and subsisted on dry food, all the while chipping off the ice that kept forming around sensitive electrics inside.

Their success shattered all previous ballooning records. But in doing so, it also demonstrated, like every notable balloon flight that preceded it, the balloon's inherent problems as a flying machine. After all, Piccard and Jones had not known when they were leaving Switzerland that they were on their way to Egypt. And even supposing that *had* been their plan, going around the world to get there was almost certainly not the best route.

It was in 1782, while watching the sparks rise from an open fire, that Joseph Montgolfier wondered whether the same force might somehow be harnessed to deliver soldiers behind the walls of an enemy fortress. This thought led him to conduct experiments with a lightweight, box-like balloon made of silk and thin wood, filled with hot air generated by burning paper. Watching from the ground, he described its ascent into the air as 'one of the most astonishing sights in the world'. A month later, in December 1782, he and his brother Étienne flew a bigger (still unmanned) device across a distance of over a mile.

OPPOSITE: **Breitling Orbiter 3.**

There was no stopping them now. In June the following year the public demonstration of a large, recognizably balloon-shaped craft made of sackcloth and paper attracted the interest of King Louis XVI. He suggested sending a pair of criminals up in a balloon (it was this sort of thing that would get him and his wife, Marie Antoinette, guillotined a few years later) but wiser heads prevailed: a sheep, a cockerel and a duck were eventually selected for a demonstration flight in the grounds of the Palace of Versailles.

With the menagerie returned safely to Earth, the Montgolfiers began work on a balloon designed to carry people. The brothers built their new 75-foot-high balloon in collaboration with a wallpaper manufacturer. That's probably why it looks as if it could have been a giant lampshade from the king's bedroom. It was decorated in blue, gold and crimson with zodiac signs, fleurs-de-lys, eagles and stylized suns featuring the king's face. On 21 November it was launched from the outskirts of Paris. On board were a doctor, Jean-François Pilâtre de Rozier, and an infantry officer, the Marquis d'Arlandes. Twenty-five minutes later they landed 5 miles away.

The effect of this first successful manned flight was electrifying. In flying for the first time, the Montgolfier brothers and their passengers had made real what had previously been the stuff of myth and dreams. For most, that alone was enough. But not all were impressed. Benjamin Franklin, the American polymath and statesman, then US ambassador to France, witnessed one of the Montgolfiers' contemporaries send an unmanned hydrogen balloon into the air. 'Interesting,' he heard a member of the crowd comment, 'but what use is it?'

'What use,' Franklin responded, 'is a newborn baby?'

In truth, though, the man whom Franklin so elegantly put down had a point. Balloons had their limitations. A year after the first flight a pair of aeronauts – as balloon pilots were known – crossed the English Channel. Just. Flying from Dover, to reach France they had to throw overboard everything that wasn't pinned down, including their brandy and even their trousers. So aeronauts had some control over whether they went up or down, but everything else was in the lap of the gods.

For another century, however, if you wanted to fly, there was no alternative to the balloon. Pleasure flights for paying passengers became popular. The military experimented with the use of balloons for observation, and they were used for scientific purposes too.

James Glaisher liked clubs. A fellow of the Royal Society, he was also president of the Royal Microscopical Society and the Photographic Society of Great Britain. But it was the club he founded in 1850 that was closest to his heart, and it was experiments on behalf of the Royal Meteorological Society that made him famous. And nearly killed him.

In 1862, he and a fellow aeronaut, Henry Tracey Coxwell, took off from Wolverhampton in a gas balloon to conduct research into atmospheric temperature and pressure. On the way up, Glaisher passed out from oxygen deprivation. Coxwell, suffering from frostbitten hands, was unable to operate the gas valve to initiate their descent. The two men continued to climb until Coxwell managed to use his teeth to release the gas and ensure their survival. They had reached an altitude of 39,000 feet – that's over 7 miles.

Glaisher and Coxwell's research flight played to the balloon's strengths. The two Britons needed only to go up and down. It was not the same for the Swedish engineer Salomon August Andrée, who decided he was going to ride a balloon to the North Pole from the Arctic island of Svalbard. With the principal scientific aims of taking meteorological observations and mapping the region using aerial photography, Andrée's first attempt in 1896 was scuppered when northerly winds confined his hydrogen balloon *Örnen* (Eagle) to the hangar. The following year the winds were more favourable, and on 11 July 1897 Andrée and his two-man crew launched from Svalbard, full of hope and ambition.

It was 10½ hours before the balloon first hit the ice, and three days until it was permanently grounded on the frozen ocean, 170 miles from land. Three months later, after trying in vain to trek back to safety across the moving pack ice on a diet of seals, walruses and polar bears, Andrée and his men were dead.

James Glaisher and Henry
Coxwell prepare to take off
from Wolverhampton gasworks
on their near-fatal flight to
an altitude of 39,000 feet.

Although balloons remain of enormous value to meteorologists and weather forecasters to this day, by the end of the nineteenth century it had become clear that it was unnecessary for passengers to venture into harm's way in the name of science. It didn't mean there weren't those who were still good at it, though. In the 1950s and 1960s a record-breaking series of balloon flights took men to the threshold of space.

By the summer of 1957 it was clear that outer space was where mankind was heading, even though Russian cosmonaut Yuri Gagarin's first orbit was still a few years away. When the US military, using manned balloons, began research into the effects of altitude and cosmic rays on the human body, its pilots were the first men to see the curvature of the Earth. The records they set over the decade that followed still stand. In 1961, two US Navy officers, Commander Malcolm Ross and Lieutenant Commander Victor Prather, flew to a height of 113,740 feet. A year earlier, Captain Joe Kittinger of the US Air Force had jumped from a balloon at an altitude of over 103,000 feet, which remains the longest freefall ever undertaken. During the descent, he plunged towards Earth at close to the speed of sound. He was wearing a version of the spacesuit NASA used for its astronauts, but Kittinger's jump gave it a much more severe test than any spaceflight. When Alan Shepard, the first American to ride a rocket into space, was asked if he would be prepared to attempt a reprise of Kittinger's jump, his response was unequivocal. 'Hell, no,' he said, 'absolutely not.'

For all Kittinger and his contemporaries' extraordinary achievements, the shortcomings of balloons as flying machines meant the future lay with civilian enthusiasts. The introduction of lightweight synthetic fabrics and safe, reliable propane gas burners meant that from the early 1960s onwards ballooning became an increasingly popular leisure activity. Colourful globes with wicker baskets slung underneath have become a familiar sight floating low in the sky at dawn and dusk.

Unused and ignored by the military and by commercial aviation – both of whom needed to know where they were travelling to and when they might get there – balloons offered a few lucky twentieth-century adventurers a chance to carve their names into the

Captain Joe Kittinger leaves the capsule on his record-breaking 1961 freefall parachute jump. That appears to be gaffer tape holding together some of his equipment.

record books. In 1978, a helium balloon called *Double Eagle II* became the first to cross the Atlantic. Six years later, Captain Joe Kittinger became the first to do the same journey solo. In 1981, two of the *Double Eagle II* crew conquered the Pacific with a flight between Japan and California. Ten years after that, the biggest hot-air balloon ever built, *Virgin Pacific Flyer*, carried the British tycoon Richard Branson and Swedish balloonist Per Lindstrand from Japan to northern Canada, a new distance record of 6761 miles. Then American businessman Steve Fossett crossed the Pacific on his own in 1995, four years before Piccard and Jones flew their balloon around the world for the first time in *Breitling Orbiter 3* – and, in doing so, pulled off what was described as 'the last great aviation challenge of the twentieth century'.

CLUSTER BALLOONING

If one big balloon can do the job, why not lots of little ones? In the brilliant 2009 Pixar animation *Up*, the house of an old widower called Carl is carried aloft by a cluster of brightly coloured balloons and great adventures follow. But that's just a movie, I hear you say. Yes, lifting a house is ambitious, but the principle is sound, as an American truck driver, Larry Walters, discovered in 1982, when he tied over forty helium balloons to his 'extremely comfortable' garden chair. He called this homemade flying machine *Inspiration 1*.

This unlikely aviation pioneer had packed sandwiches and beer for a flight he expected to take him to a few hundred feet, but at 16,000 feet, after floating past disbelieving airline pilots on their way into LA International Airport, he became concerned. Fortunately, as well as his picnic, he'd thought to pack an airgun. After drifting at altitude for some hours, he finally plucked up the courage to start shooting balloons until he began to descend.

On landing, *Inspiration 1* took out power cables and Walters was led away in cuffs. 'I've fulfilled a twenty-year dream,' he said after his remarkable flight. To which the US Federal Aviation Administration responded, 'We know he broke some part of the Federal Aviation Act and as soon as we decide which part that is, a charge will be filed.' Despite this warning, many have followed Walters's lead. What they do is called 'cluster ballooning'.

IF AT FIRST YOU DON'T SUCCEED...

Strange Shapes in the Sky (part one)

In the early years of aviation inventors struggled to find the best shape for flying machines. Trial and error was the only way, and that led to many odd designs. Some flew, some didn't. Some proved lethal, and one here, the 14 bis by Brazilian Alberto Santos-Dumont, won a prize for completing the first officially observed flight of over 25 metres.

Caproni Stipa
Italy, 1932

Blackburn A. D. Scott
UK, 1915

Papin and Rouilly Gyroptère
France, 1915

Petroczy-Karman-Zurovek PKZ
Austro-Hungary, 1918

Bonney Gull
USA, 1928

Caproni Capronissimo
Italy, 1921

Flying Doughnut
USA, 1902

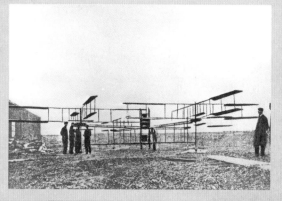

Breguet-Richet Gyroplane
France, 1907

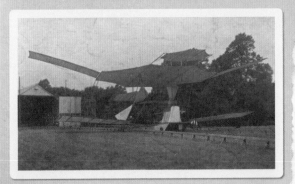

Maxim Steam Flying Machine
UK, 1894

Phillips Multiplane
UK, 1907

Phillips Multiplane
UK, 1904

Santos-Dumont 14 bis
(flying from left to right)
Brazil/France, 1906

Heavier Than Air

The Wright Brothers' First Powered Flight

Returning home one evening in the autumn of 1878, Bishop Milton Wright paused before opening the front door. He took a toy helicopter made of bamboo, cork and paper out of his pocket and twisted the rotor blades in two different directions to tighten the rubber bands attached to them. Entering the house, he kept the device hidden as he greeted his sons, then threw it gently into the air. Instead of tumbling to the ground, the spinning blades bit the air and carried it up until it nudged the ceiling. Then, as the rubber bands relaxed, it descended slowly to the floor. The boys, Wilbur, aged 11, and Orville, 7, were captivated by the toy, which they christened the 'Bat'. Although the fragile machine didn't last long, it had long-lasting effects.

Wilbur and Orville tried to build their own bigger and better replicas of the 'Bat', finding it curious that as their models increased in size, so their

ability to fly seemed to diminish. Theirs was a curiosity that would find full expression in the years to come.

It was a fascination with the death of the German gliding pioneer Otto Lilienthal in 1896 that rekindled the brothers' interest in flight. They tackled it with what they described as 'unquenchable enthusiasm'. The money they earned from a successful bicycle repair shop they'd opened four years earlier allowed them to pursue it. Teetotal and entirely happy in each other's company, they devoured books on aeronautics by pioneers such as Lilienthal, Sir George Cayley and fellow American Octave Chanute, which they borrowed from the Smithsonian Institution.

The real challenge lay in how to control aircraft. So far the most successful glider designs, like those of Lilienthal, had been controlled by the pilot shifting his weight to alter the centre of gravity. The brothers didn't believe this offered any realistic foundation for progress. Instead they took inspiration from birds. Wilbur had observed how, in order to change direction, soaring birds used the tips of their wings to alter the flow of air,

17 December, 1903. While his brother Wilbur runs alongside, Orville Wright takes off to usher in a new era of powered flight.

rather than shifting their weight. If he and Orville could somehow replicate that wing twisting, it might offer a solution to the problem of controllability.

From the turn of the century onwards they built a series of gliders to test and refine their wing-warping technique. After checking with the US Weather Bureau, the brothers decided that the Kill Devil Hills near Kitty Hawk on the North Carolina coast offered the combination of topography and strong winds they were after. In their third glider design, built with the help of a basic, homemade wind tunnel, they made more than 1000 flights over the beaches of Kitty Hawk. In working out how to control an aircraft in flight, Wilbur and Orville had invented the three-axis principle used by every aircraft since, from the Spitfire to the Space Shuttle. Their scientific, rigorous approach, application and determination had already made them the world's most experienced fixed-wing pilots, but they had not yet achieved powered flight.

To achieve that next goal they built their own 12-horsepower engine and two propellers driven by bicycle chains. These they installed on a new, slightly bigger machine, their fourth design, which they called the Flyer. Built of ash, spruce, muslin and piano wire, it combined lightness with strength. And on 14 December 1903 they tossed a coin to see who would fly her first. Wilbur won. Rising sharply after just 15 feet, he stalled and crashed into the sand. 'Due to lack of experience,' Wilbur said. Three days later, after minor repairs, it was Orville's turn.

At 10.35 a.m. on 17 December the Wright Flyer, with Orville lying prone at the controls, began its take-off run. After 40 feet it climbed into the wind, flew under full control for 12 seconds, then landed safely on wooden skids 120 feet from where it had taken off.

There were three more flights before midday, the longest (flown by Wilbur) of 59 seconds over 852 feet. That afternoon Orville sent a telegram to their father, Bishop Wright, back in Dayton, Ohio. It read:

Success four flights Thursday morning all against twenty-one mile wind started from level with engine power alone average speed through air thirty-one miles longest fifty-nine seconds inform press home Christmas

And with that the world was changed for ever.

The Red Baron

An Introduction to Manfred von Richthofen

The film *Les chevaliers du ciel* (2005) was a sort of French version of *Top Gun*. Although it was released nearly a century after the death of Manfred von Richthofen, it's the Red Baron more than anyone else who is responsible for the movie's title, which translates as *The Knights of the Sky* (but was saddled with the awkward title *Sky Fighters* on its release in English).

Richthofen is *the* iconic fighter pilot. Credited with eighty kills, he was the leading ace on any side during the First World War. And it's been his enduring reputation that has fuelled a sense that rival fighter pilots were engaging in something more noble than the brutality of war.

It's astonishing to think that he was a pilot for only two years and that, during his uncertain first flight at the controls, he crashed his aircraft. The machine was left looking, he thought, like a battered old school bus, and he was upset at being the butt of jokes from the other students. He got the hang of flying two days later. Any doubt about his skill in the cockpit had evaporated long before he scored his first official kill in October 1916, six months after he joined his first squadron.

Born in 1892 into an aristocratic family in what is now Poland, Richthofen learned to ride and hunt at a young age before beginning military training aged

11. In 1911 he joined a cavalry regiment, but with the outbreak of hostilities in 1914, it was clear that his unit was of no use whatsoever in a modern war. He was bored rigid, his main excitement coming from shooting wild pigs. When he was transferred to the supply branch, he requested a transfer to the Imperial German Army Flying Corps, complaining that he hadn't gone to war 'in order to collect cheese and eggs'.

Soon after he qualified as a pilot, Richthofen's squadron was sent to the Eastern Front to drop bombs on the Russians. Still dissatisfied, he hankered to fly on the Western Front. A meeting with Germany's

Manfred Albrecht Freiherr von Richthofen. The Red Baron.
Just 25 years old when he was killed in combat in April 1918.

A replica of Richthofen's iconic red Fokker Dr.1 triplane. Although slower than contemporary fighters – and prone to structural failure – the Dr.1 offered exceptional manoeuverability.

leading ace, Oswald Boelke, who was looking for recruits to form a new fighter unit, provided the chance he was looking for. Although Boelke died in a mid-air collision, he continued to act as an inspiration to Richthofen. Following his late CO's rules for combat, Richthofen began to rack up some impressive numbers. By January 1917, his sixteen kills had earned him the Pour le Mérite medal, known as the 'Blue Max', and command of his own squadron. In fostering his unit's esprit de corps, he encouraged pilots to paint their aircraft in bright colours. After forcing down a British Vickers two-man reconnaissance plane, he was thrilled to learn from the crew that his red-painted Albatros DIII was well known to them: they called it *Le Petit Rouge* (The Little Red). They had also treated him like the sportsman he knew himself to be. It was exactly the way he wanted to be perceived.

Despite his success, Richthofen didn't feel he'd found the ideal aircraft. He wanted manoeuvrability even at the expense of speed. It wasn't until he recovered from a bullet which grazed his skull that he settled on the Fokker Dr.1 triplane, which instantly comes to mind at any mention of the Red Baron. In this iconic fighter he scored nineteen of his eighty victories, but it was also the machine in which he died, aged just 25.

Richthofen returned to the cockpit just three weeks after having bone splinters removed from his skull following the injury that nearly killed him. Afterwards he was to suffer debilitating headaches, but the leader of the multicoloured squadron known as the 'Flying Circus' had become a talismanic figure in Germany. Accepting that, even embracing it, he believed he had no choice but to fight on. Initially, he struggled to find form, and while he never fully recovered from the head wound, through March and April the following year he added a further seventeen victims. To one of the men who survived being shot down, as he was recovering in hospital, Richthofen sent a box of cigars.

The Red Baron was shot through the chest on 21 April 1918 while trying to claim his eighty-first victim. At the time, his death was credited to a young Canadian Sopwith Camel pilot, Captain Arthur Brown, but it now seems more likely that the bullet that killed him was fired from the ground.

I prefer it this way. It seems fitting somehow that Manfred von Richthofen, the most famous fighter pilot who's ever lived, was not defeated in the air.

Richthofen was buried by the British near Amiens, and the formalities reflected his significance: six RAF officers acting as pallbearers, a fourteen-man firing party, and a bugler sounding the 'Last Post'. Photographs of the service were taken, developed and, the next day, dropped over his home airfield with a note:

TO THE GERMAN FLYING CORPS:
Rittmeister Baron Manfred von Richthofen was killed in aerial combat on April 21st, 1918. He was buried with full military honours.
From the British Royal Air Force

In a brief autobiography written in the weeks when he was recovering from his head wound, he said he hoped that the British wouldn't give up their attempts to catch him. If they did, he said, 'I would miss many more opportunities to endear myself to them.'

The irony is that, for all his ruthless efficiency as a fighter pilot, he had already done so. While the British may have wanted the Red Baron gone, his enemy also had the greatest respect and admiration for him as an adversary.

Aviation Origami
How to Make a Paper Helicopter

S o, this one's part paper dart, part science lesson, and it couldn't be simpler. Just follow the instructions below, then drop it out of an upstairs window (being careful if you really are young, rather than just young at heart, to make sure you only lean out of windows in the company of an adult). And as you watch it spin away, just remember that this is where it all began. The 'bat' that inspired the Wright brothers' passion for flight was just a toy helicopter.

HOW TO DO IT

1. Take a piece of A4 paper and cut it in half lengthways. Using a pencil, mark up one half with the template below.

2. Cut along the red lines (a, c and d).

3. Fold along the black lines (b, e, f and g).

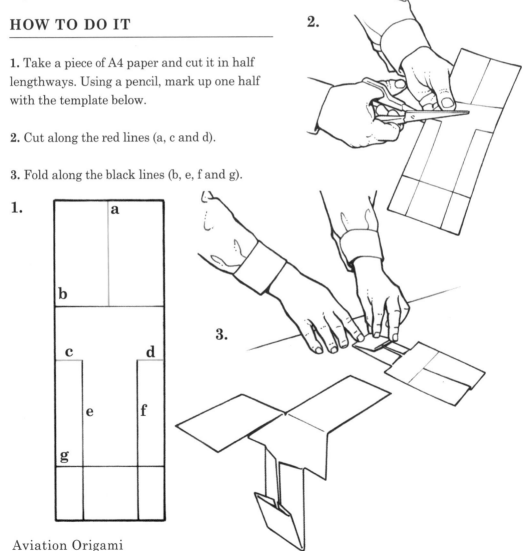

THE ROYAL CONNECTION

Both Prince William and Prince Harry are helicopter pilots. Wills flies a Sea King on search-and-rescue missions for the Royal Air Force, while his brother flies Apache gunships for the army. If your preference is for Prince William, paint your paper helicopter yellow, as shown below left. But if Prince Harry's your man, go for a dark olive green, as shown on the right.

Prince William's Westland Sea King HAR3.   *Prince Harry's AgustaWestland Apache AH1.*

On the Wing
Barnstormers and Flying Circuses

Once powered flight was established and there were sufficient numbers of aircraft and aviators, it wasn't long before air races and speed trials were set up. Machines were put through their paces, and 1912 saw the first recorded loop-the-loop and inverted flight. The First World War put a stop to the fun and games for a while, but also produced a surplus of trained pilots and capable aircraft. With the war's end, some of them wondered whether their new skills might earn them a living. And they started getting out of the cockpit. Wingwalking attracted thrillseekers – often women proved to be the biggest draw – and unsurprisingly enough it was often as life-threatening as it sounded. Fatalities were far from uncommon and neither, as a result, were job vacancies. One man sent a telegram to a potential employer that read: 'WHEN PRESENT WINGWALKER IS KILLED I WANT THE JOB'. He was soon hired, and was soon dead too, breaking his back while performing a stunt he'd dubbed the 'Bullet Drop'.

Lillian Boyer dangles one-handed. Increasing regulation forced her into retirement in 1929 and, happily, she then went on to live to the grand old age of 88.

ABOVE: *Ormer Locklear performs a handstand on the wing. A US Army Air Service flying instructor during the First World War, Locklear was killed in 1920 filming a manoeuvre for the movie* The Skywayman.

LEFT: *Watched by a huge crowd, Mabel Cody climbs from a car into a plane.*

Gladys Roy and Ivan Unger play tennis on the wing. If there was ever a ball, it didn't stay up there long enough for the photographer to capture it.

The Spin Doctors

Twelve Aerobatic Manoeuvres

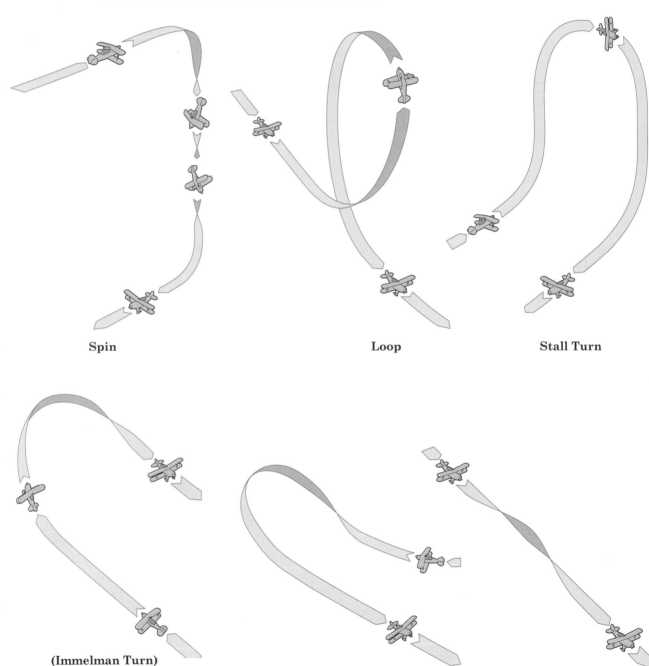

Spin

Loop

Stall Turn

**(Immelman Turn)
Half Loop and
Half Roll**

Half Roll and Half Loop

Slow Roll

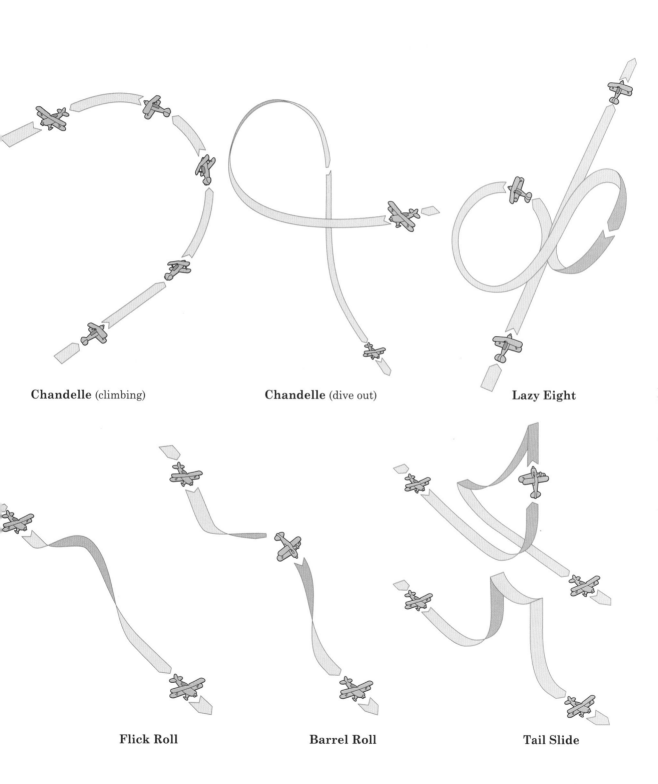

Chandelle (climbing) **Chandelle** (dive out) **Lazy Eight**

Flick Roll **Barrel Roll** **Tail Slide**

Across the Pond

Who Was First to Fly across the Atlantic?

It was night-time when he arrived. Over 33 hours after taking off from New York in his little silver Ryan Monoplane, *Spirit of St Louis*, Captain Charles Lindbergh of the US Army Air Corps Reserve picked out the lights of the London to Paris airways. He circled the airfield at Le Bourget, flew low to check the landing strip, then came in to land. Lindbergh's arrival in Paris on 21 May 1927 made him the most famous man on Earth. Over four million people – well over half the city's entire population – lined the streets for a ticker-tape parade when he returned to New York (by ship). During a subsequent tour of the United States, it's reckoned that a quarter of the whole country's population greeted him. He was the first modern global celebrity.

So, to learn that Lindbergh was *not* the first man to fly across the Atlantic is akin to being told that Neil Armstrong wasn't the first man to walk on the moon (don't worry, he was). In the eight years prior to his epic flight aboard his little monoplane, as many as ninety other people had made the journey, and many of their stories are as remarkable as Lindbergh's own.

The outbreak of the First World War ended any early hope of winning a £10,000 prize, offered by the *Daily Mail* in 1913, for the first successful transatlantic flight. But war, and the emergence of a devastating U-boat threat, prompted the development of a new US Navy flying boat designed to counter it. The big, four-engined Navy-Curtiss aircraft, known as Nancies, arrived too late for the war, but all was not lost. The admirals realized they might enjoy some return on their investment by claiming the prestige of a first aerial Atlantic crossing for the United States. In public they argued that the expense and effort were justified 'for scientific reasons'. Short of a landmark breakthrough, though, this seemed unlikely given that, in support of the attempt, they deployed a picket line of *sixty-eight* destroyers and a further five battleships along the route via the Azores to Portugal. At a reasonably brisk pace, Jesus would have been able to walk the route and enjoy a bunk and a hot meal at the end of each day. That gives the impression that it was easy. For the crews of the three flying boats that took off from Newfoundland on 16 May 1919 it was anything but.

OPPOSITE: *Charles Lindbergh poses with* Spirit of St Louis. *'Are there any mechanics here?' he asked after landing in France in front of a crowd of 150,000 people.*

'Even if we crashed on landing,' said Captain Read of the moment his Curtiss NC flying boat turned towards the Portuguese capital, 'the transatlantic flight, the first one in the history of the world, was an accomplished fact.'

Flying in open cockpits through thick fog, heavy rain and squalling winds, the Nancies were thrown around the sky. One was almost hit by a star shell from a warship trying to guide their way. Another was nearly lost when the pilot became disorientated while flying blind and was lucky to regain control. The third became so lost that the pilot landed on the rolling ocean surface so that the crew could try to get their bearings. Soon overwhelmed by the heavy seas, which damaged the aircraft's tail, they sent out an SOS and were rescued from their sinking machine by a Greek merchant ship 5 hours later.

The captain of the second Nancy, completely lost after 15 hours in filthy skies, decided to land. Smashing into the crest of a wave, the plane bounced, then crashed down again, cracking its hull on impact. Unable to take off, the crew pushed on by sea. It took them three days to sail to the Azores, backwards, using the Nancy's tail as a jury-rigged sail. For most of their 60-hour ordeal, a crewman had to sit at the end of the starboard wing providing the weight needed to keep the damaged plane's port wing out of the water. It displayed guts and seamanship, but it marked the end of another Nancy crew's ambitions.

Just one of the American flying boats, NC-4, skippered by Commander Albert C. Read, made it intact to the Azores. On 27 May – eleven days after they'd left – Read and his crew carried on to Lisbon to become the first men ever to fly across the Atlantic.

Strangely enough, the first airmail to reach Britain from North America had arrived two days earlier. When the Nancies had left Newfoundland on their long journey, they'd left behind them four British teams each hoping to be first to fly non-stop across the Atlantic. Two days behind the US Navy flying boats, Australian test pilot Harry Hawker, reputed to be the finest flyer in Britain, and his navigator, Lieutenant-Commander Kenneth MacKenzie-Grieve RN, took off from a field in their Sopwith Atlantic. Fourteen hours later, they weren't even halfway when an overheating engine forced them to ditch. After five days without word, they were officially presumed dead. The *Daily Mail* offered to provide for Hawker's daughter, while King George V offered Mrs Hawker his condolences:

> *The King, fearing the worst must now be realized regarding the fate*
> *of your husband, wishes to express his deep sympathy and that of*
> *the Queen in your sudden and tragic sorrow. His Majesty feels that*
> *the nation lost one of its most able and daring pilots to sacrifice his*
> *life for the fame and honour of British flying.*

Hawker and MacKenzie-Grieve arrived home to read their own obituaries. When it had become clear they could not stay airborne, Hawker had diverted towards the shipping lanes, where he landed in the water alongside a Danish freighter, *Mary*. Without radio, the ship had no way of telling the world that the two aviators were alive. That had to wait until *Mary*'s signal flags could be seen from shore. The exchange with coastguards was brief:

> – *Saved Hands. Sopwith Aeroplane*
> – *Is it Hawker*
> – *Yes*

The sack of drenched letters that Hawker had managed to hold on to throughout his dramatic Atlantic crossing was delivered as planned.

Another British attempt, which left an hour after Hawker and MacKenzie-Grieve, crashed on take-off, seriously injuring one of the two crewmen. That left two teams, and one of those was clearly the underdog.

When asked during a job interview at Vickers Ltd if he could navigate an aeroplane across the Atlantic, Arthur Whitten Brown simply said, 'Yes.' It was enough to win him one of two seats aboard a converted Vickers Vimy bomber that the company hoped would win it the *Daily Mail*'s £10,000 prize.

He wasn't, strictly speaking, a navigator either. He'd taught himself while enduring two years as a prisoner of war. In an era when the art of aerial navigation hadn't moved much beyond following railway lines, that meant he was well qualified.

Brown, with his pilot, John Alcock, known to all as Jack, arrived in Newfoundland to find a rival team flying a big, four-engined Handley Page V/1500 Berlin Bomber already well established. What the leader of the Handley Page team didn't realize, but what Jack Alcock had figured out, was that it was the mineral content of the local water that had clogged Harry Hawker's engine. And this same issue meant the V/1500's Rolls-Royce Eagle engines were proving problematic too. Alcock made sure the Vimy used only water that had been boiled and filtered.

At teatime on 14 June 1919, Alcock and Brown, after a swig of whisky, climbed aboard and took off. In anticipation of the gruelling journey ahead, they carried with them Fry's chocolate, Horlicks malted milk, sandwiches, two Thermos flasks of coffee and what was left of the whisky that, in Prohibition-era America, had to be prescribed for them by a doctor.

The flight through the night was largely uneventful, but at dawn the Vimy flew into thick cloud that obscured the sight of the nose from the cockpit. Unable to see and without the necessary instruments to fly blind, Alcock became completely disorientated and lost control of the Vimy. Then the big biplane stalled, literally falling out of the sky. As they tumbled, Brown watched the altimeter wind down from 3000 feet to 500. And it was not a particularly accurate measure. *We might hit the ocean at any moment*, Brown thought. He loosened his harness and tried to stash his flight log ready for a quick escape, but he knew there was little hope of survival.

Suddenly, the picture cleared as they dropped below the cloud. Brown had barely realized that they were falling sideways, the horizon at ninety degrees to their aircraft, before Alcock wrestled the Vimy back under his control.

> *When, at last, the machine swung back to level, and flew parallel with the Atlantic, our height was fifty feet. It appeared as if we could stretch downward and almost touch the great white-caps that crested the surface. Before Alcock opened up the engines we could actually hear the voice of the cheated ocean as its waves swelled, broke, and swelled again.*

Next they faced horizontal rain, hail, snow and sleet. And with its arrival, a crucial fuel gauge became iced up, forcing Brown to unstrap, leave the safety of the cockpit and climb out on to the fuselage, kneeling in the slipstream, as the hail attacked his back like buckshot. He was forced to carry on with this until the storm was gone. He was safe, he thought, *as long as Alcock kept the machine level.* But he also knew that with the ice jamming the flight controls, there was very little Alcock could do to guarantee it. The Vimy would either stay level, or she wouldn't.

Sixteen and a half hours after taking off they landed inelegantly in an Irish bog. And the country went wild. 'ALCOCK ANNIHILATES SPACE AT 120 MPH,' exclaimed one enthusiastic headline. Another speculated that their flight paved the way for commercial transatlantic flights. A fortnight later that possibility looked to have come a whole lot closer.

William Ballantyne, a young airship rigger, was excited that 'Tiny', as the R34, Great Britain's latest great airship, was called by those who worked on her, was on her way to America, but disappointed not to be part of the crew. Although the R34 was bigger than a battleship, the numbers she could carry on the first east–west aerial transatlantic crossing were limited to thirty, and Ballantyne had not made the cut. Rather than miss out, he, together with the airship's mascot, a kitten called Whoopsie, hid on top of a girder between two gas bags. Twelve hours later, cramped and nauseous, Ballantyne made himself known. It was too late to put him overboard by parachute, so for the rest of the four-day passage to New York he was made to cook for the crew. On arrival, the crew of the R34 were greeted by huge crowds cheering from

Just 16½ hours to go. Alcock and Brown take off from Newfoundland on their way to becoming the first people to fly non-stop across the Atlantic.

grandstands, then fêted for three days before climbing back aboard their 643-foot airship and returning home – leaving Ballantyne behind in New York. Over the 75-hour journey they ate hot meals, slept in hammocks and listened to jazz on a gramophone record player. Little wonder that Arthur Whitten Brown, who'd endured the spartan discomforts of the Vimy's open cockpit, was sure that airships pointed the way towards commercial transatlantic flights carrying fare-paying passengers.

So why, after the success of the NC-4, the Vimy and the R34 in 1919, does Charles Lindbergh remain the most famous transatlantic aviator of them all?

I think it's to do with the purity, perfection and romance of Lindbergh's effort. The US Navy Nancy hopped and skipped its way across the Atlantic, supported by a fleet of warships nearly the same size as today's entire Royal Navy. Alcock and Brown bulled their way across and ended up nose first in a bog with their tail in the air. And the R34 carried thirty people – and a cat – across the pond while they listened to music and put a stowaway to work. All were remarkable, courageous efforts, but none possessed the poetry of Lindbergh's solo flight. Alone in his silver slip of a plane he took off in New York and, 33½ hours later, landed in front of a clamouring crowd of 150,000 people. *Alone*, that was the key. An editorial in the New York *Sun* got it right:

> *Alone?*
>
> *Is he alone at whose right side rides Courage, with Skill within the cockpit and faith upon the left?*
>
> *Does solitude surround the brave when Adventure leads the way and Ambition reads the dials? Is there no company with him, for whom the air is cleft by Daring and the darkness made light by Emprise?*
>
> *True, the fragile bodies of his fellows do not weigh down his plane; true, the fretful minds of weaker men are missing from his crowded cabin; but as his airship keeps its course he holds communion with those rare spirits that inspire to intrepidity and by their sustaining potency give strength to arm, resource to mind, content to soul.*
>
> *Alone?*
>
> *With what other companions would man fly to whom the choice were given?*

Who Were You?

Insignia of Yesterday's Air Forces

In recent years many air forces have all but abandoned their traditional national insignia, a practical decision, given that daubing bright colours all over your warplanes has never helped hide them from the enemy. But it's not so bad. A lot of the brightest and the best disappeared years ago anyway, killed off by changing regimes and redrawn borders. So let's celebrate the James Deans and Marilyn Monroes of the roundel world. There are some corkers below that were gone too soon. I shouldn't have to point out that an admiration for, say, the roundel sported by Democratic Kampuchea does not imply any enthusiasm for Pol Pot, but to avoid any misunderstanding, let me clearly state that my interest is purely artistic.

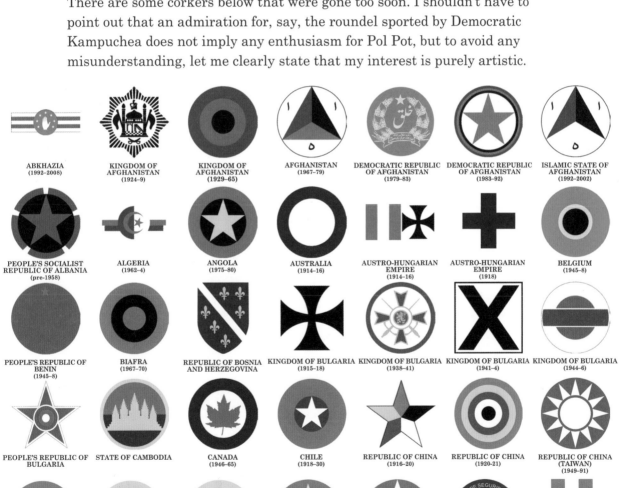

ABKHAZIA
(1992–2008)

KINGDOM OF
AFGHANISTAN
(1924–9)

KINGDOM OF
AFGHANISTAN
(1929–65)

AFGHANISTAN
(1967–79)

DEMOCRATIC REPUBLIC
OF AFGHANISTAN
(1979–83)

DEMOCRATIC REPUBLIC
OF AFGHANISTAN
(1983–92)

ISLAMIC STATE OF
AFGHANISTAN
(1992–2002)

PEOPLE'S SOCIALIST
REPUBLIC OF ALBANIA
(pre-1958)

ALGERIA
(1962–4)

ANGOLA
(1975–80)

AUSTRALIA
(1914–16)

AUSTRO-HUNGARIAN
EMPIRE
(1914–16)

AUSTRO-HUNGARIAN
EMPIRE
(1918)

BELGIUM
(1945–8)

PEOPLE'S REPUBLIC OF
BENIN
(1945–8)

BIAFRA
(1967–70)

REPUBLIC OF BOSNIA
AND HERZEGOVINA

KINGDOM OF BULGARIA
(1915–18)

KINGDOM OF BULGARIA
(1938–41)

KINGDOM OF BULGARIA
(1941–4)

KINGDOM OF BULGARIA
(1944–6)

PEOPLE'S REPUBLIC OF
BULGARIA

STATE OF CAMBODIA

CANADA
(1946–65)

CHILE
(1918–30)

REPUBLIC OF CHINA
(1916–20)

REPUBLIC OF CHINA
(1920–21)

REPUBLIC OF CHINA
(TAIWAN)
(1949–91)

COLOMBIA
(1920–4)

COLOMBIA
(1924–7)

COLOMBIA
(1928–53)

PEOPLE'S REPUBLIC OF
CONGO

COSTA RICA

COSTA RICA
(1964–94)

USTAŠE CROATIA
(1941)

USTAŠE CROATIA
(1941–5)

CROATIA
(1991–4)

CUBA
(1955–9)

CUBA
(1959–62)

CZECHOSLOVAKIA
(1918–20)

CZECHOSLOVAKIA

EAST GERMANY

KINGDOM OF EGYPT
(1939–45)

KINGDOM OF EGYPT
(1945–58)

FINLAND
(1918–44)

FRANCE
(1912–45)

FREE FRANCE

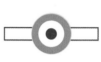
FREE FRANCE
(Alternative)

GERMAN EMPIRE

NAZI GERMANY

GHANA
(1964–6)

HAITI
(1961–4)

HAITI
(1964–86)

HAITI
(1986–94)

HUNGARIAN SOVIET
REPUBLIC

HUNGARIAN SOVIET
REPUBLIC
(1919)

KINGDOM OF HUNGARY
(1938–41)

KINGDOM OF HUNGARY
(1942–5)

SECOND HUNGARIAN
REPUBLIC

PEOPLE'S REPUBLIC OF
HUNGARY
(1951–90)

HUNGARY
(1990–1)

INDIA
(1947–9)

INDONESIA
(1946–9)

IRAQ
(1931–2003)

IRISH FREE STATE

REPUBLIC OF IRELAND
(1939–54)

ISRAEL
(Early version)

ITALY
(1915)

FASCIST ITALY

ITALIAN SOCIAL
REPUBLIC

DEMOCRATIC
KAMPUCHEA

PEOPLE'S REPUBLIC OF
KAMPUCHEA

KATANGA

KHMER REPUBLIC

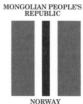
KINGDOM OF LAOS

LAOS
(Painted over RLAF
insignia)

LATVIA
(1918–40)

LATVIA (NATIONAL
GUARD)
(1993–2000)

LIBERIA

KINGDOM OF LIBYA

LIBYAN ARAB REPUBLIC

GREAT SOCIALIST
PEOPLE'S LIBYAN ARAB
JAMAHIRIYA

LITHUANIA
(1920–1)

LITHUANIA

MALAYSIA
(1963–82)

MALTA
(1980–8)

MANCHUKUO
(Air Force)

MANCHUKUO
(Air Transport)

MONGOLIAN PEOPLE'S
REPUBLIC

NETHERLANDS
(1914–21)

NETHERLANDS
(1943–6)

NEW ZEALAND
(1943–6)

NICARAGUA
(1942–62)

NICARAGUA
(1962–79)

NORTH YEMEN

NORWAY
(1937–40)

OTTOMAN EMPIRE

POLAND
(1918–21)

POLAND
(1921–93)

PORTUGAL
(1915–16)

(SOUTHERN) RHODESIA
(1939–54)

RHODESIA (FEDERATION
OF RHODESIA &
NYASALAND (1954–63)

(SOUTHERN) RHODESIA
(1963–70)

RHODESIA
(1970–80)

KINGDOM OF ROMANIA
(1941–4)

SOCIALIST REPUBLIC OF
ROMANIA
(1947–85)

RUSSIAN EMPIRE

SERBIA
(1912)

SERBIA
(1915)

SEYCHELLES

SINGAPORE
(1968–73)

SINGAPORE
(1973–90)

SLOVAK REPUBLIC

SLOVENIA
(1991–6)

UNION OF SOUTH
AFRICA
(1920)

UNION OF SOUTH
AFRICA
(1927–47)

UNION OF SOUTH
AFRICA
(1947–57)

SOUTH AFRICA
(1957–94)

SOUTH AFRICA
(1994–2003)

SOUTH KOREA
(1949–2005)

SOUTH VIETNAM

SOUTH YEMEN

SECOND SPANISH
REPUBLIC
(1931–6)

SECOND SPANISH
REPUBLIC
(1936–9)

SPANISH STATE
(Variant 1)

SPANISH STATE
(Variant 2)

SRI LANKA
(1951–2010)

REPUBLIKA SRPSKA
(Variant 1)

REPUBLIKA SRPSKA
(Variant 2)

SUDAN
(1956–70)

SWEDEN
(1914–15)

SWEDEN
(1927–37)

SWEDEN
(1937–40)

SWITZERLAND
(1914–47)

SYRIA
(1948–58)

TURKEY
(1918–72)

UKRAINE
(1991)

USSR
(1922–43)

USSR, RUSSIA
(1943–91, 1991–2010)

UNITED ARAB REPUBLIC

UNITED KINGDOM
ROYAL NAVAL AIR
SERVICE
(1914–15)

UNITED KINGDOM
(1937–42)

UNITED KINGDOM
SOUTH EAST ASIA AIR
COMMAND (1942–6)

UNITED KINGDOM
(1942–7)

UNITED STATES
(1918)

UNITED STATES
(1917–18, 1921–42)

UNITED STATES
(1942–3)

UNITED STATES
(1943)

UNITED STATES
(1943–7)

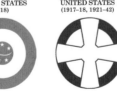

UNITED STATES MARINE
CORPS
(1912)

UPPER VOLTA

KINGDOM OF YEMEN

KINGDOM OF
YUGOSLAVIA
(1923)

KINGDOM OF
YUGOSLAVIA
(1929–41)

REP. OF YUGOSLAVIA

REP. OF YUGOSLAVIA,
SERBIA AND
MONTENEGRO

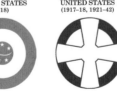

ZAIRE

Romeo and Juliett
An Introduction to the Phonetic Alphabet

In an age of call centres and telebanking, what's officially known as the NATO phonetic alphabet is so well known that it's difficult to imagine that it hasn't always been with us. In fact, its adoption and standardization are relatively recent developments. Between 1924 and 1942 the Royal Air Force used the following alphabet:

> ACE > BEER > CHARLIE > DON > EDWARD > FREDDIE > GEORGE > HARRY > INK > JOHNNIE > KING > LONDON > MONKEY > NUTS > ORANGE > PIP > QUEEN > ROBERT > SUGAR > TOC > UNCLE > VIC > WILLIAM > X-RAY > YORKER > ZEBRA

Meanwhile, US flyers had their own alphabet:

> ABLE > BAKER > CHARLIE > DOG > EASY > FOX > GEORGE > HOW > ITEM > JIG > KING > LOVE > MIKE > NAN > OBOE > PETER > QUEEN > ROGER > SUGAR > TARE > UNCLE > VICTOR > WILLIAM > X-RAY > YOKE > ZEBRA

From 1943 the RAF adopted the US phonetic alphabet, but it was the rapid development of civil aviation after the Second World War that led to the creation of the standardized phonetic alphabet we use today. And with English being the lingua franca of the air, regardless of aircrews' nationality, it needed to retain clarity in a wide variety of accents from non-native English speakers.

The first stab at it, introduced in 1951, missed the mark. The International Civil Aviation Organization tried:

> ALFA > BRAVO > COCA > DELTA > ECHO > FOXTROT > GOLF > HOTEL > INDIA > JULIETT > KILO > LIMA > METRO > NECTAR > OSCAR > PAPA > QUEBEC > ROMEO > SIERRA > TANGO > UNION > VICTOR > WHISKEY > EXTRA > YANKEE > ZULU

Delta, Nectar, Metro, Victor and Extra were regularly muddled. Other words became unclear through poor reception and static. Coca, Metro, Nectar, Union and Extra were all replaced. By 1965, when the International

Maritime Organization signed up, the form we're used to now had been nailed down. Not, however, without a few regional variations that remain in use today. Here it is (with Morse code thrown in for good measure):

ALFA · — Not 'Alpha' because of potential confusion over the pronunciation of 'ph'. **BRAVO** — · · · **CHARLIE** — · — · **DELTA** — · · Replaced by 'Data', 'David' or 'Dixie' at some North American airports, where Delta Airlines – callsign 'Delta' – is the main user. **ECHO** · **FOXTROT** · · — · **GOLF** — — ·	**HOTEL** · · · · **INDIA** · · Replaced by 'Italy' in Pakistan because they can't quite bring themselves to speak the name of their neighbour and frequent enemy. **JULIETT** · — — — Internationally it's 'Juliett' with a double 't' because a single 't' would be silent to French speakers. **KILO** — · — **LIMA** · — · · Replaced by 'London' in Brunei, Indonesia, Malaysia and Singapore, where 'lima' means 'five'.	**MIKE** — — **NOVEMBER** — · **OSCAR** — — — **PAPA** · — — · **QUEBEC** — — · — **ROMEO** · — · **SIERRA** · · · **TANGO** — **UNIFORM** · · — **VICTOR** · · · —	**WHISKEY** · — — Not Scottish 'whisky' as that manages without the 'e' used by the rest of the world. Nor any whiskey at all in Saudi Arabia, where the very mention of it, wherever it's from, goes against the grain. 'Washington' is used instead, which in itself is probably considered by some Saudis to be a bit close to the bone. **X-RAY** — · · — **YANKEE** — · — — **ZULU** — — · ·

On a few occasions the phonetic alphabet has become familiar beyond the world of radio communication. In 1954, a BOAC de Havilland Comet registered as G-ALYP became famous as 'Yoke Peter' after breaking up over the Mediterranean. A Chinook helicopter known as Bravo November has become perhaps the most well-known aircraft in the Royal Air Force after surviving the Falklands War, leading the British air assault on Iraq in 2003 and providing the cockpit for two DFC awards.

SAS callsign Bravo Two Zero became universally well known after the success of Andy McNab's book of the same name. Bravo Zulu has become naval slang for 'well done', and then there's Foxtrot Oscar, which doesn't mean well done at all …

War Minus the Shooting

A History of Air Racing

In later life US Air Force General Jimmy Doolittle claimed that the Granville Brothers' Gee Bee R1 racer 'was the most unforgiving plane I ever flew'. As a younger man, Doolittle had set world speed records, flown manoeuvres others had thought impossible, and led the legendary US raid against Tokyo in retaliation for the bombing of Pearl Harbor. His logbook was full and varied, but he singled out the Gee Bee.

The Gee Bee was a completely uncompromising design, built during the Great Depression of the 1930s to win cash prizes at air races that might save its makers from bankruptcy. It was little more than a flying engine. No plane looked as if it cared less about anything other than bludgeoning its way through the sky than the Gee Bee racer, and that lack of finesse meant it was lethal. The smallest unchecked control input could send the unstable machine cartwheeling into the ground.

The first two Gee Bees crashed, killing their pilots, and a third came to grief in 1933. In 1935 a fourth, made of parts salvaged from the second and third machines, also crashed and killed the pilot. When Doolittle was asked why he wanted to fly a killer like the Gee Bee, his answer was simple: 'Because it was the fastest thing going.'

With that unassailable logic, Doolittle had put his finger on the visceral appeal of air racing. It was the very thing that he and the United States had been instrumental in bringing about.

The Schneider Trophy was Europe's pre-eminent air race. The competition's creator, the Frenchman Jacques Schneider, believed that the future belonged to aircraft that operated from water, so his trophy was solely for aeroplanes that could do so. In 1922 a British pilot called Henri Biard edged out the Italians to win the trophy. His little Supermarine Sea Lion II flying boat was far from sophisticated, but after two years with Italy winning the trophy unopposed, the closeness of the race captured the public's imagination.

It also caught the eye of the US Navy. Until this point, the Schneider Trophy had been a slightly amateur affair contested by national flying clubs. The US Navy campaign, though, left nothing to chance, training hand-picked pilots and dispatching them with every bit of kit and equipment they needed specially produced for the job. Fielding a version of the Curtiss Racer, which had just won the annual Pulitzer Air Race in the USA, they had every reason to be confident, and their confidence turned out not to be misplaced. When, on race day, the American Curtiss CR-3 racers comfortably took first and second places in the competition, *The Times* sniffed that 'British habits do not support the idea of entering a team organized by the State for a sporting event'.

The British government disagreed, however, and bought a number of the exceptional Curtiss D-12 engines that had been key to the US victory, and told Rolls-Royce to make one that was even better. But new engines weren't ready in time for the next race in 1924, which was won even more convincingly by US Army Air Service pilot Jimmy Doolittle in a record-breaking 232.6 mph run. Doolittle's aggressive flying, and his rare ability to resist the high G-loads his hard cornering generated, thrilled the crowds and cemented his position as a national hero.

Supermarine S.6B, winner of the 1931 Schneider Trophy and holder of the world air-speed record. Its designer, R. J. Mitchell, went on to design the Spitfire.

It was said that the Granville Gee Bee racer resembled 'a section of sewer pipe that had sprouted wings'. In 1932, legendary aviator Jimmy Doolittle described it as the 'sweetest ship I've ever flown'. An opinion he would go on to qualify.

The British realized that to win the trophy they would need service support and hence, following the American example again, a High Speed Flight was set up within the RAF. The 1926 trophy was left to the Italians, who carried out Mussolini's orders to win 'at all costs' against an American team shorn of government support.

The British, using an outdated engine to power their Supermarine S5 seaplane, were lucky to win in 1927. Then, late in 1928, while walking on the beach with three colleagues, Sir Henry Royce began sketching a new V-12 engine in the sand with his walking stick. The finished design incorporated the lessons learned from the American D-12, and used a supercharger to increase the power. Built, tested and installed in Supermarine's new S6 with just a month to spare before the 1929 race, the 'R' engine proved to be outstanding. Britain won its second Schneider Trophy on the trot.

Rolls-Royce squeezed another 500 horsepower out of the 'R' engine and, in September 1931, flying a blue, silver and red Supermarine S6B float plane, Squadron Leader John Boothman of the RAF's High Speed Flight won the Schneider Trophy again. The rules stated that with a third victory in five years, the competition had now been won outright. The trophy was Britain's to keep. Watching Boothman complete the seven 50-kilometre laps at an average speed of over 340 mph was a crowd reckoned to be well over half a million strong. What was absent was any competition.

The Italians, unable to get their truly magnificent Macchi MC.72 ready in time after a fatal accident in testing, could not compete. The MC.72 eventually proved to be supremely fast, raising a 407.5 mph air speed record set by the S6B to 440 mph.

Unlike the British, though, the Italians seemed to do nothing with what they'd learned through racing. By contrast, R. J. Mitchell, the S6B's designer, said that without the competition, the 'R' engine 'would have taken at least three times as long to produce'. It was of crucial importance to Mitchell, the designer of the Spitfire, because the 'R' engine led directly to the one used by that war-winning fighter the Merlin, of which nearly 150,000 were built.

Which brings us back to racing.

Whereas, before the Second World War, participation in air racing had been of great benefit to the military, the tables were turned in the post-war decades. In aviation's early years it was relatively straightforward to build an aeroplane. The First World War accelerated the pace of change, but failed to place it beyond the technical or financial grasp of private individuals or companies. The last years of the Schneider Trophy made it clear that this state of affairs would not continue. Then the rapid advances made during the Second World War finished the job. From now on, the cutting edge of aircraft development streaked out of sight.

Behind it, the scraps the military no longer wanted or needed provided the very best and fastest air racing could lay its hands on. And top of the shopping list was the Rolls-Royce Merlin engine.

If you were in the market for a seaplane racer then I imagine this would've been a pretty persuasive advert.

In the USA there was a revival of the two series that had replaced the Pulitzer: the Thompson Trophy, in which entrants lapped a 10-mile closed-course circuit, and the Bendix, a 1000-mile transcontinental point-to-point. Merlin-engined P-51 Mustangs won all four of the post-war Bendix Trophies at speeds nearly 200 mph faster than the quickest pre-war times.

While race pilots in America went at each other with all the spit and belligerence of opposing football teams, their British counterparts were more akin to cordial golfers. What the British decided they needed was a race with a bit more maths in it, so 1949 saw the revival of the King's Cup, a cross-country race originally established by King George V in 1922. A handicap system in which slower, less powerful aircraft were given a headstart meant that, theoretically, everyone, regardless of what they were flying, had an equal chance of winning. Although smartly painted warbirds such as Princess Margaret's Hurricane, *The Last of the Many*, competed, they often spent more time on the ground than in the air. Thankfully, the 1967 race was won by a P-51 Mustang.

In America the P-51s were now the rule rather than the exception. After four good years, both the Bendix and Thompson trophies fell by the wayside. But since 1964 the National Championship Air Races have been held annually near Reno, Nevada. It's the world's fastest motorsport.

Every year P-51s, Sea Furies, Bearcats and Yaks, all modified, prepped and polished to eke out every last inch of speed, compete in Reno's Unlimited Class. There have been attempts to establish other competitive events, such as the 1970 California 1000, which even saw a big DC-7 airliner racing wingtip to wingtip with the old warbirds, but it's only Reno that's survived.

As many as 250,000 people a year take part in an annual pilgrimage to Reno. It's easy to see why. Banking at nearly 90 degrees just 50 feet above the desert floor, the Unlimiteds in full cry, jostling for position in three dimensions, are like no other sight in sport. Then there's the noise from the redlined piston engines, a meaty, percussive roar that makes the heart beat faster.

In the nose of each P-51, the old Merlin engine is pumped up to the point of self-destruction, churning out more than double the 1600 horsepower it was designed to. But the pilot Skip Holm, who flew a streamlined, red and gold clipped-wing Mustang called *Dago Red* to victory in 2002 and 2003 at speeds of over 500 mph, wouldn't have it any other way. The Merlin, he says, is a work of art. Its more powerful Rolls-Royce replacement, the Griffon, he dismisses as nothing more than a tractor engine.

During the Korean War, propeller-engined Hawker Sea Furies showed they were capable of shooting down MiG-15 jet fighters. Now ex-Space Shuttle astronaut and Top Gun graduate Robert 'Hoot' Gibson races this one, Riff Raff, *for fun.*

Holm is one of Reno's big figures. With a CV that includes combat tours in Vietnam and test flying classified prototypes out of Lockheed's top-secret Skunk Works, he's reckoned to be one of the best pilots ever to have flown there. He competes against other combat veterans, test pilots and astronauts in gleaming, brightly coloured aircraft carrying sponsors' logos and names such as *Riff Raff*, *Dreadnought*, *Strega* and *Red Baron*. It's the perfect spectator sport.

The audience knows it's watching the best of the best. Like the Olympics, Reno's appeal is in ultimate performance. Who's fastest? Who's strongest? In Europe, after the Schneider Trophy, air racing gave up on this and instead evolved into a participation sport. Competitive, certainly, but polite. Reno is anything but. Tom Dwelle, pilot of a souped-up red and black Sea Fury called *Critical Mass*, summed it up: 'It's combat and the thing is to know where all those guys are at all times. OK, if somebody dies out there – sayonara, man. Tough, you know – you're big boys. If you're afraid to die you got no business out here. This ain't no puss game. This is the real thing.'

Or, as Jimmy Doolittle put it more succinctly, 'the fastest thing going'.

Chicken or Beef?
The Story of Airline Food

'So, what's the deal with airline food?' Jerry Seinfeld once asked on *Saturday Night Live*, in a knowing reference to a line held to be the last refuge of the bad stand-up comedian; a clichéd observation about something so universally and completely reviled that it can't fail to connect with a restless audience. Airline food wasn't always as bad as it is now, but it did have to get better before it got worse again.

Passengers on German Zeppelins were treated to champagne as early as 1914, and onboard chefs and dining rooms had been introduced on big airships by the 1920s. However, this wasn't something it was possible to replicate on the aircraft of the day.

In 1919 the company Handley Page Transport began offering cold boxed lunches to passengers on its service flying between Cricklewood and Brussels, but often the prospect of food had to be abandoned because of turbulence. Even when it wasn't terrifying, flying as a passenger inside the barely enclosed cabin of an early biplane was not particularly conducive to fine dining. When, in 1921, KLM installed a galley on board one of its aircraft, they'd only been airborne for 15 minutes when it fell on top of a passenger after vibrations shook loose the screws holding it to the fuselage.

As it had been first with drinks on the Zeppelins, so Germany was also first to provide proper hot meals when Lufthansa introduced its 'Flying Dining Car' service in 1928. But, flying relatively low in bumpy air and breathing cabin air that was often thick with the smell of oil and kerosene, sickness was a problem for everyone on board. A chef hired by Air France from the Ritz said, 'Like most passengers, I became ill. While caring for them, I would run to the bathroom and throw up.' Small wonder that the first stewardesses employed by American Boeing Air Transport in 1930 were all nurses. Along with placing a paper bag behind the seat in front, it seemed to be a sensible precaution.

Advances in aircraft design went hand in hand with improved catering. As the aircraft themselves became more sophisticated, so too did the food.

OPPOSITE: *Passengers on board an Imperial Airways Handley-Page W8b flying between Croydon and Paris enjoy a silver service meal. The 12-seat airliner was also the first to have been designed with an onboard lavatory.*

In 1936, one passenger aboard an Imperial Airways flight to the Far East wrote: 'By far the best part of the journey has been the food. I have feasted from London to Mandalay on foie gras and ox tongue, roast beef and spiced lamb, lime jellies and the best pêche Melba I have ever eaten.'

This golden age could last only as long as airliners got better and passenger numbers stayed small. On board an Imperial Airways 'Empire Class' flying boat there were only twenty-four passengers to look after, but as new designs emerged, especially after the Second World War, the numbers on board each aircraft were beginning to creep up.

Into the 1950s, with no more than seventy-five passengers aboard their Boeing Stratocruisers, Pan Am and BOAC were offering steaks cooked to

Quite apart from spoiling passengers with the food on offer, Pan Am menus also offered cigarettes, medical kits, dominoes and benzedrine inhalers.

Breakfast in economy. Somewhere at 30,000 feet. Recently.

order. Breakfast could be protracted though, depending on altitude. At 9000 feet an egg took 20 minutes to cook.

To cope with increasing passenger numbers on jet airliners like the 707, airlines began to rely more on flight kitchens on the ground. But the rot really began when the Boeing 747 Jumbo Jet took off for the first time on a rainy day in February 1969. Flying as many passengers in one go as KLM had flown during the whole of 1920 meant that in-flight catering had to change. Simplicity, industrialization and weight became crucial considerations. In the 1920s Imperial Airways had used slender 14-year-olds to serve food, but that wasn't an option for BOAC when its first 747 was delivered in 1970. With every extra pound in weight costing £17 a year in fuel, china crockery was out and trolleys and trays were in.

Airline catering became a numbers game dominated by a few big providers. One of the biggest, LSG Sky Chefs, serves over 450 million meals a year to over 300 airlines. John Besh, a New Orleans-based chef who has consulted for the company, sums it up: 'The real issue is the sheer, vast quantities of food ... food is going to lose a touch of soul in the process.'

LSG Sky Chefs itself says it's trying to grapple with 'rising passenger expectations and airlines' pressure to cut costs'. I'm not sure that first bit is a real problem any more ...

Dead Heat

The Zeppelin Race

Commander Charles Rosendahl was America's most senior airshipman. An ex-commander of the United States Navy's most successful airship, USS *Los Angeles*, he was now commandant of Naval Air Station Lakehurst in New Jersey, the country's premier airship facility. On the evening of 6 May 1937 he watched as one of the world's newest, largest airships, the *Hindenburg*, made its final approach to his base's mooring mast. He'd flown around the world aboard her predecessor, the *Graf Zeppelin*, but he'd never been on board the *Hindenburg*. Nor would he ever get the chance.

At 7.25 p.m. he noticed a flame on top of the vast, cigar-shaped silver aircraft, just forward of the vertical tail fin. 'It was a brilliant burst of flame resembling a flower opening rapidly into bloom,' he later recalled. 'I knew at once the ship was doomed.' Then, as 7 million cubic feet of hydrogen went up, there was a loud *whumph* like the sound of an igniting gas ring.

The airship story is one that needs to begin at the end, and the age of the airship died in the 34-second blaze of the *Hindenburg*. There had been other, more deadly airship disasters, but none that had been broadcast live, as the *Hindenburg* had been. None that had so vividly and irrevocably demonstrated that the big hydrogen-filled airships were, essentially, flying bombs.

When the British scientist Henry Cavendish first discovered hydrogen in 1766 he called it 'flammable air', and its properties were well known to the designers of the *Hindenburg* and every airship filled with the gas before her. What on earth were they all thinking?

Helium, the alternative option, now seems the obvious choice and is used to keep today's blimps in the air. An inert gas so safe it's even used as a fire suppressant, it is also – after hydrogen – the second most abundant element in the whole universe.

Admittedly helium is twice as heavy as hydrogen, but because both gases are so much lighter than air, helium still provides 93 per cent of hydrogen's lifting capacity. That drops to about 88 per cent in real-world conditions

OPPOSITE: *USS* Macon *under construction in Akron, Ohio. She and her sistership carried a squadron of five biplane fighters which they launched and recovered in mid-air.*

as it's impossible to guarantee absolute purity, but airship designers still reckoned that every 1000 cubic feet of hydrogen would provide 68 lb of lift compared to helium's 60 lb. Given the relatively small difference, why did airship designers use hydrogen at all?

The existence of helium wasn't confirmed until 1895, when a small sample was produced from Norwegian uranium ore. The amount wouldn't have lifted a paper bag, and manned hydrogen balloons had already been flying for over a century. So when Count Ferdinand von Zeppelin flew his 410-foot-long airship *LZ1* in 1900, no consideration was ever given to using anything but hydrogen. For all practical purposes, helium might as well not have existed.

It wasn't until 1903 that substantial quantities of helium were found in natural gas reserves beneath the American Great Plains. Extracting it took time, though, and by 1921 US gas fields had produced just 200,000 cubic feet of helium – barely enough to fill a couple of Olympic-sized swimming pools.

The Vickers R.100 moored at Cardington, Bedford. With a large formal dining room and a promenade deck she could carry 100 passengers in cruise-ship comfort. She cost £350,000.

By that time, Zeppelin's machines had made their mark. The old count died in 1917 knowing that, until 1916 at least, the British had no defence against the bombing raids that had introduced the First World War to Britain's civilian population. However, the British then started to use incendiary bullets. Hydrogen may have proved to be the Zeppelins' undoing as bombers, but not before they had angered Britain enough to want to kill off the German airship industry.

The United States took a different view. When work began on the US Navy's first rigid airship, USS *Shenandoah*, the design was copied from a German Zeppelin that had been forced down during the First World War. As part of the post-war settlement imposed on Germany, it saw an opportunity to have a brand-new airship built by the world's leading manufacturer. The US Navy, of course, had one major advantage over the Germans, the British and indeed anyone else who wanted to fly airships: it could use helium.

When *Shenandoah* first flew in 1923, her 2.1 million cubic feet of helium that filled gas bags made from the outer membranes of (a lot of) calves' stomachs represented more or less the world's entire supply of the gas. In 1924 the US Navy's new German-built airship, USS *Los Angeles*, crossed the Atlantic filled with hydrogen that was later replaced with recycled helium from the emptied *Shenandoah*. There still wasn't enough helium available to run two airships.

The transatlantic delivery flight of the new airship made Dr Hugo Eckener, the head of the Zeppelin company, a celebrity. In the USA President Calvin Coolidge held a reception for him at the White House. At home a newspaper described him as 'Germany's greatest and only diplomat'.

The British seemed to have an ambivalent view of the airship (despite being first to cross the Atlantic in one when His Majesty's Airship R34 crossed east to west and back again in 1919), perhaps as a result of it falling between the two stools of navy and air force. But Eckener's success even appeared to stir London into action. In 1924 the Imperial Airship Scheme was proposed to provide better transport and communications between the countries of the British Empire. Initially, two designs were signed off: one, the R100, to be built by private industry; the other, the R101, to be built by the government-owned Royal Airship Works. Both would be bigger than any airship yet built anywhere in the world. Both would offer lavish multi-deck passenger accommodation that had more in common with a luxury liner than with aviation. And they were both deliberately innovative. There, though, the similarity ends.

The Vickers R100, designed by Barnes Wallis (who during the Second World War built the bouncing bomb of Dam Busters legend), was a beautiful piece of engineering, elegantly simple and therefore light for its size and easy to maintain. In July 1930, despite encountering violent storms en route, the R100 made a record-breaking journey to Canada and back.

On the other hand, the government-built R101 was an overcomplicated dog, half-baked and underpowered. Prematurely granted a Certificate of Airworthiness, she was dispatched to India before the necessary flight-testing was complete. Eight hours after take-off she crashed in northern France, killing forty-eight of the fifty-four people on board. Hydrogen ensured that she was immediately consumed by fire. Britain took fright, cancelled and scrapped the exceptional R100, and walked away from airships for good.

By contrast, the loss of the USS *Shenandoah* in a storm in 1925 did nothing to dampen American enthusiasm for the airship. Of the forty-five people on board, twenty-nine survived the break-up of the ship, riding to the ground on sections still buoyant with gas. Encouragingly, none were killed by fire. Consequently, in 1928, the Goodyear-Zeppelin company began work on two vast new airships for the US Navy.

At the time of their contraction the USS *Akron* and USS *Macon* were the largest airships in the world. Capable of staying aloft for a week to scout for enemy ships, they also carried a 'heavier-than-air unit' of fixed-wing fighter planes in an internal hangar, which allowed them to extend the range of their search and defend themselves from attack. Lowered through an opening in the airship's belly in order to launch, the little blue and yellow Curtiss Sparrowhawk biplanes returned by hooking back on to the 'trapeze'. Brilliant!

Sadly, it was too good to be true. In fleet exercises the airships, fighters or not, were judged to be getting shot down with alarming regularity. And by the end of 1935 both airships had crashed at sea. Of *Akron*'s seventy-six crew, only three survived the cold of the North Atlantic. There had been no lifejackets on board. Two years later, lesson learned, just two of *Macon*'s crew died. With their loss, the airship became, as one historian put it, 'the first twentieth-century weapons system to pass into oblivion'.

For Germany, now the only country still in the airship business, it was clear 'noble gas' should be used instead of hydrogen. Since 1928, Dr Eckener's 'dream machine' *Graf Zeppelin* had been giving airships a good name. She had circumnavigated the globe, flown to the Arctic and established a regular transatlantic passenger service to Brazil. Buoyed with confidence, Eckener began work on the largest flying machine the world had ever seen

– the behemoth called *Hindenburg*, which he planned to fill with helium. Unfortunately for him, the United States – still the world's only supplier of helium – had passed the Helium Control Act in 1927, which banned the export of their rare, precious gas. With a heavy heart, Eckener was forced to fill *Hindenburg* with hydrogen instead.

You can't credit Adolf Hitler with being right about much, but when it came to the Zeppelins, sadly, he hit the nail on the head:

> *The whole thing always seems to me like an inventor who claims to have discovered a cheap new kind of floor covering which looks marvellous, shines for ever and never wears out. But he adds that there is one disadvantage. It must not be walked on with nailed shoes and nothing hard must ever be dropped on it because, unfortunately, it's made of high explosive.*

The tragedy is that the awesome *Hindenburg* was supposed to be different, yet her destruction became the airship's defining image.

Hindenburg over Manhattan. She remains the biggest flying machine ever built but is remembered for the terrifying fireball that prompted radio reporter Herbert Morrison to cry, 'Oh, the humanity . . .'

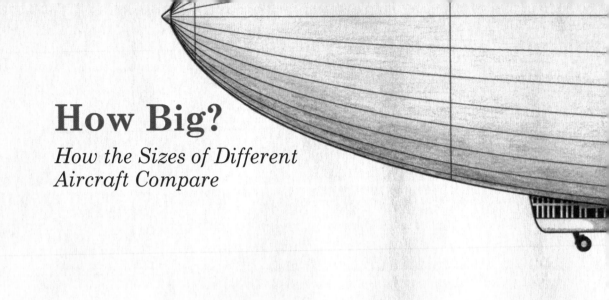

How Big?

How the Sizes of Different Aircraft Compare

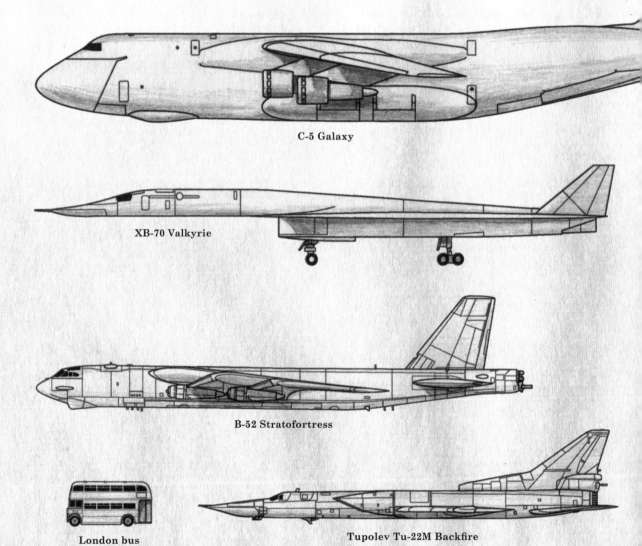

C-5 Galaxy

XB-70 Valkyrie

B-52 Stratofortress

London bus

Tupolev Tu-22M Backfire

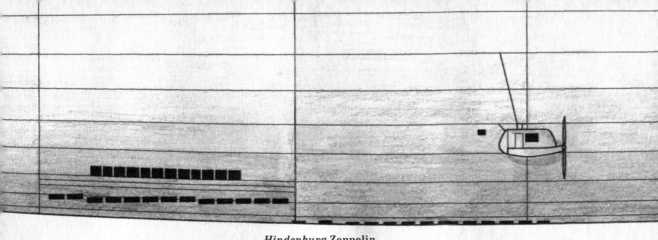

Hindenburg Zeppelin

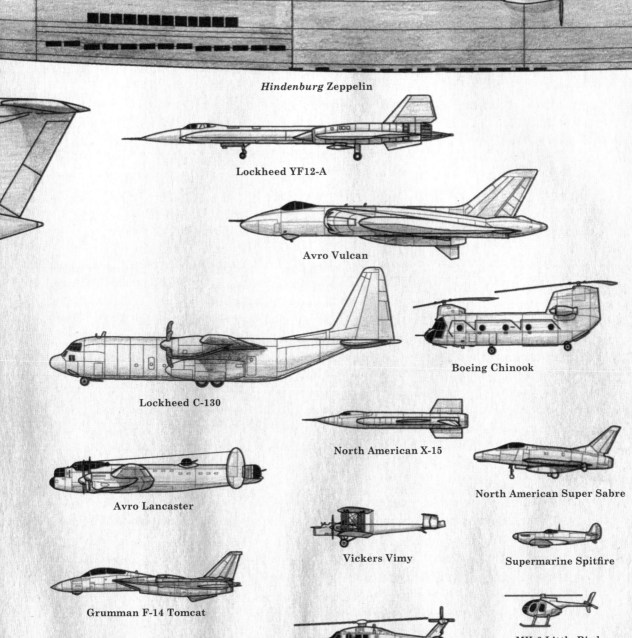

Lockheed YF12-A

Avro Vulcan

Lockheed C-130

Boeing Chinook

North American X-15

North American Super Sabre

Avro Lancaster

Vickers Vimy

Supermarine Spitfire

Grumman F-14 Tomcat

Sikorsky Blackhawk

MH-6 Little Bird

Lockheed Martin F-22 Raptor

Fokker triplane

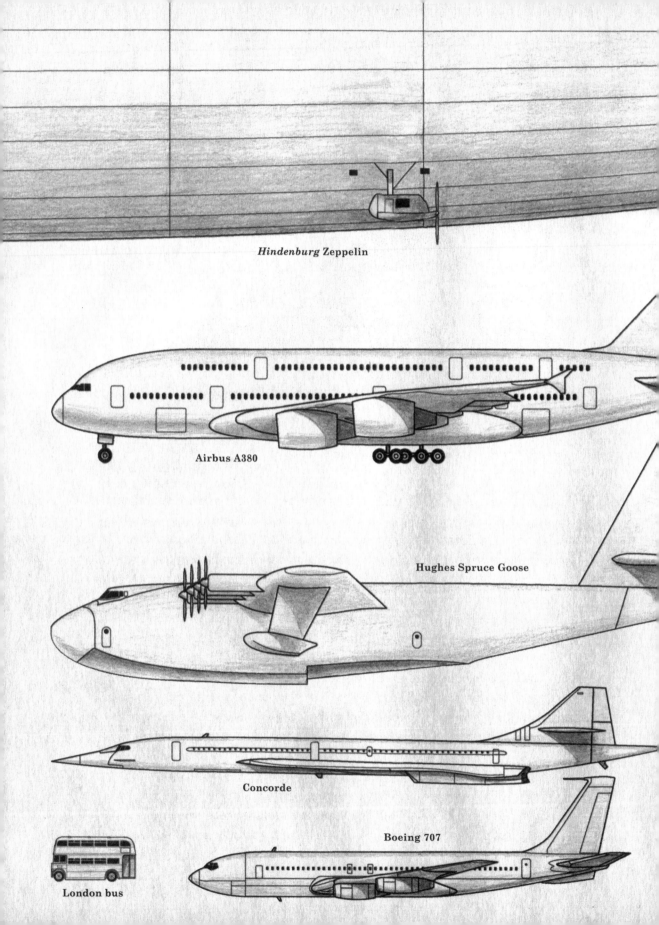

Hindenburg Zeppelin

Airbus A380

Hughes Spruce Goose

Concorde

Boeing 707

London bus

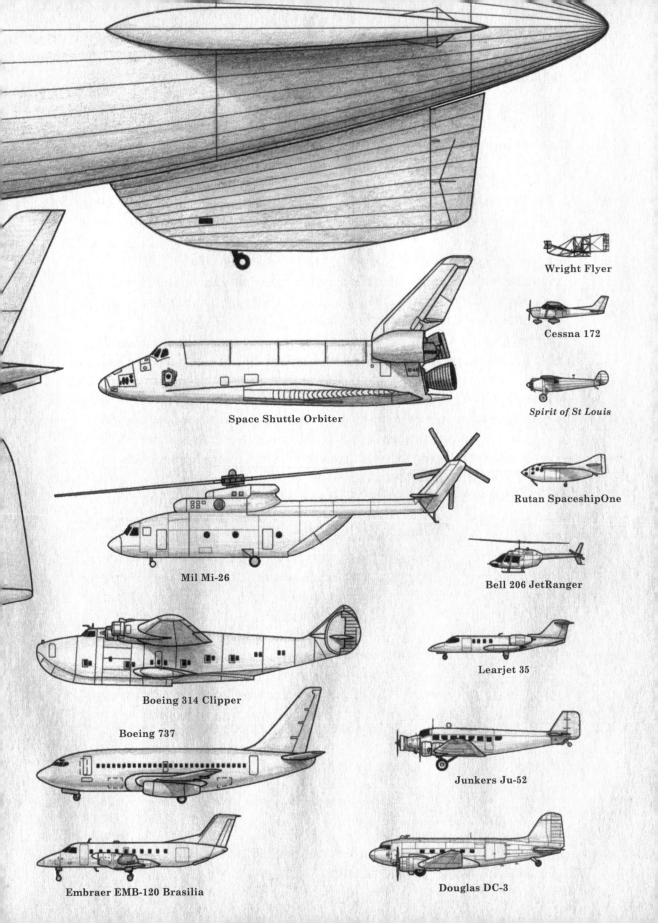

Wright Flyer

Cessna 172

Spirit of St Louis

Rutan SpaceshipOne

Space Shuttle Orbiter

Mil Mi-26

Bell 206 JetRanger

Boeing 314 Clipper

Learjet 35

Boeing 737

Junkers Ju-52

Embraer EMB-120 Brasilia

Douglas DC-3

The Wind Beneath My Wings
The Story of Gliding

We learned how to glide long before we learned to fly. By launching themselves from high ground, nineteenth-century pioneers such as George Cayley, Otto Lilienthal and the Wright brothers offered a tantalizing glimpse of what lay ahead. Yet although the ability to glide predates powered flight, ultimately it took much longer to develop.

After demonstrating powered flight, Orville and Wilbur Wright continued to improve their gliding skills, but it took until 1921, two years after powered aircraft had first crossed the Atlantic, for their 1911 endurance record of 9 minutes and 45 seconds to be broken in Germany. There was good reason for it happening where and when it did. That gliding was once more enjoying the attention of some of aviation's best minds and most talented flyers was a happy unforeseen consequence of the Treaty of Versailles (a less happy one being the Second World War).

Banned by the treaty from developing fighter aircraft, German designers turned their considerable skill and invention to the development of gliders. It led to a boom. Over the next two decades, increasingly sophisticated glider design advanced with a greater understanding of the ways in which gliders could find lift. To ascend, a glider, always losing height, must do so through a body of rising air. Early glider pilots had realized that wind scooped up the side of a hill produced ridge lift at the top, and this was used for most early endurance flights. By the mid-1930s, thermal lift – found in columns of rising warmer air, and wave lift – created in the lee of the steady flow of wind over a mountain, were also contributing to record-breaking flights. In 1931 new records for distance (169 miles) and endurance (23 hours and 34 minutes) were set, the latter in Hawaii by a US Army fighter pilot.

By 1937 there were 50,000 trained glider pilots in Germany. And as a result of German lobbying following the inclusion of gliding as a demonstration sport in the 1936 Berlin Olympics, it was to be included in the 1940 Tokyo Olympics. Of course, owing to the outbreak of the Second World War, Germany's hopes

OPPOSITE: *The most efficient modern gliders have a glide ratio of 50:1 or more, meaning they can travel as far as 50 feet forward for every single foot of altitude they lose. By contrast, a 747 airliner manages a glide ratio of about 15:1, a Cessna 172 about 9:1 and the Space Shuttle, which had to glide in after every mission, just 6:1.*

ABOVE: *The cover of a brochure, produced for the 1936 Berlin Olympics, that describes the inclusion of gliding as a demonstration sport.*

of winning gold in the specially produced 'Olympia' glider were never realized. War, however, brought its own momentum to glider development.

Before the war the Soviet Union had embraced gliding as enthusiastically as Germany, and by 1939 had a greater number of glider pilots and most of the sport's world records. Since the early 1930s, it had also developed larger military gliders as troop transports, an idea quickly adopted by the Luftwaffe, which in 1940 launched a completely successful surprise attack against a Belgian fortress using over forty ten-man gliders. The Allies soon developed their own gliders, and during Operation Market Garden at Arnhem in 1944 used over 2500 in a massive airborne operation. As well as being built by aircraft manufacturers, US Waco CG-4 gliders used in the assault had also been produced by cabinet-makers, coffin-builders and piano manufacturers.

After the war, only the Soviet Union persisted with military gliders with any great enthusiasm, keeping them in service until the mid-1960s and even, in April 1954, landing four Yakovlev Yak-14s on the Arctic ice to deliver men and supplies – including a bulldozer! – to their North Pole drift station. But with the arrival of bigger and better military helicopters, gliding returned to its civilian roots.

Stimulated to a degree by large numbers of trained pilots leaving the military who wanted to continue to fly, membership of gliding clubs swelled throughout the 1950s, while technological innovation saw new records set. The altitude record, set by Steve Fossett and Einar Enevoldson in 2006, now stands at over 50,000 feet. The two pilots, looking like astronauts, wore full USAF pressure suits for the attempt.

The distance record of over 1400 miles is held by a German pilot, Klaus Ohlmann, and today Germany remains at the heart of gliding, leading the way in both manufacturing and pilot numbers, accounting for nearly a quarter of the world's flyers.

It's an intriguing legacy of decisions made nearly a century earlier, and evidence that gliding, that most pure and unbelligerent form of manned flight, is in its own way as inextricably linked to the history of conflict as any other.

BELOW: *Essentially disposable, the Yakovlev Yak-14 (known as 'Mare' to NATO) was often the only way of carrying heavy loads to remote parts of the Soviet Union throughout the 1950s.*

G-AHCZ

BRIT...

Great Planes

Douglas DC-3

Maybe the greatest of all time? Certainly in terms of its impact. The Douglas DC-3 was arguably more important to victory in the Second World War than any fighter, bomber, tank or warship. And don't just take my word for it. That was D-Day commander General Eisenhower's view. But in addition, it was also the aircraft that ushered in the modern era of mass air travel. So it won the Second World War and was the first modern airliner. What more do you need? Oh, all right then: it's still flying and working today, and will be for decades.

First flight: December 1935
Principal operator: TWA (followed by the *entire world's* air forces and airlines)
Last operational flight: Still in service

MURRAY

Eye in the Sky

The Story of Aerial Reconnaissance

On 1 August 1798, Rear Admiral Sir Horatio Nelson routed the French fleet in the Battle of the Nile. Ashore, a French Army officer, Captain J.-M.-J. Coutelle, was powerless to help. Nelson's attack had come before he and his company of *aérostiers* had been able to unload and deploy their observation balloons.

Had they had time to unpack, Coutelle, the world's first military aviator, might have been able to provide advance warning of the attack. Instead, the French defeat dramatically shifted the balance of naval power in the Mediterranean in favour of the Royal Navy. Coutelle's pioneering unit was disbanded the following year, despite his successful contribution to the battles of Fleurus and Sprimont four years earlier. But it had been a start.

The key to any military victory is intelligence. And spies in the sky, from balloons to satellites, became one of the very best ways of providing it.

Over the century that followed Coutelle's first mission, developments in aerial reconnaissance were slow. Experiments were carried out attaching cameras to kites, artillery shells, rockets and even pigeons, but the balloon remained the most practical method of seeing over the horizon. That changed in the early years of the twentieth century.

'We believe that the principal use of a flyer,' wrote Orville Wright four years after he became the first person to achieve powered flight, 'at present is for military purposes.' It was the Italian army that, in 1912, first put Wright's theory to the test.

Fighting the Turks for control of what is now Libya, Italian airmen were the first to fly aeroplanes in war, the first to take aerial photographs from a fixed-wing aircraft, and the first to film enemy positions, which they did from an airship.

When Britain's Royal Flying Corps (RFC) came into existence the same year, reconnaissance was their top priority. However, two years later, when the First World War began, they were still not particularly good at it. When discoloured roads were recorded as columns of troops, and tombstones as

OPPOSITE: *A print celebrating the world's first air force, the French* aérostiers *and their balloon,* L'Entreprenant *or* Enterprise. *The image at the bottom right shows soldiers varnishing a balloon at the School of Military Ballooning.*

TRANSPORT DE L'ENTREPRENANT
DE MAUBEUGE À CHARLEROI

LE COMMANDANT COUTELLE

COMITÉ DE SALUT PUBLIC
13 Germinal An II.

CRÉATION DE L'ÉCOLE DE MEUDON

ÉCOLE DE MEUDON, VERNISSAGE DES BALLONS

LES AÉROSTIERS DE LA PREMIÈRE RÉPUBLIQUE

enemy positions, army commanders on the ground were probably right to treat the RFC's intelligence with a pinch of salt.

By the end of the war, however, the situation could not have been more different. Dedicated photographic reconnaissance units had been set up – French success informing British efforts – and new technology and techniques were developed. A massive, continually updated aerial map of the Western Front kept tabs on German movements.

For some pilots it all seemed to lack the cut and thrust of flying fighters. One pilot compared photo-reconnaissance to 'the routine of going to the office daily, the aeroplane being substituted for the suburban train. The officer does his daily job and goes home; the board sit in debate over the profit and loss account.'

As it turned out, he was almost completely wrong. It was often recce pilots who flew the most interesting, dangerous and daring missions of all – a fact another First World War aviator understood only too well.

Sidney Cotton was a maverick. Born in Australia, he came to Europe in 1915 to fight and fly after the sinking of the *Lusitania*. After a clash with his superiors, he left the Royal Naval Air Service in 1917. For the next twenty years he flew and raced cars. He also developed a photographic company, but by 1938 the business was stumbling. That was when he got a call from MI6. Using business trips as cover, Cotton began to fly secret photo-reconnaissance sorties over Germany in a modified Lockheed 12A Electra. Under the noses of – and sometimes in the company of – senior German military figures, including the deputy führer, Reichsmarschall Hermann Goering, he recorded the build-up of the Nazi war machine.

Cotton's was the last civilian aircraft to leave Berlin before war was declared. Arriving back in Britain after overflying German bombers that were en route to Poland, Cotton told British Customs where he had just flown in from. 'Left it a bit late, haven't you?' came the reply. Just a month later, Cotton had been commissioned into the RAF and was running a dedicated reconnaissance unit flying a pair of camera-carrying Spitfires.

A former commander-in-chief of the German Army had claimed: 'The next war will be won by the military organization with the most efficient photographic reconnaissance.' And throughout the Second World War, Allied units like Cotton's proved crucial, discovering evidence of German radar sites, the Italian fleet in harbour at Taranto, and production of V1 and V2 rockets, as well as mapping the Normandy

The British de Havilland Mosquito was used as a spyplane by both the Royal Air Force and the US Army Air Force. Made of wood, in 1941 it was the world's fastest operational aircraft. 'When I see a Mosquito,' said Herman Göring, head of the Luftwaffe, 'I turn green and yellow with envy.'

beaches in advance of the D-Day landings. Flying alone and unarmed, pilots relied on speed, height and camouflage to protect themselves. Alongside RAF Spitfires, the USAAF flew Spitfires of its own in the photo-reconnaissance role, next to homegrown Lockheed P-38 Lightnings. But it was the wooden-built de Havilland Mosquito that, for both the British and Americans, proved to be the outstanding photo-reconnaissance platform of the war.

Despite the vital contribution made by Allied reconnaissance squadrons to winning the Second World War, it was during the Cold War that spyplanes took centre stage. Height, speed or a combination of the two remained the spyplanes' only defence. Although Spitfires continued to fly operational reconnaissance missions for the RAF until well into the 1950s, soon after the war new jet designs emerged. Overflights of both the Soviet Union and China were authorized, and between 1952 and 1955 American and British crews flew RB-45 Tornados, RB-47 Stratojets and Canberras deep into Soviet airspace.

They were not made welcome and a number returned to base damaged by enemy fire. 'What did you think they would do?' USAF General Curtis LeMay asked one crew member who'd told of how enemy fighters had tried to shoot him down, 'Give you an ice cream cone?'

Even as crews risked their lives over the Soviet Union, in America, in conditions of absolute secrecy, a new aircraft was being developed that it was hoped would place them out of harm's way. Instead, the Lockheed U-2 found itself at the centre of the most famous spy-in-the-sky story of all.

The Lockheed U-2 was essentially a jet-powered glider designed to fly at heights of over 70,000 feet – or twice the height at which today's jet airliners cruise. At this height it was supposedly out of reach of both enemy fighters and missiles. But on 1 May 1960, CIA pilot Francis Gary Powers was shot down over Russia. By nightfall he was a prisoner in Moscow's infamous Lubyanka prison, the home of the KGB.

Two years later American spyplanes were taking pictures of a threat that was rather closer to home. While RF-101 Voodoo and RF-8A Crusader reconnaissance jets streaked low over Cuba to monitor the build-up of Soviet

OPPOSITE: *When a CIA U-2 was shot down over Russia, the US painted NASA on the tail of another U-2 in an effort to pretend it was just a civilian research plane that had wandered off course. The game was up when the Soviet Union revealed they'd captured the pilot. The jet remains the archetypal spyplane.*

missiles, U-2s flying high overhead made it a belt-and-braces effort. Then, on 27 October 1962, another U-2 was shot down and her pilot killed. While a combination of judgement, restraint and excellent intelligence provided by the recce pilots allowed President John F. Kennedy to face down and defuse the Cuban Missile Crisis, it was clear that America needed a machine that could outperform the U-2. Fortunately, it already had one.

For six months an extraordinary machine called the Lockheed A-12, code-named 'Oxcart', had been conducting flight tests from an airfield called Groom Lake, a secret facility also known as Area 51, which the US government still does not acknowledge exists (although the speed with which an internet search for Groom Lake, Nevada, brings up something that looks a lot like a secret airbase suggests the cat's out of the bag). Designed and built for the CIA by the team behind the U-2, the A-12 was like nothing else in the sky.

Capable of flying at more than three times the speed of sound and at an altitude of over 80,000 feet, the A-12's construction relied on the unwitting cooperation of the enemy she was designed to keep in check. The heat generated by flying at such high supersonic speeds meant that conventional aluminium construction was out of the question. To avoid melting from her own top speed, the A-12 was over 85 per cent titanium. As it happened,

the best-quality titanium came from the Soviet Union, so, using a front company to disguise its true purpose, the CIA acquired all it needed to build its revolutionary jet.

In 1965, a development of the A-12 called the YF-12A seized the world air speed record back from the USSR with a top speed of over 2070 mph. This was broken again in 1976 by the ultimate A-12 model, the legendary SR-71A Blackbird. The record – 2193 mph or Mach 3.3 (3.3 times the speed of sound) – still stands.

Top secret. The Lockheed A-12 Oxcart takes off from Groom Lake on an early test flight in April 1962. This remarkable machine, and the SR-71 Blackbird it spawned, remain the high watermark in high-performance jet aircraft.

But this was by no means as fast as she could fly. And one crew, detecting missile launches during a mission over Libya in 1986, took her to a speed of Mach 3.5 as they made their escape.

For thirty years spacesuited aircrews flew their black jet over the Baltic, North Vietnam, Cambodia, Laos, Lebanon, Yemen, Egypt, Syria, Iran, Cuba, Nicaragua, North Korea, China, South Africa, Bosnia and even the Falkland Islands. And despite being fired on nearly 4000 times, no Blackbird was ever shot down.

The USAF, however, didn't quite have a monopoly on remarkable reconnaissance missions. Between 1971 and 1972, Soviet MiG-25 Foxbats were recorded flying over Israeli-held Sinai at heights of up to 75,000 feet, and on one occasion at a speed of Mach 3.2. The trouble was that the Foxbat's engines weren't up to it. One run at this speed destroyed them, leaving them good for nothing but scrap. The Blackbird, on the other hand, could do it over and over again.

But the days of dedicated reconnaissance jets have gone the way of the Cold War itself. Perhaps they needed each other. After being retired, brought back and then retired again, the Blackbird was gone by 1998. The RAF's high-flying Canberra PR9s went to war one last time in 2006 in Afghanistan, nearly fifty years after joining the air force, and were then retired. Delta-winged French Mirage IVs went the year before that. And the MiG-25 Foxbat is all but gone from squadron service. Only the U-2 remains in military service – and, with unmanned drones snapping at its heels, only by the skin of its teeth. It's now an anachronism.

Satellites, unmanned drones and multi-role fighters carrying cameras and sensor pods have nearly made the dedicated high-altitude reconnaissance jet redundant. Nearly, but not completely.

A single pair of big-winged RB-57F Canberra reconnaissance jets, descendants of a British design that first flew in 1949, remain in the service of NASA. Their day job includes – *seriously* – collecting 'cosmic dust'. But every so often one of them, stripped of serial numbers and NASA markings, travels east from its home base in Houston, Texas, to Kandahar, Afghanistan. And once there, it does what spies in the sky have always done – it gathers information that keeps its side out in front.

Aerial reconnaissance is as important now as it was when Coutelle's company of *aérostiers* first took to the sky in their balloons over two centuries ago.

REPUBLIC XF-12 RAINBOW
High-speed, high-altitude reconnaissance

In an age of satellites, GPS and Google Maps it's easy to lose sight of just how difficult it used to be to know what was going on beyond the horizon. It was a particular problem for US military commanders fighting Japanese forces in the Pacific during the Second World War. They simply had no means of knowing what the enemy was up to. As early as 1943 there were plans to use long-range bombers flying out of India and China against the Japanese mainland, but they had no reconnaissance aircraft with the range to get there and back, nor the speed and high-altitude capability necessary to stay out of trouble if they could. So they asked US manufacturers for a machine that could do it all.

In response, Republic Aviation, the company behind the butch-looking P-47 Thunderbolt, came up with one of the most beautiful aircraft ever designed. Perfectly streamlined and elegantly proportioned, Republic's XF-12 Rainbow looked like a step into the future.

Its performance too was every bit as good as it looked. Hauled through the air by four hugely powerful Pratt & Whitney Wasp Major turbo-supercharged radial piston engines each capable of generating 3500 horsepower, the Rainbow could outrun most contemporary fighters.

The trouble was, when the prototype Rainbow was revealed in December 1945, the USAAF no longer had the same pressing need to spy on Japan. Fortunately, the maker had designed it with a view to converting it for commercial air travel. After all, what could be more prestigious for an airline than flying what was, in effect, the Concorde of its day? Both Pan Am and American Airlines placed orders, but in the austere times that followed the war, passengers and airlines were prepared to forgo speed and exclusivity, so bigger, slower, cheaper rivals, such as the Douglas DC-6, cleaned up. Not a single Rainbow airliner was ever built.

The XF-12 remains the fastest four-engined piston-engined aircraft ever built and the only one capable of exceeding 450 mph in level flight. But just like Concorde she turned out to be the wrong bet.

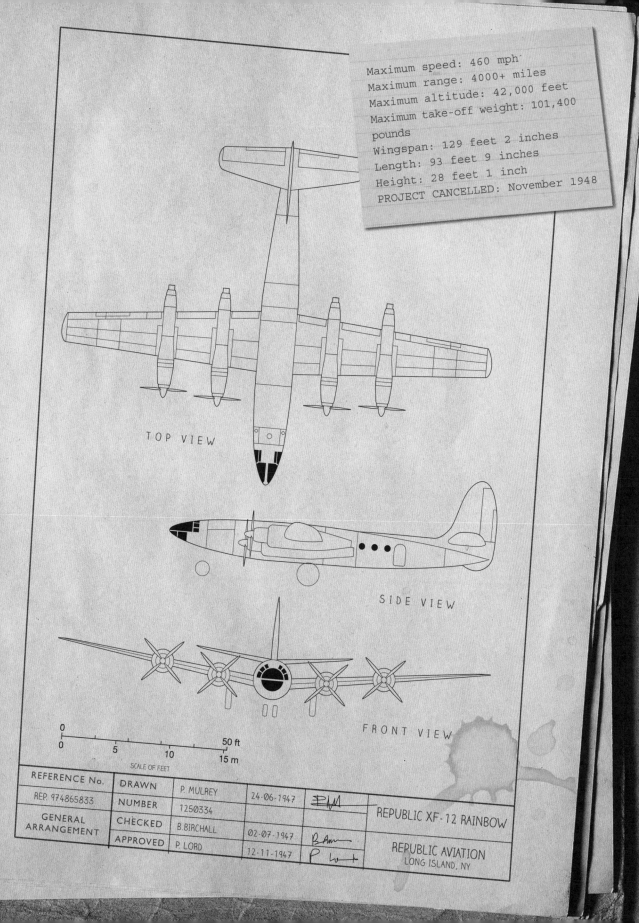

Maximum speed: 460 mph
Maximum range: 4000+ miles
Maximum altitude: 42,000 feet
Maximum take-off weight: 101,400 pounds
Wingspan: 129 feet 2 inches
Length: 93 feet 9 inches
Height: 28 feet 1 inch
PROJECT CANCELLED: November 1948

TOP VIEW

SIDE VIEW

FRONT VIEW

0
0   5   10   15 m
                              50 ft
SCALE OF FEET

REFERENCE No.	DRAWN	P. MULREY	24-06-1947	P.M.	REPUBLIC XF-12 RAINBOW
REP. 974865833	NUMBER	1250334			
GENERAL ARRANGEMENT	CHECKED	B. BIRCHALL	02-07-1947	B.Am	REPUBLIC AVIATION
	APPROVED	P. LORD	12-11-1947	P.Lord	LONG ISLAND, NY

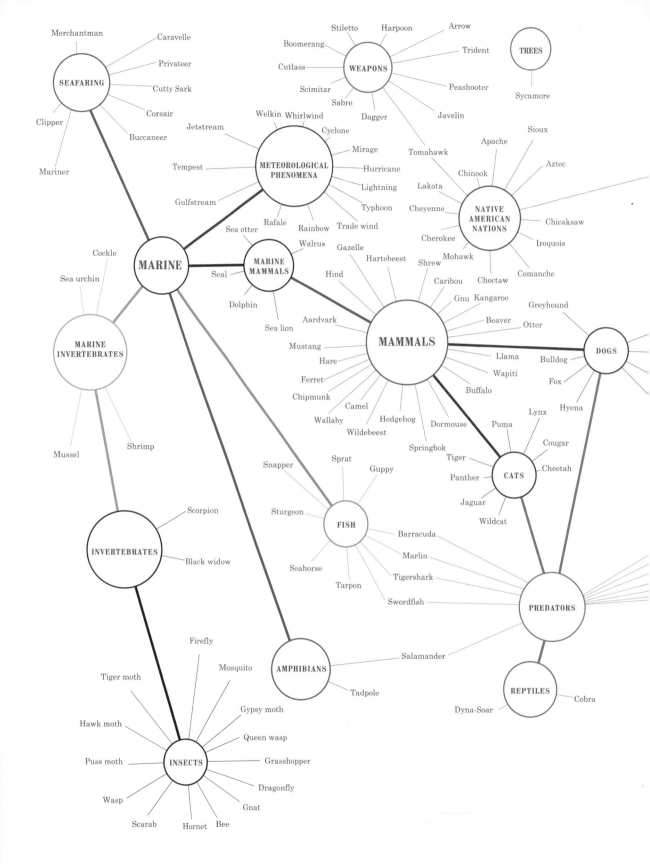

88   Animal, Vegetable or Mineral?

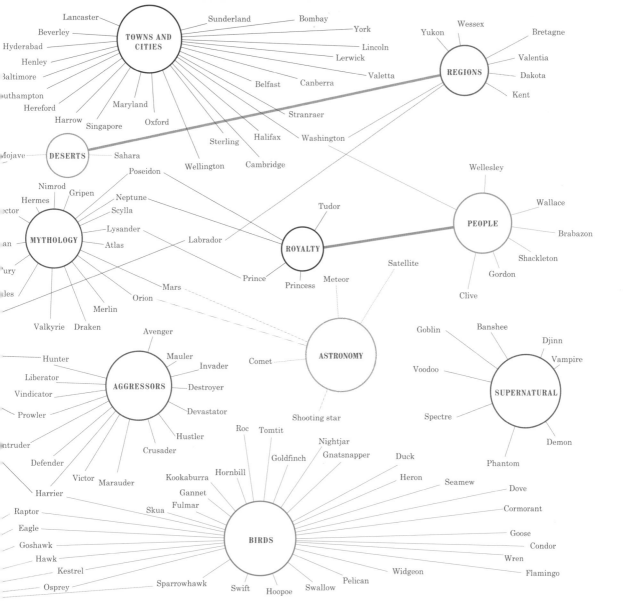

Animal, Vegetable or Mineral?

A Few Things Aircraft Have Been Named After

There seems to be almost nothing that manufacturers won't name aircraft after. The graphic above is a nowhere near comprehensive collection that will give a flavour of the wide variety of names used. There are obvious sources of inspiration. I've barely scratched the surface of the number of birds' names used. But you'll also see just how random some of the choices have been. I mean, when you haven't used up all the birds in the world, let alone all the birds of prey, why go for the Gnatsnapper?! Then, when you're out of birds, it would surely be a long time before Gnu made it on to anyone's shortlist. You'd think. And, honestly, what were Short Brothers thinking when, in 1926, they decided to bless their new monoplane racer with the name of a shellfish and call it the Mussel?

Corsairville

The Rise and Fall of the Flying Boat

Just five years after Alcock and Brown crossed the Atlantic in a wood and fabric biplane, new designs, such as the Dutch Fokker F.VII and the similar, all-metal Ford Trimotor, made their aircraft look like a relic from a bygone age. The new models were monoplanes capable of carrying ten passengers in the relative comfort of an enclosed cockpit. It seemed clear that they represented the future of commercial air transport. By the early 1930s American manufacturers were beginning work on designs such as the Boeing 247 and Douglas DC-2, the former usually recognized as the first genuinely modern airliner. Streamlined and sleek, these two aircraft were capable of carrying passengers at speeds of 200 mph.

Such sophisticated designs made the decision by Imperial Airways of London to order eight 100-mph Handley-Page HP.42 biplanes seem extraordinarily reactionary. But there was method in their madness.

Rapid technological advances made bigger, heavier and faster airliners possible, but a by-product of this was that landing speeds also increased. Higher landing speeds required longer, smoother runways, but in 1928, when Imperial issued their specifications for the HP.42, there wasn't a single paved runway in the world. Added to that, Imperial served India, Africa and the Middle East, and were often operating from scrub that had barely been cleared of stones and goats. Flying from rough strips across the British Empire, Imperial Airways simply wasn't able to take advantage of the latest technology. The solution was to take to the water.

A flying boat, minus wheels and with a fuselage shaped like the hull of a speedboat, can land and take off on any stretch of smooth water. If they opted for flying boats, Imperial (and their American counterpart Pan Am, who flew to South America and had designs on longer transoceanic Pacific routes) could build aircraft that were more than a match for the land-based alternatives.

In 1936 Imperial Airways put the beautiful four-engined C-Class Empire flying boat into service. Luxuriously appointed for just twenty-four passengers, the Empire had been built by Short Brothers without first constructing a

OPPOSITE: *Billed by Imperial Airways as 'the most luxurious flying boats in the world', everything about Empire-class service evoked glamour, comfort and style.*

prototype, but it conformed to the old belief that if it looked right, it was right. Capable of 200 mph, it was the fastest flying boat in the world. Each of the elegant silver machines was given a name beginning with 'C', such as *Calypso*, *Caribou*, *Canopus* and *Cleopatra*.

On 14 March 1939, Corsair took off from Lake Victoria in east Africa bound for Juba, 350 miles away in southern Sudan. The journey was scheduled to take a couple of hours, but owing to a piece of faulty navigation equipment, the crew got thoroughly lost and were still flying around four hours after take-off. With just 15 minutes of fuel left in the tanks, there was no option but to land where they could. In a piece of skilful flying, the flying boat's captain – brother of Jack Alcock who, in 1919, had been first to fly non-stop across the Atlantic – put her down gently, only for a submerged rock to tear the hull. In danger of sinking, Alcock gunned the throttles and managed to beach *Corsair* in the thick mud at the side of the river. But which river? It transpired that they'd flown south-west and were in the Belgian Congo, miles from civilization. Nine months later, after a road, a dry dock, a dam and an artificial lake had been built, the repaired *Corsair* was refloated and took off. She left in her wake Corsairville, a settlement built to house the Congolese workers employed to help salvage her.

Lacking really long range, the Empires were designed to leapfrog their way from one destination to the next as they flew from Southampton to Cape Town or Brisbane. This constraint posed a problem for Pan Am's Martin M-130 flying boat on the California to Hawaii route as there were few stops available. Even making it across the Pacific meant carrying no more than eight passengers. Pan Am built just three of these aircraft – *China Clipper*, *Hawaiian Clipper* and *Philippine Clipper* – and while they undoubtedly won the airline prestige, they didn't make it money. What's more, the only commercial transatlantic service that had ever been operated, until the *Hindenburg* blew up in 1937, was by Germany's Zeppelin airships.

In an effort to address the problem of range, Pan Am and Imperial both conducted survey flights across the North Atlantic in 1936. While the Pan Am

flying boat arrived at Foynes in southern Ireland with enough fuel to fly another 1500 miles, the shorter-ranged Imperial C-Class craft had to carry extra fuel tanks just to make it to Newfoundland. By 1939, both airlines took delivery of new flying boats built specially to make the 'water jump'.

Pan Am's giant new Boeing 314 was the biggest airliner in service with any airline in the world, its wings so thick that the flight engineer could crawl through them and make adjustments to the four 1600-horsepower engines in flight. The new Clippers carried twenty-two passengers, looked after by a twelve-man crew. There had never been – nor will there likely ever be again – a more luxurious commercial airline service. The big Clippers, with their distinctive triple tails and the Stars and Stripes emblazoned on the slab sides of their 'hound-dog' nose, were instant icons.

The British machine, Short's G-Class, flew for the first time in July 1939, less than a month after Pan Am's Clippers had started carrying passengers across the Atlantic. It was a similarly impressive machine, just 5 feet shorter in length, but capable of the same speed and range. Recognizably a scaled-up version of the Empire boats, it could fly four times further. Imperial ordered three of them, the first of which, named *Golden Hind*, was delivered at the end of September. In every way, though, it was already too late.

With the outbreak of the Second World War earlier in the month, all three of Imperial's new G-Class flying boats were requisitioned by the Air Ministry and pressed into service for maritime reconnaissance. But the war hastened the end of the big passenger-carrying flying boats more radically and permanently. The writing had been on the wall since 1938, when a new German airliner had flown non-stop from Berlin to New York. It wasn't the range of the Focke-Wulf Fw-200 Condor that threatened the dominance of the British and American flying boats – it was more that she wasn't a flying boat at all.

The ability to land on water meant long-range flying boats could travel more or less anywhere in the world and put down safely. But if the world were to be covered in runways, as happened during the war, landing on

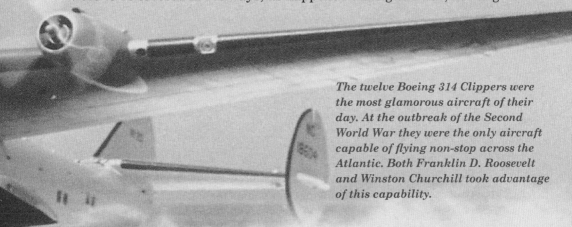

The twelve Boeing 314 Clippers were the most glamorous aircraft of their day. At the outbreak of the Second World War they were the only aircraft capable of flying non-stop across the Atlantic. Both Franklin D. Roosevelt and Winston Churchill took advantage of this capability.

A machine out of time, the big, beautiful Saunders-Roe Princess overflies the 1953 Farnborough Air Show. The two Princess prototypes were eventually broken up and the cockpit of one of them was used, for a while, as an office at a scrap yard.

water no longer offered any kind of advantage. By the end of the war, Britain alone had spent £600 million, the equivalent of about £24 billion today, on airfield construction.

It took just a few years for the idea to sink in that there was simply no need for flying boats any more. Post-1945 saw the emergence of designs that had been started before or during the war. They were often magnificent.

In the United States, billionaire Howard Hughes persevered with what was the largest aircraft ever built. The H-4 was known as the Spruce Goose because of its all-wooden construction (and because 'spruce' rhymed with 'goose', while 'birch', which it was made of, didn't). Hughes hauled the behemoth into the air – just – in 1947 for less than a minute during what was supposed to be a taxi test. I'm pleased he got that incredible beast into the air.

Similarly, I'm happy that French manufacturer Latécoère, when asked to build a transatlantic flying boat in 1939, came up with the enormous, stunningly beautiful six-engined 631, despite the inconvenience of having been invaded. The first prototype was confiscated by Germany. The second 631 was built, dismantled, hidden around Toulouse for the remainder of the war, then assembled once the coast was clear. It flew in March 1945, and immediately after the war was the only French aircraft capable of carrying passengers across the Atlantic so, for reasons of national prestige, flew under the banner of Air France. A crash off Cameroon in 1955 prompted the final retirement of these wonderful-looking, but not entirely safe, machines.

It was the British who seemed most reluctant to let go of the flying boat. The Short Solent first flew in 1946. Although smaller than the 1939 G-Class, she was faster, and in 1948 BOAC's small fleet of Solents took over the three-times-a-week service to Johannesburg. As the silver flying boats, Union flags painted on their tails, accelerated through the swell, it must have seemed to nostalgics that nothing had changed. But the last flight to South Africa was flown in November 1950.

As final as that appeared to be, it wasn't quite the end of Britain's love affair with the flying boat. One British manufacturer, Saunders-Roe, was proclaiming its own vision of the future that seemed reliant on the idea that Britain built wonderful flying boats, so the rest of the world had better get in step.

'Disembarkation into a small craft in choppy water is not a fitting end to a comfortable journey by flying boat,' claimed a Saunders-Roe advertisement. But instead of building an airliner with wheels to make use of all the new wartime runways, they proposed constructing a 'waterdrome' – an airport terminal built around a huge artificial inland lake – and more flying boats. There was simply no telling them.

I'm glad they didn't listen. If their predictions hadn't been so completely wrong, they'd never have built the wonderful Princess. This ten-engined flying boat was genuinely unique, marrying two different generations of aircraft design that the rest of the world regarded as mutually exclusive. Second in size only to Howard Hughes's record breaking H-4, the Princess, even as she was being built, was a magnificent, anachronistic cul-de-sac.

Amazingly, that didn't stop Saunders-Roe thinking about what might follow the Princess, and this took the shape of an elegant design for a six-engined jet flying boat they called the Duchess. She never left the drawing board.

But even that wasn't the end of it. After the Princess was cancelled and the three airframes wrapped in weatherproof cocoons, like a dying millionaire cryogenically frozen in the hope of future revival by as yet undiscovered medical advances, the Saunders-Roe design team were still pitching ambitious new flying boat ideas. The most exotic of them – indeed, about as exotic an aircraft design as there's ever been – was for a 24-engined, V-tailed, four-deck flying boat designed to carry 1000 passengers – that's twice as many as today's A380 Super Jumbo – for the cruise line P&O.

It's easy to mock, but there's something desperately sad about the way Saunders-Roe clung on to the dream. For barely ten years, most of which were disturbed by war, the big flying boats of Pan Am and Imperial Airways represented the very pinnacle of civil aviation. There was a never-to-be-repeated romance about them. The world is a better place for their brief, evocative existence, and in that assessment I include – maybe most of all – the lovely, doomed Saunders-Roe Princess.

From CDG to LAX via LHR
Some of the Better Airport Three-letter Indentifiers

The first man to cross the English Channel carrying both a passenger and an animal was killed on 31 December 1910 when his aircraft crashed in New Orleans. The place where John Moisant broke his neck became a cattle yard and was named Moisant Stock Yards (MSY) in honour of him. When the site was bought for development it retained the name, and in 1962 became New Orleans International Airport. But over 100 years after Moisant's death, his legacy remains – in the airport's three-letter identifier, MSY.

In the early days of flight it didn't matter. There were no airports, just fields. But as the aviation industry grew, so too did the need for organization, bureaucracy and standardization.

Initially, airlines in the United States copied the two-letter codes used by the National Weather Service. But not every city in America provided the weathermen with information. And as the airline industry grew exponentially between the wars, it became clear that something more comprehensive was necessary.

The introduction of three-letter codes provided 17,576 possibilities, and it's often straightforward to see how and why the letters have been assigned – for instance, the first three letters of a city's name – BER/Berlin, CHA/Chattanooga, SYD/Sydney or DUB/Dublin. But it isn't always that simple.

First of all, those cities with weather stations often got to keep their two letters and just had an 'X' tacked on the end. LAX in Los Angeles is one such example.

Sometimes the letters were allocated because of the *name* of an airfield rather than its location. In Paris you have CDG (Charles de Gaulle) and ORL (Orly). Other times, as with London Heathrow (LHR), the letters were drawn from a combination of both name and location. Often, though, as in the case of New Orleans International, it's a little more interesting, and the results more fun. Opposite are a few examples.

AAA The first code on the list belongs, with some justification, to Anaa, a tiny Pacific atoll in French Polynesia.

FAT Fresno Yosemite International Airport used to be Fresno Air Terminal. And although a new code was requested when the name changed, the US Federal Aviation Administration (FAA) declined to alter it.

FFA Officially, this airfield is in Kill Devil Hills, North Carolina, but just to the north is the Kitty Hawk Woods Coastal Reserve, and that reveals the story behind the three-letter identifier. In 1903, the name Kitty Hawk became famous as the site of the Wright brothers' first powered flight. Today, the little airstrip managed by the US National Parks Service is called First Flight Airfield.

HPN White Plains, New York. The letters 'K' and 'W' were originally reserved first letters for radio and television stations, so White Plains simply used its second letter, as does Key West in Florida, which is EYW. For the same reason, Kansas City in Missouri is MKC.

JFK It's actually rare for an airport to change codes, but New York International Airport, which opened on the site of Idlewild Golf Course in 1948, was renamed in honour of John F. Kennedy a month after the president's assassination in November 1963. The FAA quickly sanctioned the code change from IDL to JFK.

NKX This one belongs to the home of 'Top Gun' Naval Air Station Miramar, aka 'Fightertown, USA'. The US Navy was quick to claim 'N' as its own, so a disproportionate number of identifiers beginning with 'N' are US Navy Air Stations, while Newark, New Jersey, was forced to go with EWR.

OGG Kahului airport in Hawaii claims its three letters from Captain Bertram J. Hogg, a local aviation pioneer and the first man to fly a commercial inter-island flight after the Japanese attack on Pearl Harbor.

ORD The world's busiest airport, Chicago O'Hare, was named after local war hero 'Butch' O'Hare, so no clues to the airport code there. But the airport was originally the site of an aircraft factory called Orchard Place, which probably explains things.

SUX Sioux City, Iowa. City officials have twice tried to get the code changed. They made more progress than their counterparts at Fresno, and the FAA offered a number of alternatives. One of them was GAY. Sioux City decided to stick with SUX and embrace it. 'Fly SUX' T-shirts and mugs are now for sale. (Incidentally, GAY now belongs to Gaya in India.*)

YZZ Toronto, Canada. After most first letters had been hoovered up by American airports, Canada got first dibs on the letter 'Y'. Among the many other Canadian cities with 'Y' codes are Montreal (YMX), Vancouver (YVR), Edmonton (YEG), Ottawa (YOW), Big Trout (YTL) and Snake River (YXF). You get the picture.

ZAK 'Z' was often reserved for 'special purposes', so ZCW, for instance, is an air traffic control centre near Washington, DC. But ZAK appears to have been allocated to a bus station in Italy ...

ZZV There is no ZZZ, so Zanesville, Ohio, is the last code in the alphabetical list. However, it is rivalled for 'Z's by Zanzibar, which is ZNZ.

* Other airports that, one imagines, have considered a code change are:
BUM – Butler County Regional Airport, Missouri, USA
VAG – Varginha, Brazil
SEX – Sembach, Germany
PEE – Perm, Russia
POO – Poços de Caldas, Brazil
KAK – Kar, Papua New Guinea
ARS – Aragarcas, Brazil

Great Planes

Supermarine Spitfire

Designer R. J. Mitchell's masterpiece, the Spitfire, is a 1930s aircraft that still looks sleek today. It was the first fighter built for the RAF that was really ahead of the game. Over 20,000 were built, and they put in a war-winning performance. For me, it's those beautiful lines in tandem with the meaty roar of the Rolls-Royce Merlin engine that make it so special. How is it a machine can *move* you?

First flight: 5 March 1936
Principal operator: Royal Air Force
Last operational flight: 1962 (RAF air combat trials against a Lightning F3)

'Never, in the field of human conflict ...'

The Second World War in the Air

Seven years before the outbreak of the Second World War, the British prime minister, Stanley Baldwin, told Parliament, 'It is well for the man in the street to realize that there is no power on Earth that can prevent him from being bombed ... the bomber will always get through.'

And it wasn't as though the powers that be weren't trying to prevent just that. The Air Ministry offered a £1000 prize to anyone who could build a 'death ray' capable of killing a sheep at a distance of 100 yards, but were forced to conclude that such a weapon was beyond the technology of the day. The research, though, led to the discovery that radio energy could be used to bounce back off the surface of an approaching bomber to reveal its position rather than destroy it. Thus was radar born, and it was enthusiastically supported by Air Marshal Hugh Dowding, later head of Fighter Command, which bore responsibility for protecting Britain against the Luftwaffe.

The German Air Force had never faced anything like it. What's more, Dowding's use of radar, combined with central command and control, allowed him to husband his resources, deploying his fighters where they were needed to counter German attacks, rather than maintaining inefficient standing patrols. The two sides were evenly matched until, provoked by British bomber raids against Berlin, the Luftwaffe was ordered to switch its emphasis from attacks on the RAF to the destruction of British cities. It was a decision that saved Britain. The more finite resources of the air force simply didn't have the same capacity to absorb destruction as the nation's cities.

The Royal Air Force believed strategic bombing – that is, attacking the enemy's industrial infrastructure and means to make war – was the route to victory. The problem was that, in the early years of the Second World War at any rate, it wasn't very good at it. If its small, slow Fairey Battles and Bristol Blenheims flew high enough to stay out of reach of German flak, their bombs were hopelessly inaccurate. If brave crews flew low enough to hit the target,

Often overshadowed by the Spitfire, the rugged Hawker Hurricane was a capable fighter plane and accounted for a greater proportion of enemy kills during the Battle of Britain than its faster, more elegant rival.

they got shot down. Capable of launching, at most, around 150 aircraft, Bomber Command simply wasn't capable of making any kind of significant strategic impact, let alone bombing an enemy into submission.

The year 1942 proved to be a turning point. Efforts at precision bombing were abandoned in favour of 'area bombing', in which whole landscapes were smashed. And the entry into service of two new four-engined heavy bombers, the Avro Lancaster and the Handley Page Halifax, finally gave Bomber Command the aircraft it needed to pursue its devastating new approach.

By the summer, fleets of as many as 1000 heavy bombers flew against targets in Germany. More importantly, Bomber Command's new machines and new tactics were reinforced by the arrival in England of the United States Eighth Army Air Force. It led to a round-the-clock bombardment of Germany. By night, the Lancasters and Halifaxes of RAF Bomber Command attacked. By day, formations of US Army Air Force B-17 Flying Fortresses and B-24 Liberators took over. Until the invasion of Italy in September 1943 and D-Day the following year, bombers remained the only means by which the Allies could take the fight to the enemy.

However, it's too easy, when you're the biggest and the best, to underestimate the enemy. And in December 1941 it was clear that both America and Great Britain had severely underestimated Japan. Faced with the overwhelming strength of the US Navy in the Pacific, Japan had been forced to innovate. At a time when the supremacy of the battleship was unquestioned, Japan paid attention to her aircraft carrier fleet. In

The Douglas SBD Dauntless dive-bomber spearheaded the US Navy's crucial victory at the Battle of Midway, destroying or crippling all four of the Imperial Japanese Navy's aircraft carriers.

1941, other countries in the world had devoted much time and thought to developing an effective naval air force. Operating squadrons of modern fighters, dive-bombers and torpedo bombers – Zeros, Kates and Vals – the Imperial Japanese Navy launched a surprise attack against the American fleet at Pearl Harbor on 7 December 1941. And as if this devastating exhibition of naval air power wasn't clear enough, three days later two British ships, HMS *Prince of Wales* and HMS *Repulse*, were sunk by Japanese torpedo bombers.

With the destruction of her battleships, the US Navy now had no choice but to rebuild her Pacific fleet around the aircraft carriers that had escaped the Japanese attack. It set the scene for a series of epic naval battles in which the main offensive weapons used by both Japanese and US forces were not the big guns of their capital ships, but fighters and bombers from their carriers. And at the Battle of Midway, just six months after the attack on

Pearl Harbor, US Navy carriers scored a decisive victory over their Japanese counterparts. Midway was designed by the Japanese to be a conclusive showdown, but two months earlier American intelligence had broken the Japanese Navy codes. This time the US Pacific fleet would not be ambushed, and of the five Japanese fleet carriers sent to Midway, four were destroyed by aircraft from the US carriers (all four had taken part in the attack on Pearl Harbor). Following victory at Midway, American plans to build more battleships were torn up. Instead, by the end of July, she had *131* new aircraft carriers under construction and on order. And let's not forget the air groups. Over 12,000 Grumman F6F Hellcats, 12,000 Vought F4U Corsairs and nearly 10,000 Grumman TBF Avengers were built to fly off them.

Indisputably, the greatest economy on Earth manufactured her way to victory. From turning out fewer than 500 planes in 1939, American aircraft manufacturers began to produce an average of 60,000 a year. On top of this, by the end of 1940 British factories alone were turning out more aircraft than Germany. Despite extraordinary efforts, neither Germany nor Japan could compete.

On day one of Operation Barbarossa, the German invasion of the Soviet Union, the Soviets lost over 1200 aircraft. By mid-August 1941, just two months later, four of the Luftwaffe fighter wings had each destroyed at least 1000 Soviet aircraft. German fighter aces flying Messerschmitt Bf-109s were racking up impossible scores of hundreds of kills. But it wasn't enough. Not even close. The country was too big, the population too large and the winter too cold. The Soviet Union's ability to soak up punishment was too great. After the blitzkrieg advance of 1941, there was stalemate. When, in the summer of 1943, the German army tried once more for a breakthrough, at Kursk, there were 2100 frontline aircraft in support of the tank attack. Against them were 4600 Soviet aircraft and another 2750 in reserve. As well as now possessing outstanding fighters, such as the Yakovlev Yak-9, the Soviet Air Force also had vast numbers of the Ilyushin Il-2 Sturmovik, an extremely rugged, armoured machine designed to provide close air support for ground forces. Low-flying swarms of these heavily armed attack aircraft – alongside what must have seemed to the Germans like limitless numbers of tanks – were integral to the Soviet victory at Kursk.

Effective use of aircraft in support of ground forces had been a blind spot for the Allied forces. In Europe the British and American 'Bomber Barons' – air force leaders, such as Carl Spaatz and Henry Arnold of the USAAF and the RAF's Arthur Harris – were so convinced that strategic bombing alone would win the war, they virtually ignored the need to develop tactical forces

The tough, armoured Ilyushin IL-2 Sturmovik was designed specifically for ground attack. In contrast to the Soviet Union and Germany, Britain and the United States were slow to grasp the importance of close air support for the army.

in support of the fighting on the ground. Instead, it was left to the man commanding the RAF Desert Air Force in North Africa, Air Vice Marshal Arthur Coningham, to work out how to do it. His first task was to patch up relations with the army. Only then could he explain that, like Fighter Command during the Battle of Britain, the Desert Air Force had to be under central command and control rather than at the beck and call of each and every army unit on the ground. Crucial to success was the introduction of fighter-bombers. Dedicated ground-attack aircraft, such as the Junkers Ju-87 Stuka dive-bomber and Il-2 Sturmovik, tended to be slow and vulnerable to enemy fighters. By actually using fighter planes, such as Hurricanes and American Curtiss P-40 Kittyhawks armed with bombs and heavy-calibre guns for close air support, Coningham had a force that could do the job on the ground but also *look after itself*. American forces joined the fight in North Africa in November 1942. By February the following year, they too placed their fighter-bombers under Coningham's command. On 12 May 1943 the war in North Africa was won.

In Europe the Allied strategic bombing campaign had yet to achieve the same objective. While the relentless Allied bombing was soaking up German resources in defence of the Fatherland, German aircraft production had still to reach its peak. The Bomber Barons were, in effect, making the same mistake the Germans had made during the Battle of Britain when they abandoned the fight against the RAF in favour of attacks against British cities. Until the Allies put the Luftwaffe out of action, the war would not be won. So far they'd failed to stop Germany building aircraft. That left either destroying the Luftwaffe in the air or preventing them from taking off in the first place. In 1944 both strategies began to be used in earnest.

When USAAF fighters first escorted American bombers into German airspace, the Luftwaffe high command was in no doubt about its significance. As well as defending the country, German fighters now also had to defend themselves. Initially, Berlin was still beyond the range of American fighters. The bombers had to complete the last – and most dangerous – leg of their journey alone. But when the big Republic P-47 Thunderbolt was joined by the even longer-ranged North American P-51 Mustang – perhaps the war's most complete fighter plane – the game changed. 'When I saw Mustangs over Berlin,' said Hermann Göring, 'I knew the jig was up.' Even more disastrous for the Luftwaffe was a change in Allied tactics. Instead of staying close to the bombers the escort fighter pilots were charged with defending, Mustang pilots were ordered to go on the offensive and actively hunt their Luftwaffe counterparts. The effect was staggering. The Luftwaffe lost 17 per cent of its pilots in a week, 30 per cent in a month and another 30 per cent the following month. In the first six months of 1944, Göring lost 2262 of the 2395 fighter pilots who began the year. Added to that, attacks on Germany's oil production seriously affected its fuel reserves. At the beginning of 1944 she was producing nearly 200,000 tons of aviation fuel a month. By the end it was near zero.

In search of a silver bullet, the Luftwaffe threw cruise missiles, ballistic rockets, V-1s and V-2s, and radical new jet and rocketplane designs, such as the Messerschmitt Me-262 and Me-163, into the fight, but they were simply overwhelmed.

Supported by fighter-bombers, Allied ground forces fought their way east after the D-Day landings. With troops on the ground, Coningham's close air support doctrine proved its worth beyond the North African desert. Over northern Europe, heavily armed P-47s and Hawker Typhoons echoed the success of the Soviet Sturmoviks, while fighter-bombers also attacked precision targets with a success and an accuracy that the advocates of strategic bombing could only dream about.

In the Pacific too a new generation of fighter aircraft was crucial to the success of US Marines fighting a horrifically bloody campaign to recapture islands that were stepping stones towards the Japanese mainland. The distinctive gull-winged Vought F4U Corsair, lugging bombs, rockets and napalm, proved to be as effective against targets on the ground as it was against fighters like the Zero.

While the Allies, spearheaded by the US Navy and US Marine Corps, island-hopped their way towards Japan, above them the US Army Air Force was flying a machine capable of fighting the kind of war the Bomber Barons had always imagined, but never been able to carry out. In the Boeing B-29 Superfortress the USAAF had a bomber that could fly above the flak and beyond the reach of all but a handful of Japanese fighters. Ironically, it was by flying at low level, from islands recaptured in 1944, that the B-29s proved their worth. Against Japanese cities built of wood and paper the US bomber dropped thousands of tons of incendiary bombs, generating firestorms that created their own weather systems. One of the B-29s, flying late in the stream, was whipped up by a powerful thermal from 5000 feet to 12,000 feet, barrel-rolled, then tumbled back down to low altitude. When the pilot finally regained control at 4000 feet, his aircraft was travelling at nearly 500 mph, her damaged wings looking like corrugated iron. The damage done to cities like Tokyo, Osaka and Kobe was appalling. On one night alone 19 square miles of Tokyo was gutted. In six months of fire raids over half a million civilians were killed, nearly as many as had died in over four years of attacks on Germany. But for all the unsustainable devastation

The Boeing B-29 Superfortress represented a quantum leap forward in bomber design when it was introduced in 1944. Used only in the Pacific campaign during the Second World War it went on to remain in frontline service until the 1960s.

of the firestorms, Japan's leaders seemed no closer to surrender. Instead they were planning ahead, hiding away 9000 fighter planes to use for kamikaze suicide attacks against an Allied ground invasion. Unable to win, Japanese Imperial Headquarters made the sacrifice of 100 million people by 'charging the enemy to make them lose the will to fight' their strategy.

It took two air raids, two B-29s and two bombs, and the instant deaths of over 100,000 people, to prevent that greater catastrophe.

The dropping of two atomic bombs on Hiroshima and Nagasaki on 6 and 9 August 1945 allowed the emperor to announce his country's surrender, citing the 'new and most cruel bomb' and its potential to lead to the 'ultimate collapse and obliteration of the Japanese nation'.

In the end it was a numbers game. As some historians have observed, once Germany opened a second front against the Soviet Union, and Japan had forced a reluctant USA into the war with her attack on Pearl Harbor, the industrial strength, resources and manpower available to the Allies made them unbeatable, however long and costly the war might be. I don't disagree, but at the same time I think there were two crucial air battles over the six years of war upon which *everything* that followed was balanced. Both could easily have been lost by the side that won. One lasted four months, the other just two days.

If, in 1940, the Royal Air Force had been defeated in the Battle of Britain, Germany – whether she invaded the United Kingdom or not – would have won the war in Europe and shaped the peace. Two years later, the US Navy won the vital battle at Midway. Had US naval aviators lost this knife-edge fight, had America lost her carriers, it's far harder to imagine any subsequent campaign to dislodge Japanese forces – who'd have won time to consolidate and strengthen their presence across the western Pacific – being successful, whatever industrial advantages America enjoyed.

By the time of the Japanese surrender, military aviation had changed beyond all recognition. The calibre of men who fought the war in the air didn't alter greatly. Men of every nation displayed great courage, skill and, throughout the war, varying degrees of experience. Certainly their tactics evolved and improved over six years. But the revolution was in the machinery available to them. It was a six-year transformation. The war began with biplanes serving in frontline squadrons and ended with jet fighters, precision-guided bombs and ballistic missiles. Virtually all subsequent aviation development, from the jet engine to the moon landings, was forged in the crucible of the Second World War.

Ducks and Drakes and Bouncing Bombs

How Skipping Stones Inspired the Dam Busters

One of the most famous and dramatic air attacks in history took place during the night of 16/17 May 1943. Nineteen Lancaster bombers from 617 Squadron took off from RAF Scampton in Lincolnshire to destroy three German dams. The operation, codenamed CHASTISE, would require enormous skill and courage, and the use of technology not yet combat proven.

The brainchild of a British aircraft engineer named Barnes Wallis, the weapon that was key to the success of the dams raid was a bouncing bomb inspired by the childhood game of ducks and drakes, in which a spinning stone skips across the surface of the water.

Wallis's spherical bomb was expressly designed to attack targets such as hydro-electric dams, or warships hiding in Norwegian fjords, as it would simply bounce over the top of their protective torpedo nets and explode right up against them. This ensured that the blast would be effective, rather than being dissipated by the distance of even a near miss. The very nature of the bomb's arrival would contribute to its accurate delivery and, as a result, its destructive power.

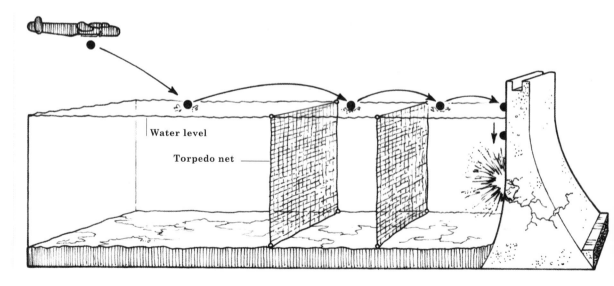

Water level

Torpedo net

The two converging beams of light shining from the bottom of the Lancaster's fuselage were used by the pilot to ensure he flew at exactly the right altitude to drop his bomb.

Delivering Wallis's weapon, though, demanded both great skill and courage. Flying low and straight over the water on their attack run, the Lancasters exposed themselves to withering anti-aircraft fire. Of the nineteen aircraft taking part, eight were lost. Fifty-three men were killed. But the attack succeeded in destroying the Möhne and Edersee dams in the heavily industrialized Ruhr valley, and forced an already overstretched enemy to divert resources it could ill afford to their reconstruction. For his leadership during the raid, Squadron Leader Guy Gibson was awarded the Victoria Cross.

By the time the classic movie about the raid was released in 1955, 617 Squadron was already the most famous unit in the Royal Air Force, known to all simply as the 'Dam Busters'.

It was always with thoughts of the Dam Busters in mind that, as a boy, I forced myself to learn how to skip a stone across the surface of a pond. I'm sure I wasn't alone. And even if the exploits of Guy Gibson and his men are far from the minds of children learning how to play ducks and drakes today, it remains a rite of passage.

Of course, there's now a ducks and drakes world championship. While I always reckoned anything more than four or five bounces was pretty good going, the world record, held by Russell 'Rock Bottom' Byars, stands at fifty-one. Quite a feat, for sure. But, you know, if it's all the same to Mr 'Rock Bottom', I think I'll stick with Guy Gibson for inspiration.

HOW TO SKIM A STONE

1. Look for the smoothest, flattest, most circular stone you can find.

2. Hold the stone like a disc, resting it on your middle finger with your thumb on top, and keeping your index finger curled round the edge. Keep your grip loose. Soft hands are important.

 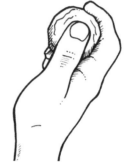

3. Perhaps crouch down a little. Pull your arm back, then chuck the stone using a flick of the wrist. You want to feel as if you're throwing the stone flat, rather than angling it down towards the surface. As you throw, use your index finger to give the stone a tweak to get it spinning horizontally like a discus (or a flying saucer).

4. Ideally – scientific research apparently confirms this! – the stone needs to hit the surface of the water with the front edge angled up 20 degrees above horizontal. This will ensure that it presents its broad, flat underside to the surface of the water, not the narrow leading edge (which will have it diving beneath the surface rather than skipping). The same research has shown that, as satisfying as it is to get the stone spinning as you launch it, spin is less important in multiple bounces than forward speed and angle of attack.

5. Keep practising until you have fifty-one bounces in your sights, then be sure to contact Guinness World Records.

Ducks and Drakes and Bouncing Bombs

Never Coming Home

RAF Losses since 1945

In the European theatre of war during the Second World War, the RAF lost over 22,000 aircraft. It's a horrific number, of course, as it meant the deaths of terrible numbers of airmen, killed in their prime. But we were at war for six years, so despite all the individual tragedies, perhaps the scale of the sacrifice is no surprise. But how many aircraft has the air force lost since then?

In 1991 alone the figure was twenty-two. Of that total, seven were lost during the Gulf War, so perhaps it's unrepresentative. How many, then, have been lost in years since the end of the Second World War? Seven hundred? A thousand? Those estimates might be about right. It was peacetime after all.

In fact, between the end of hostilities in 1945 and the end of the twentieth century the RAF had lost 7419 aircraft and 4850 crew. But after the carnage of the 1940s and 1950s, the number of deaths decreased sharply. It wasn't just that fewer aircraft were being lost – although that was significant; it was also because the widespread introduction of the ejection seat meant that crews had a fighting chance of escape.

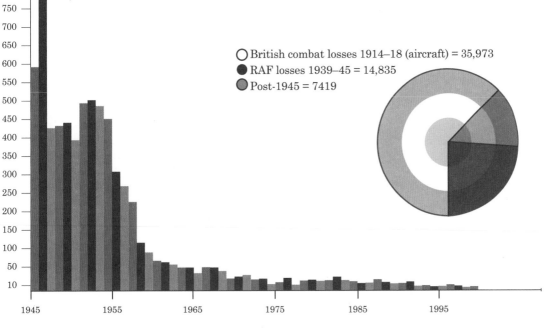

○ British combat losses 1914–18 (aircraft) = 35,973
● RAF losses 1939–45 = 14,835
◐ Post-1945 = 7419

VICKERS VALIANT B2 'PATHFINDER'
Low-level penetration bomber

In 1959 a U-2 spyplane flown by Gary Powers was shot down by a missile over the Soviet Union. It was immediately clear that flying at great altitude offered Britain's V-bombers no protection against enemy defences, so the RAF began training to go in under the radar instead. But the strain of flying in the thicker air at low level led to cracks in the wings of the RAF's Vickers Valiant B1s, and they were quickly retired. The irony is that Vickers had already designed and built an aircraft that was perfectly suited to the switch in tactics.

In 1951, alongside the standard Valiant, the Royal Air Force had ordered a one-off variation on a theme. Based on its experience in the Second World War, the Air Staff wanted an aircraft that could fly ahead of the main bomber force to accurately mark the target. The result was the Valiant B2.

Beefed up to cope with flying fast and low, the Pathfinder was tested over the English Channel at speeds of up to 640 mph. That's comparable to the low-level maximum of the USAF's swing-wing B-1B Lancer, which first flew nearly thirty years later and remains in service today.

Low down at 600 mph, condensation seemed to wrap the Pathfinder in its own whipping, billowing cloud. It added menace to an already imposing presence that the test pilot Brian Trubshaw had been instrumental in creating. When he saw the bomber's muscular shape in the Vickers design office, he signalled his approval, then added: '… and paint the f**ker black'.

Maximum speed: Mach 0.85/640 mph
Maximum range: (at least) 3500 miles
Maximum altitude: (greater than)
54,000 feet
Maximum take-off weight: (greater
than) 140,000 pounds
Wingspan: 114 feet 4 inches
Length: 112 feet 9 inches
Height: 32 feet 2 inches
PROJECT CANCELLED: September 1952
(although production of the sole B2
prototype was allowed to continue)

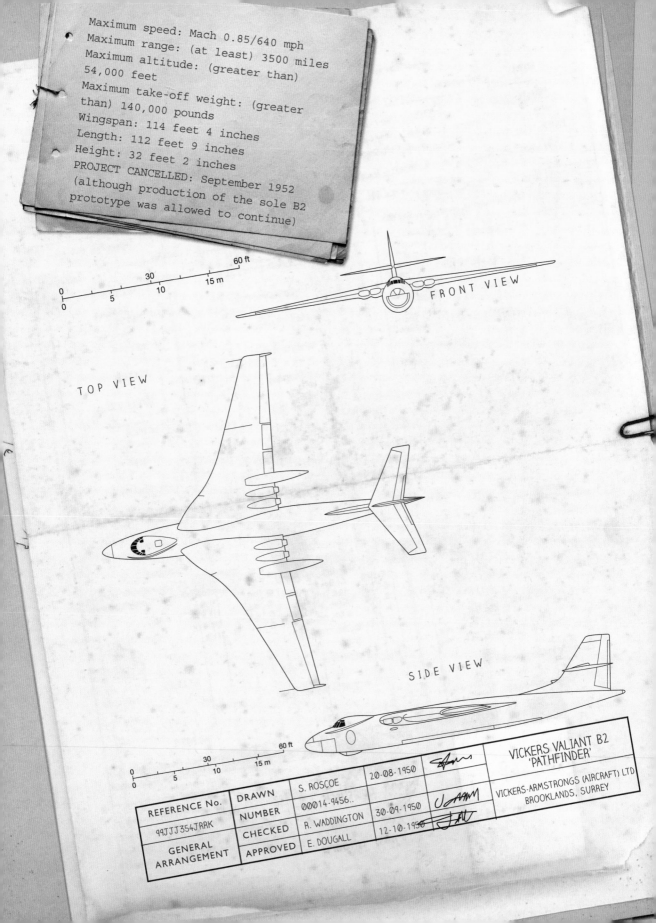

FRONT VIEW

60 ft
30
15 m
10
0
5
0

TOP VIEW

SIDE VIEW

60 ft
30
15 m
10
0
5
0

VICKERS VALIANT B2 'PATHFINDER'			
		20·08·1950	VICKERS·ARMSTRONGS (AIRCRAFT) LTD BROOKLANDS, SURREY
REFERENCE No.	DRAWN	S. ROSCOE	
	NUMBER 00014·9456··		30·09·1950
99JJJ354JRRK	CHECKED	R. WADDINGTON	12·10·1950
GENERAL ARRANGEMENT	APPROVED	E. DOUGALL	

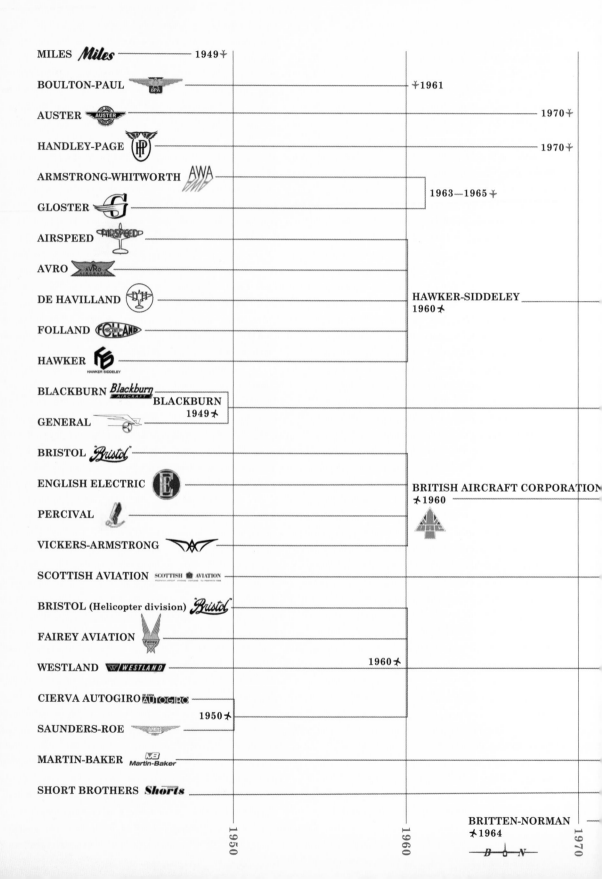

MILES *Miles* ——————— 1949✝

BOULTON-PAUL ————————— ✝1961

AUSTER ————————————————— 1970✝

HANDLEY-PAGE ——————————— 1970✝

ARMSTRONG-WHITWORTH ———

GLOSTER ——————— 1963—1965✝

AIRSPEED

AVRO

DE HAVILLAND ——————— HAWKER-SIDDELEY
1960✈

FOLLAND

HAWKER

BLACKBURN *Blackburn* BLACKBURN
1949✈

GENERAL

BRISTOL *Bristol*

ENGLISH ELECTRIC BRITISH AIRCRAFT CORPORATION
✈1960

PERCIVAL

VICKERS-ARMSTRONG

SCOTTISH AVIATION

BRISTOL (Helicopter division) *Bristol*

FAIREY AVIATION

WESTLAND 1960✈

CIERVA AUTOGIRO
1950✈

SAUNDERS-ROE

MARTIN-BAKER

SHORT BROTHERS *Shorts*

1950   1960   1970

BRITTEN-NORMAN
✈1964

And Then There Were Four

The Disappearance of Britain's Aircraft Manufacturers

At the end of the Second World War, there were over twenty-five aircraft manufacturers dotted around the UK. Some, like Avro and Hawker, or Vickers and Supermarine were already conjoined, but although part of the same group, still built aircraft under their own names.

Despite Hawker Siddeley's acquisition of Avro before the war, for instance, the Vulcan bomber was always the Avro Vulcan. The record-breaking Swift was always the Supermarine Swift, not the Vickers-Armstrong Swift. Some quickly retired from the scene. After the outstanding MB.5 fighter failed to attract an order, Martin-Baker turned its attention to building ejection seats. Miles was wrapped up soon after the cancellation of the promising M.52 supersonic research jet. Even ten years after the war's end, the extraordinary sequence of government-enforced mergers and acquisitions that was on the horizon would have seemed unlikely to those in the industry. But by the mid-seventies, though, there were just four companies still making aircraft in the UK.

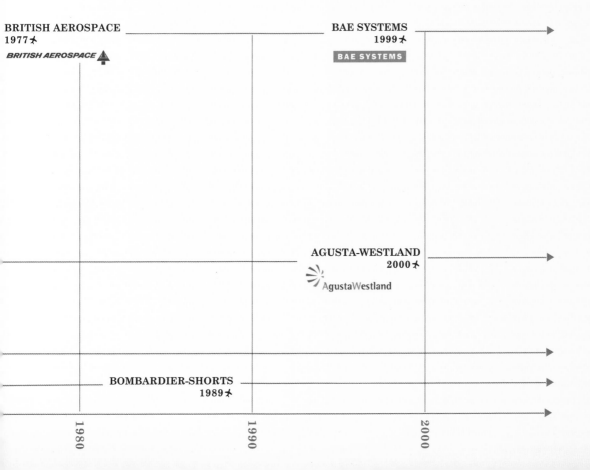

Paper Plane
The Perfect Paper Dart

Just as making the perfect cake requires trial and error, so does creating the perfect paper dart. The design illustrated here is the result of many hours of patient research with my children, including a weekend spent trialling subtly different variations, all flight-tested from one end of the hall to the other (my wife was away). The best of them were chosen for a more advanced test flight programme from an upstairs bedroom window.

A snub-nosed design won the day, offering the required combination of speed, stability and distance. The key is balance, and the heavy folds of paper in the nose, as inelegant as they might look next to your stereotypical needle-nosed dart, proved crucial. The upturned wingtips gave it a more rakish look, and helped make sure it went where we wanted it to. Then we added roundels, tailflashes, shark's mouth and afterburners. The perfect paper dart.

HOW TO DO IT

1. Take a piece of plain A4 paper and, using a ruler and pencil, mark out the lines illustrated on the right. Now fold it according to the steps shown opposite. The shaded parts indicate the area(s) to be folded, while the dotted lines indicate the folds themselves.

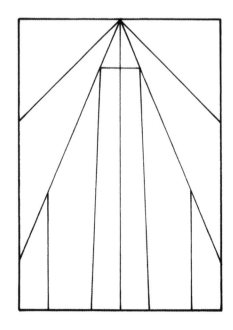

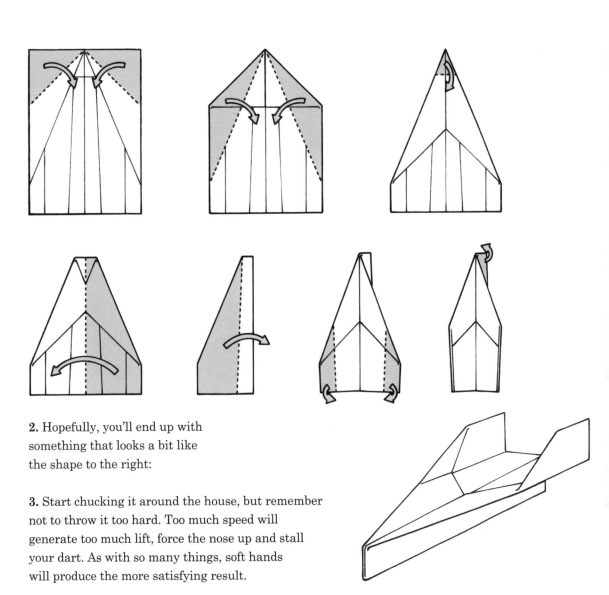

2. Hopefully, you'll end up with something that looks a bit like the shape to the right:

3. Start chucking it around the house, but remember not to throw it too hard. Too much speed will generate too much lift, force the nose up and stall your dart. As with so many things, soft hands will produce the more satisfying result.

4. Now it's time to decide who you want to be flying for and get the coloured pencils out. The one below looks as if it should have been in the RAF in the late 1950s.

A Dirty Distant War

Eleven Significant Air Battles

Since the end of the Second World War, the skies have hardly been at peace and yet, with a few major exceptions, aerial engagements between opposing fighter aircraft have been rare. There remains, though, something undeniably compelling about the gladiatorial nature of a dogfight. And that's been my criterion for inclusion here. I've tried to steer clear of the obvious, so air wars in Korea, Vietnam, the Falklands and Israel are absent. Nor have I included civil wars. That said, I've bent the rules to include the Cuban Bay of Pigs incident and the long-running face-off between China and Taiwan. I've included them because they're interesting, but I don't suppose either Cuba or Taiwan considered they were fighting civil wars.

Bay of Pigs – Cuba/USA 1961
Hawker Sea Fury / Douglas B-26b

Cuba's motley collection of vintage fighters made mincemeat out of the US-trained counter-revolutionary air force.

The Football War – Honduras/El Salvador 1969
Vought F4U Corsair / North American F-51 Mustang

The last time that Second World War-era fighters met in combat ended with the Honduran Corsairs shooting down three Mustangs.

The Cenepa War – Peru/Ecuador 1995
Sukhoi Su-22 / Dassault Mirage F-1

Ecuador's Mirages and Kfirs comprehensively outclassed their Peruvian opponents in this brief war.

War of Independence – Egypt/Israel 1948

Supermarine Spitfire / Supermarine Spitfire

This was the last time the RAF, caught in the middle because of Britain's responsibility for Palestine, scored an aerial victory, when it shot down a pair of Egyptian Spitfires.

Ethiopia/Eritrea 1999

Mikoyan MiG-29 / Sukhoi Su-27b

A conflict that saw the latest Russian fighter designs meet in combat (the advantage lay with Ethiopia's big Sukhois) and the first jet-on-jet victory by a female fighter pilot.

Iran/Iraq 1980–8

Grumman F-14 Tomcat / Mikoyan-Gurevich MiG-25

The F-14 Tomcat, flown by Tom Cruise in *Top Gun*, has scored more aerial victories with the Islamic Republic of Iran Air Force than it ever did with the US Navy.

Egypt/Libya 1977

Mikoyan Gurevich MiG-21 / Mikoyan-Gurevich MiG-23

After years of taking Egypt's side against Israel, the ever unpredictable Colonel Muammar Gaddafi tried a different tack.

Second Straits Crisis – Taiwan/China 1958

North American F-86 / Mikoyan-Gurevich MiG-17

The combat debut of the Sidewinder heat-seeking missile meant that Taiwanese Sabre pilots got the better of this conflict with over thirty confirmed kills.

India/Pakistan 1965 and 1971

Lockheed F-104 / Mikoyan-Gurevich MiG-21

India and Pakistan's well-trained, well-equipped air forces met on two occasions.

Ethiopia/Somalia 1977–8

Northrop F-5 / Mikoyan-Gurevich MiG-17

Ethiopia's F-5s, flown by Israeli mercenary pilots, quickly established their superiority over the Somalian MiGs.

The Border War South Africa/Angola 1966–90

Dassault Mirage F-1 / Mikoyan-Gurevich MiG-21

South Africa's two air-to-air victories were gun kills against MiGs flown by Cuban pilots.

Great Planes

North American P-51 Mustang

The prototype Mustang was completed just three months after the contract was signed. And, somehow, it was a classic: fast, long-ranged, well armed, beautifully balanced and exceptionally easy on the eye. The Mustang was credited with nearly 5000 kills during the Second World War, and was still dogfighting in South American wars as late as 1969.

First flight: 26 October 1940
Principal operators: US Army Air Corps, US Air Force, Royal Air Force and nearly thirty other air forces
Last operational flight: 1984 (with the air force of the Dominican Republic)

Eject! Eject! Eject!

The Unsung Hero of the Ejection Seat

Bernard Lynch is not generally well known as one of aviation's pioneers or heroes, but there's no doubt that he belongs on the list. His unsung bravery has helped to save the lives of extraordinary numbers of military aircrew.

During the latter years of the Second World War, it became clear that increasing performance meant that unassisted escape from a stricken aircraft was becoming less and less practical. After the death during a test flight of his business partner, Captain Valentine Baker, James Martin of the Martin-Baker aircraft company made it his mission to bring into service a successful ejection seat, and reorganized the company to achieve it.

While the US military was experimenting with spring-loaded downward ejection seats, research conducted by the Royal Aircraft Establishment in Great Britain suggested that the use of an explosive charge to fire the seat upwards was better. The trouble was that there was simply no information about what sort of upward acceleration the human body could stand. And that was where Bernard Lynch, a fitter in the Martin-Baker factory, came into the picture.

In January 1945, for the first time, an experimental rig fired a chair carrying a 200 lb dummy into the air along two vertical guide rails. Just four days afterwards, Lynch strapped himself in and the trigger was pulled. With admirable restraint, the engineers arrested Lynch's ascent just 4 feet 8 inches from where he'd left, but that wasn't enough to ensure escape from the cockpit of a failing aircraft. Consequently, having survived that first shot in one piece, Lynch got back into the hot seat for further tests. With each firing, the power of the gun's cartridge was increased. On the fourth firing, after reaching a height of over 10 feet, the stoic fitter reported 'considerable physical discomfort'. I'll bet.

Nonetheless, this didn't stop Lynch from climbing into the back seat of a Gloster Meteor jet fighter in July 1946 and being ejected as the aircraft

OPPOSITE: *When, during a flight in 1962, an engine fire burnt through the flight controls of his Lightning aircraft, test pilot George Aird ejected. Although he suffered multiple fractures and cuts after crashing through the roof of a greenhouse, he survived.*

streaked across Chalgrove Airfield in Oxfordshire at 8000 feet and 320 mph. Two years later he was even ejecting from the company's Meteor for the benefit of cheering crowds during an air pageant at Gatwick Airport.

It's possible that by this time Lynch was no longer quite the man he once was, for the force of an ejection compresses the spine. A number of Martin-Baker clients lost an inch or more of height after pulling the handle. Today, if aircrew eject more than once, they're not allowed to strap into an ejection seat again. Often they'll transfer to flying helicopters, which tend not to have ejection seats. Obviously.

But for all the inherent physical stress and danger in using ejection seats, they have made a dramatic impact on military flight safety.

And, since James Martin's response to his partner's death and Bernard Lynch's bravery, Martin-Baker has become the market leader. Its seats are used by military aircraft from ninety-three countries across the world, including, most recently, in America's new Joint Strike Fighter, the Lockheed Martin F-35 Lightning II. At the time of writing, Martin-Baker's seats have saved nearly 7500 lives.

Strapped into an experimental ejection seat test rig, Bernard Lynch prepares for 'considerable physical discomfort'.

THE FLYING EJECTION SEAT

During the Vietnam War, the US Navy lost over 500 aircraft in combat, as a result of which nearly 200 aircrew became prisoners of war. Alongside them, the US Air Force suffered three times as many aircraft losses. In every case there were aircrew who had either

been killed, captured or were in need of rescue. And while rescuing aircrew from behind enemy lines was given top priority, the challenge was considerable. Dedicated USAF squadrons flying Sikorsky HH-3 'Jolly Green Giant' helicopters, supported by heavily armed, piston-engined Douglas A-1 Skyraider attack aircraft, flew dangerous extraction missions, which, of course, put even greater numbers of aircrew at risk.

This prompted the navy and air force to ask, 'What if downed aircrew had the means to fly themselves back into friendly territory?' Three different aircraft companies accepted the challenge of coming up with an answer. The results were worthy of a Transformers movie: ejection seats that, on firing their occupant out of a stricken aircraft, unfolded, extended and locked themselves into mini-flying machines. Bell Aerosystems suggested a jet-powered hang-glider that suspended the pilot, face down and still strapped to his seat, beneath it. Fairchild-Hiller also suggested a glider, but theirs was a sort of pop-up machine made of cloth stretched over a spring-loaded metal frame. My favourite is the gyrocopter designed by Kaman Corps. On ejecting, a two-bladed rotor unfurled above the pilot's head, while a tail and a micro turbofan jet flicked up behind him. And the name given to this invention? Stowable Aircrew Vehicle Escape Roto-seat – or SAVER for short.

How practical any of these ideas really were for aircrew disorientated and sometimes injured by the violent act of ejection itself remains a matter for conjecture as none, sadly, made it into service. But that they were dreamt up at all merits a hat tip to the creativity and ingenuity of aircraft designers – and to the importance that the USA attaches to bringing its soldiers home.

MARTIN-BAKER MB5
Fighter

The Martin-Baker company is one of the most successful and enduring names in aviation. This is because it is the world's leading manufacturer of ejection seats. You wouldn't have bet on its survival. It's been nearly seventy years since the company last built an aircraft, and it never put an aircraft into production. The tiny handful of prototypes it did build are well known only to committed aviation enthusiasts. All of which represents something of a tragic waste.

In 1929 an Ulsterman, Jimmy Martin, decided that he wanted to build great aircraft. The self-taught son of a farmer, he really had no qualifications for doing so except self-belief and a God-given genius for aircraft design. In 1934, with his friend the First World War flying ace Valentine Baker, he set up Martin-Baker Aircraft. Their first aircraft, the MB1, pioneered new construction techniques. But Martin wanted to build fighters. In the minds of the Air Ministry, that was a job for the established big boys like Hawker, Supermarine or Gloster. And I suppose you can see the ministry's point. With war looming, it must have seemed risky to divert money and resources to a cottage industry like Martin-Baker. It was a bad decision, though.

Working on a shoestring and forced to use a temperamental Napier Sabre engine that was not of his choosing, Martin designed an outstanding fighter, the MB3, which was heavily armed, fast, manoeuvrable and easy to maintain. But when that troublesome engine failed, the MB3 crashed, killing Val Baker. Despite the devastating loss of his friend, James Martin persevered. And the next design to be built, the MB5, turned out to be his masterpiece, an aircraft considered by many to be the finest piston-engined fighter ever. As one contemporary noted, the sleek MB5 'looked like a cross between a Mustang and a V2 rocket'.

The test pilot Eric Brown pronounced it 'outstanding', saying he felt so completely at home after climbing into the cockpit for the first time that 'I might have already flown hundreds of hours in it – a compliment I could pay to no other new type of advanced aircraft.'

But piston-engined perfection came too late. Lacking the support and investment that might have hastened its construction, it was already clear in May 1944, when Martin's wonderful machine first took to the air, that the jet age had begun.

I'm pleased that the Martin-Baker company makes the world's best ejection seats, but it's a thought always tinged with regret that, given the opportunity, it might also have built some of the world's best aeroplanes.

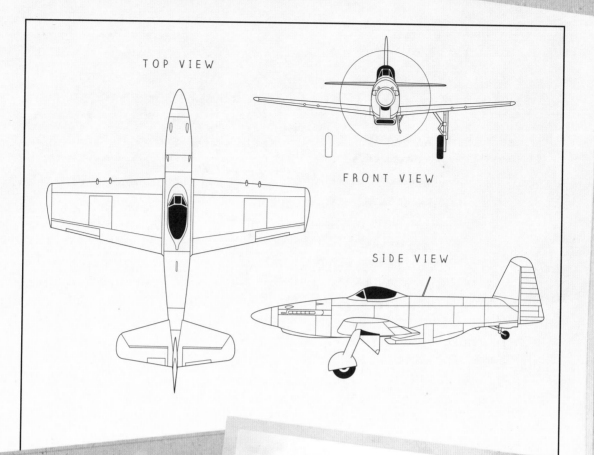

TOP VIEW

FRONT VIEW

SIDE VIEW

Maximum speed: 460 mph
Maximum range: 1236 miles
Maximum altitude: 40,000 feet
Maximum take-off weight:
12,090 pounds
Wingspan: 35 feet
Length: 37 feet 9 inches
Height: 15 feet
PROJECT CANCELLED: 1945*
*Any hope of an order probably
died when, during a demonstration
in front of Winston Churchill,
the engine failed on the only
occasion during the MB5's test-
flying career.

0   5   10   15   20   25 ft
0   2   4   6   8 m
SCALE OF FEET

REFERENCE No.	DRAWN	C. WYATT	11-12-1943		MARTIN-BAKER MB5
123 KKFJHH 556	NUMBER	12 4443			
GENERAL ARRANGEMENT	CHECKED	G. POTTLE	12-12-1943		MARTIN-BAKER AIRCRAFT CO. CHALGROVE, OXFORDSHIRE
	APPROVED	C. CHARALAMBIDES	03-01-1944		

The Bermuda Triangle
Fact or Fiction?

In the opening scene of Steven Spielberg's science-fiction classic *Close Encounters of the Third Kind*, scientists discover five propeller-driven US Navy torpedo bombers parked in a neat circle in the south-western desert of the United States. 'They look brand new,' someone remarks. As they would, I expect, if they'd been looked after well by aliens who'd taken them thirty-two years earlier. But while their discovery in the Sonoran Desert was fantasy, the planes themselves were real. And so too was their disappearance.

On 5 December 1945, Flight 19, a formation of US Navy Grumman TBM Avengers, vanished without trace off the coast of Florida. The five aircraft took off from Fort Lauderdale Naval Air Station at a quarter to two for a training mission out over the western Atlantic. Apart from practising low-level bombing, it was also a navigation exercise. The bombing went well, the navigation less so. Flight 19 dropped its last bomb at around three o'clock. Three and a half hours later its last radio transmission was heard. Lost and out of fuel, the flight leader thumbed his radio and reported, 'We'll have to ditch.' Within a few hours of that last transmission, a Martin PBM Mariner flying boat launched to find them had also been lost.

The story of what happened that night has become one of the foundation stones of the legend of the Bermuda Triangle. And along with the Roswell Incident and the Philadelphia Experiment, it became part of a sort of holy trinity of conspiracies laid at the door of the US military.

Of course, it wasn't just the 'unexplained' disappearance of Flight 19, or that of their would-be rescuers, that built the legend of the triangle. There were other mysteries ...

In a magazine advertisement for Britain's Avro Tudor airliner, the boss of British South American Airways claimed, 'It is one of the finest propositions ever known in the field of long-range air transport.' It was anything but. After a crash in 1947 that killed the man who'd designed it, another Tudor vanished in the Bermuda Triangle in January 1948, then another a year later. No trace of either aircraft was found. In 1950 a USAF Globemaster was lost. In 1954 a US Navy Constellation vanished. Two years later the US Navy lost a Martin Marlin flying boat, and in 1962 a USAF KB-50 tanker disappeared. Reportedly, no wreckage was found from any of these aircraft. I could go on, heaping incident upon incident until you felt sure that something inexplicable was going on in this mysterious patch of water. This is more or less what Charles Berlitz, the author of the global bestseller *The Bermuda Triangle*, does.

What he fails to mention is that, according to the United States Coast Guard, there's nothing statistically unusual in the number of aircraft and ships lost in the Bermuda Triangle. Or that the Avro Tudor was a terrible aircraft, rejected by BOAC, prone to fuel leaks and with an unreliable cabin heating system that ran off aviation fuel bled from the engines' tanks. Or even that in the 1940s and 1950s planes went down with frightening regularity, and that

'*Some say it's UFOs. Others say it's a lost civilization. You may decide it's both.*' Hmmm.

in the huge expanse of the Atlantic Ocean, it was *easy* to find no trace.

Berlitz touches on a US Navy investigation into 'electromagnetic gravitation and atmospheric disturbance'. The US Navy confirmed that Project Magnet was an effort to survey the Earth's geomagnetism for navigational charts. UFO enthusiasts drew the conclusion that the real purpose was to detect the presence of aliens by tracing the disruption caused by the anti-gravity engines of their flying saucers. Berlitz and others certainly fuelled this kind of speculation.

In his book Berlitz follows one chapter called 'Is there a logical explanation?' with another titled 'Space-time warps and other worlds'. The answer to the question he poses is, I'm afraid, 'yes'. Much as I'd love to learn of proof of alien visitation, the discovery of Atlantis or even some top secret military research programme, it's just wishful thinking. And even wishing really, *really* hard, won't, sadly, make it otherwise.

Aliens Among Us?

The Peculiar Story of the Roswell Flying Saucer

On 8 July 1947 the residents of Roswell, New Mexico, woke up to the news of a UFO, or unidentified flying object. 'RAAF CAPTURE FLYING SAUCER ON RANCH IN ROSWELL REGION' announced the headline in the *Roswell Daily Record*.

Certainly something had fallen from the skies.

A rancher called William 'Mac' Brazel had found debris on his land and reported it to the police. They handed the problem over to the nearby Roswell Army Air Field (RAAF). Intelligence officers sent to Brazel's homestead collected the wreckage and took it back to Roswell with them, issuing a statement to say that a flying disc had been found. The find was then sent on to the headquarters of the Eighth Air Force at Fort Worth in Texas. The next day the Eighth Air Force commander offered further clarification. The bits and pieces found by Brazel, he said, were the remains of a weather balloon. He even invited reporters to come along and see the material for themselves. That should have been that. It was, until at the end of the 1970s conspiracy theorists decided to stir things up. In 1980 Charles Berlitz, author of *The Bermuda Triangle*, wrote a book called *The Roswell Incident*. It had a similar impact to his earlier tome. Suddenly, people wanted to believe something otherworldly had taken place at Roswell. And once that happened, there seemed to be no shortage of people who started to recall events in 1947 slightly differently. Rubber, tin foil and paper became material that could only have been extraterrestrial in origin. Then a mortician who'd been working at the Roswell funeral home in 1947 watched a TV programme about Roswell and decided to phone a hotline to say he'd witnessed an alien autopsy. I don't suppose there was anyone more surprised than he was when, in 1995, film of an alien autopsy emerged.

Even this, though, was not the most bizarre attempt to explain what happened at Roswell. That has to be a story that manages to combine Joseph Stalin, Josef Mengele and secret Soviet overflights of America inspired by the Orson Welles radio play of *War of the Worlds* and designed to spread panic throughout a credulous population. The only believable thing about it was that it didn't involve aliens. On that front, at least, it has *something* in common with the USAF's account.

In 1995 the Air Force, in an effort to put a stop to all the nonsense, published a detailed report on the Roswell Incident. Containing photographs and documents, many of which had been declassified for the first time, it ran to 1000 pages and revealed that the Eighth Air Force statement claiming the Roswell 'flying saucer' was a weather balloon had not been true. But in 1947 the truth had had to remain top secret.

At that time the greatest priority for the US military was establishing whether or not the USSR had the atom bomb. But in an era before spy satellites or reconnaissance jets it was a fiercely difficult thing to be sure of. A classified programme called Project Mogul was initiated in the hope that 600-foot-tall high-flying balloons carrying sensitive acoustic sensors might detect the distant rumble of a nuclear explosion or missile launch.

The USAF report was clear: the debris recovered from 'Mac' Brazel's ranch was not from outer space but from barely 100 miles to the south-west; the fourth of a series of Project Mogul balloons launched from what is now Holloman Air Force Base, New Mexico.

Just as *The X-Files* would have us believe, the truth is out there ...

Just to be clear, this picture doesn't provide any kind of evidence for the existence of flying saucers.

The Right Stuff
Breaking the Sound Barrier

In the autumn of 1947, Captain Chuck Yeager, a young United States Air Force test pilot, finished dinner with his wife before the two of them saddled up a pair of horses for a night ride. It was a moonless night and, racing back to the ranch where they'd eaten, Yeager hit a gate and was thrown off his horse. His wife immediately diagnosed the stabbing pain in his chest as a broken rib. A visit to a local doctor confirmed it. He'd bust two of them.

Yeager was in the middle of a test-flying programme that was on the cusp of flying faster than the speed of sound – or Mach One – for the first time.

The sound barrier, as it was known, had earned an almost mythical status. No one was entirely sure what the effect of trying to fly through it might be, but pilots had been killed as they approached it. British test pilots from the Royal Aircraft Establishment, Farnborough, flew Spitfires in near-vertical full-power dives to try to understand better the buffeting and loss of control that afflicted contemporary piston-engined aircraft as they approached the speed of sound.

What was needed was an aircraft specifically designed for the job. Work began on a British design, the Miles M.52, in 1943. Crucial to its possible success were thin, low-drag wings and an innovative all-moving tail instead of the usual elevators on the trailing edge. The research was shared with the American Bell Corporation in 1944. The British M.52 was cancelled just a few months before it was due to fly in the summer of 1946, but that all-moving tail proved to be crucial.

In the summer of 1947 Chuck Yeager thought the X-1 project had run aground. At Mach .94 the little bullet-shaped rocket plane encountered exactly the same loss of elevator control that had plagued test pilots at Farnborough. Without pitch control, Yeager knew he could go no faster in the X-1. What he didn't realize, though, was that built into the Bell's design was the provision for an all-moving tail. So far it had only been tested on the ground, but by operating it from the cockpit in the air, Yeager was able to take the orange-painted X-1 he'd christened 'Glamorous Glennis', after his wife, safely beyond Mach .94. The attempt to break the sound barrier was on again. And then he went riding after dinner.

But Yeager, as he might have put it himself, was a tough s'mbitch'. Shot down in France during the Second World War, he escaped over the Pyrenees to Spain. When he returned to combat, he proved to be an outstanding fighter pilot who, in scoring five victories in a single mission, became an 'ace in a day'. Also one of the first pilots to shoot down a Messerschmitt Me-262 jet, he was not a man you'd bet against. And he decided he wasn't going to let a pair of broken ribs stop him from trying to break the sound barrier.

'If I can't, I won't. If I can, I will,' he told Glennis. The only other person Yeager admitted the injury to was fellow test pilot Jack Ridley, the X-1 programme's flight test engineer. Between them they worked out a way for the incapacitated Yeager to lock the cockpit door of the X-1 without needing his right arm, using a piece of sawn-off broom handle.

On 14 October 1947, at 20,000 feet over the Mojave Desert, Yeager made the painful climb down the ladder from the B-29 mothership to the cockpit of the X-1. He locked the door, stowed the broom handle, then completed his pre-flight checks. Was he ready to go? 'Hell, yes,' he told the pilot of the mothership. 'Let's get this over with …' The X-1 dropped from the belly of the B-29.

The Bell X-1 in flight. The little rocket plane was painted bright orange.

At Mach .96 Yeager experienced the usual heavy buffeting, but as he continued his accelerating climb, it seemed to smooth off. In front of him, the machmeter, the instrument recording his speed relative to the speed of sound, began to flick wildly before the needle spun clockwise.

On the ground the world's first sonic boom echoed across the desert.

For 20 seconds Yeager flew the X-1 above Mach One before shutting down the rocket engine and gliding back to land on the dry lake bed below. From launch to landing, the X-1's historic flight had lasted just 14 minutes.

The aircraft, with an elated Yeager standing on the wing, was towed behind a jeep back to the operations building. Waiting inside, one of the scientists who'd feared the pilot might not survive the flight picked up a textbook and threw it into a rubbish bin. He put his arm around Jack Ridley and said, 'Let's go rewrite the book, Jackie.'

WHAT IS THE SOUND BARRIER?

As an aircraft flies, it creates pressure waves that radiate out from it in all directions like ripples from a pebble thrown into a pond. Unlike those on the surface of the water, these waves travel at the speed of sound. At subsonic speeds an aircraft makes up a little ground on the waves travelling ahead of it. At the speed of sound the waves radiating out ahead can't outrun the aircraft and are compressed into a single strong shock wave – the cause of the buffeting experienced by Chuck Yeager. A supersonic aircraft can pierce this and travel faster than the shock waves ahead. These then bend back behind the aircraft into a shock cone trailing in its wake. The sonic boom on the ground is the sound of that shock cone as it like the – very fast – shadow of a cloud. Rather than being a single crack, the sonic boom actually travels along the ground behind the aircraft in what's known as a boom carpet.

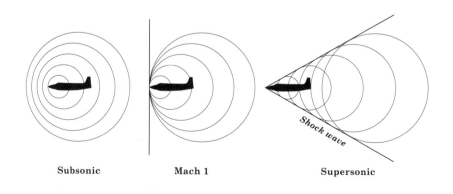

| Subsonic | Mach 1 | Supersonic |

F. A. B. Scott

A Few Island Airbases

Trawling through a dusty box of old magazines in a second-hand bookshop, there was a copy of the *Illustrated London News* that immediately caught my eye. On the cover was a photograph of an island bisected from end to end by a runway. The headline described it as 'THE RAF'S LONELIEST OUTPOST'. That got me. I've always thought there's something about an island airbase that promises either daring, seat-of-the-pants flights, or attempts to take over the world.

Perhaps it was Tracy Island from *Thunderbirds* that fed my imagination. Or maybe it was the lure of the villain's lair in a James Bond film. Whatever the case, there's a romance about an island airstrip that's seductive. Like discovering that there really are dragons, it's the appeal of fiction made fact. And, as often as not, the real-life stories of the world's island airbases are as extraordinary and unlikely as anything that might spring from the imagination. A few of the most interesting ones are described overleaf.

International Rescue's Thunderbird 1 *launches from its hangar beneath Tracy Island's retracting swimming pool.*

INDIAN OCEAN

MALDIVES

INDIAN OCEAN

RAF Gan

0° 41' 29" S, 73° 9' 22" E

This is the one: 'the RAF's loneliest outpost'. Located on Addu Atoll in the Maldives, the airfield on Gan Island was built by Royal Navy engineers for the Fleet Air Arm during the Second World War. Six hundred miles south-west of Sri Lanka, it's little more than a speck in the ocean, fringed with palm trees and white sand. In 1957, however, it transferred to the RAF and became a vital staging post en route to Britain's shrinking colonial commitments in the Far East.

One airman stationed there described it as 'a cross between Devil's Island and a holiday camp'. That just about nailed it. One station commander expressed a hope that his men would take more interest 'in things like painting, pottery and classical music'. It was a vain hope. As one airman pointed out, 'Everything revolves round the beer can. What else is there to do?'

In 1970 there were 600 RAF personnel there and one woman, a WRVS volunteer. 'They like to have a woman to talk to,' she said. I imagine the queue to talk to her from men serving 10½-month unaccompanied tours was a long one.

Diego Garcia

7° 18' 48" S, 72° 24' 40" E

It was the sixteenth-century Spanish explorer Diego García de Moguer who gave his name to the largest of the Chagos Archipelago islands when he discovered it lying 2000 miles east of Africa and 1000 miles south of India. But it was the French who populated it with people they shipped from Madagascar in the eighteenth century to work the plantations that they established there. With the defeat of Napoleon in 1814, the islands became British and remain so.

Aircraft first arrived in 1942, when the RAF established a flying-boat base to counter the threat from German and Japanese submarines. But it was not until 1971, when the British government agreed to let the USA use Diego Garcia as a military base, that a runway was built. It grew rapidly over the next twenty years, until it was capable of sustaining large-scale raids by B-52s, B-1s and B-2 Stealth bombers in support of US operations in Iraq and Afghanistan.

Alongside around 3500 American military personnel and support workers, the British presence is a token one. Fewer than fifty Royal Marines and sailors make up Naval Party 1002 and have responsibility for policing and customs, and for registering births, deaths and marriages. But no descendants of the original plantation workers remain. The Chagos islanders were evicted from their home to make way for the airbase. They're still fighting for the right to return to the island.

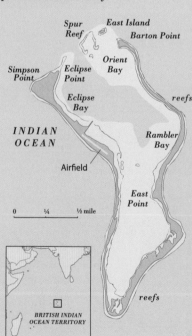

BRITISH INDIAN OCEAN TERRITORY

Tinian Island

15° 0' N, 145° 38' E

Part of the Mariana chain found by Ferdinand Magellan in 1521, Tinian Island lies in the Pacific, about 4000 miles west of Hawaii. Since being claimed for the Spanish crown, it was also possessed by Germany and Japan before, in the summer of 1945, being captured by US forces.

Tinian's original claim to fame was as the first place where napalm was used in the Pacific campaign. Then it became about the most important place in the world.

On 6 July 1945, a Boeing B-29 Superfortress with a modified bomb bay landed at Tinian's North Field airstrip. A month later, the bomber, named *Enola Gay* after the pilot's mother, dropped the first atom bomb on the Japanese city of Hiroshima. Three days later another B-29, called *Bockscar,* dropped a second atom bomb, this time on Nagasaki.

On 14 August Emperor Hirohito announced his country's surrender, but not *all* his subjects laid down their arms. The last Japanese soldier on Tinian wasn't finally captured until 1953.

Ascension Island

7° 56' S, 14° 22' W

If you're looking for a real-life Tracy Island, you won't do better than Ascension. Rising in splendid isolation from the Atlantic Ocean about halfway between Brazil and West Africa, it's got it all. The product of a now dormant volcano, this spectacular place is home to petrified lava flows, golden beaches, spawning turtles, giant land crabs and a tropical cloud forest. Her history includes visits from Portuguese navigators, pirates and Charles Darwin aboard the HMS *Beagle*, and, in 1815, the arrival of a British garrison following Napoleon's imprisonment on St Helena, 800 miles to the south-east.

Her runway was built by US Army engineers during the Second World War and first used by Royal Navy Swordfish biplanes. Later, after the sinking of the *Laconia* by a U-boat, it was used by American bombers. The high point of Ascension's contribution to aviation history should have been her role as a diversion airfield for NASA's Space Shuttle. But it wasn't.

Her starring role finally came in 1982. On the night of 31 May, a month after Argentina invaded the Falkland Islands, a fleet of RAF aircraft roared away from the runway into the night sky. Sixteen hours and one cratered target later, the single Avro Vulcan bomber returned from what was the longest bombing raid in history.

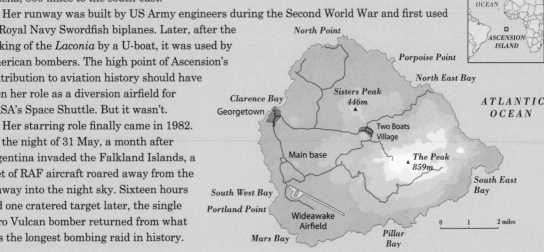

Freight Dogs
The Story of Air Cargo

At first, the United States limited her military involvement in Afghanistan to the use of air power and Special Forces in support of local forces. It wouldn't last. As the US footprint deepened following the overthrow of the Taliban, so too did the requirement for an increasingly substantial and complex infrastructure. That alone would present a formidable challenge, often reliant on private contractors. But when a massive electricity generator had to be moved from Bagram to where it was needed in remote, inaccessible and hostile territory in the south, there was no one willing to take on the job, even for the $60,000 fee on offer. The trouble was there wasn't an aircraft able to operate from the rough strip that was capable of carrying the weight, *and* getting there and back without refuelling. And there was no fuel. Then an ex-Soviet Air Force crew from Byelorussia said they'd take on the contract for $2 million. Up front. With nowhere else to turn, America paid up.

As agreed, the Byelorussian crew loaded the generator in their big Ilyushin Il-76 transport jet, unloaded it at the destination, then sat down for a cigarette, apparently unconcerned about flying out again. They were soon picked up by Afghans driving an old bus.

'How will you get the plane back?' one of the US soldiers asked.

'We won't,' came the reply, 'we're ditching it here.' They'd bought a barely airworthy old crate for $500,000, flown her and the generator on a wing and prayer, and now, $1.5 million better off, were driving home. What chutzpah!

'Freight dogs' – the badge of honour claimed by those hauling cargo around some of the worst places on Earth – have always had to have their wits about them. When air freight was in its infancy, the crew of an Aero-union Liore 213 biplane coaxed two circus horses to climb aboard by playing the music that normally accompanied their entrance into the big top.

It's probable that British pioneer John Moore-Brabazon was the first pilot to carry a live cargo when, in 1909, he decided to see 'if pigs could fly'.

OPPOSITE: *Built to carry the Buran space shuttle on its back, the six-engined Antonov An-225 Mriya is the largest, heaviest winged aircraft ever built. Only a single example has ever been completed.*

He strapped a wastepaper basket to the wing of his biplane, loaded it with a small pig and took it for a spin with no ill consequences. By 1924, KLM managed to airlift a prize bull from Rotterdam to Paris. But, generally speaking, with space and weight at a premium, cargo usually gave way to airmail. Even today, live cargo accounts for only 1 per cent of all air freight.

Initially the only goods sent by air were either very perishable or very urgent. Around 500 tons of newspapers travelled between London and Paris every year, and fresh flowers represented 40 per cent of the traffic through Amsterdam airport. Low-volume, high-value cargo also worked. After the Wall Street Crash in 1929, KLM operated six flights a day transporting gold between European Central Banks.

But the development of a network was slow. This mattered less to Europe and the USA, which enjoyed efficient rail, road and sea connections, than to those parts of the world still reliant on pack mules. Air freight was a godsend in places such as Central America. And in New Guinea, an open-cast gold mine barely accessible via a gruelling ten-day overland journey was supplied exclusively by three Junkers G-31 transport planes, *Peter*, *Paul* and *Pat*, for twelve years until the Japanese invasion in 1942. The world was at war again.

In March 1931, a Guinea Airways Junkers G31 trimotor began the first airlift in history. Over the next 11 years, three G31s carried over 37,000 tons of cargo to and from New Guinea's Bulolo gold fields.

And war, once more, proved to be the greatest catalyst for advances in aviation. No more so than in the field of air cargo.

Prior to the outbreak of the Second World War, the US Army Air Force simply had no meaningful air transport capability. By the end of the war, though, Brigadier-General William Tunner, commanding operations in India, said his men could fly 'anything, anywhere, anytime'.

Although the two countries had been fighting since 1937, China formally declared war on Japan after the attack on Pearl Harbor in December 1941. With China's own industry destroyed by the Japanese, her war effort was dependent on resupply from the USA. But with Japan now in control of Burma, and the Soviet Union refusing access through Kazakhstan, the only way to do it was by air. That meant US and Chinese pilots making risky crossings of 'The Hump', the eastern Himalayas blocking the route between India and China.

Flying day and night in all weathers, in a collection of unarmed cargo planes which, fully loaded, couldn't even clear the peaks, the pilots had to twist through the mountain passes, courageously facing Japanese fighters en route. Small wonder the India-China Wing of Air Transport Command (ATC) earned the Presidential Unit Citation for their bravery, the only non-combat unit to do so. Over three years the ATC flew about 750,000 tons of cargo across 'The Hump' in aircraft such as the DC-3, the Curtiss C-46 Commando and the C-87 Liberator Express (a stripped-out transport version of the B-24

Liberator), which could, at most, carry around 6 tons each. But *every single thing* used by US forces in China – from bullets and fuel to food and toilet paper – was flown in. Over 1300 crew and passengers paid with their lives, and at least 500 aircraft were lost. It was an astonishing effort, the scale of which had simply never been seen before. However, it would pale in comparison with what was coming.

On 24 June 1948 the Soviet Union closed all surface routes in and out of Berlin, a city divided into East and West at the end of the Second World War. Only the air corridors from West Germany remained open. The city's 2.1 million inhabitants had enough flour for seventeen days, powdered milk for twenty-six days, and a month and a half's worth of potatoes. To keep going, it was estimated that West Berlin would need 13,000 tons of supplies a day – every day. There was really only one man to run the show: Hump commander General William Tunner.

USAF pilot Grant Halverson was told his squadron needed to get four of its C-54 transport planes en route to Berlin the next morning. He had his reservations about the mercy mission because Germany had been the enemy. The first time he flew in carrying 10 tons of flour he was transfixed by the moonscape of bombed-out Berlin. *How*, he wondered, *can two million people live in a place so devastated?*

Planning to film the conveyor belt of aircraft coming in and out, Halverson made his way to the perimeter of the airfield. Kids, also watching the planes, were pressed against the other side of the barbed wire. 'Don't give up on us,' they told him. Moved, Halverson passed sticks of gum through the wire, which the children shared. Those who missed out were content to smell it.

'Come back here tomorrow,' Halverson told them, 'and when I come in to land, I'll drop enough gum for you all.' For the next three weeks, Halverson, after wiggling his wings, dropped chocolate and gum tied to handkerchief parachutes. But when 'The Candy Bomber' made the front page of the newspapers, Halverson expected trouble. 'Keep doing it,' he was told. General Tunner was quick to appreciate the great value of Halverson's initiative. There was soon a whole squadron of Candy Bombers, and over the months that followed they dropped 21 tons of sweets.

For over a year, aircraft, often harassed by Soviet fighter planes, flew around the clock. The Americans soon settled on a standardized fleet of 300 C-54 transporters. The British used whatever they could lay their hands on, from Sunderland flying boats operating from Lake Havel to converted Lancaster bombers. Beaten, the Soviet Union lifted the siege of Berlin on

12 May 1949. When the airlift ended four months later, nearly 2.5 million tons of supplies had been flown in. Just to put that in perspective, the total annual weight of freight flown from North America to Europe *today* is less than 1.5 million tons, and the total annual weight coming in to Europe from Africa is less than half a million tons.

The Berlin Airlift was a staggeringly impressive operation and, for my money at least, must stand as the Cold War's finest hour.

A significant chunk of the British effort had been civilian, using surplus RAF aircraft crewed by Second World War veterans flying for a burgeoning collection of small charter airlines. A similar air cargo scene was developing in the USA, where freight outfits, such as Slick and Flying Tiger Line, were bringing the 'anything, anywhere, anytime' attitude to civilian flying. Often business took a back seat. When Flying Tiger Line hired its first accountant and he asked to see the books, 'What books?' came the reply. But although only those with a nose for business would survive, this devil-may-care approach came to characterize the Freight Dogs. Squeezed by the big, established airlines, they took their money where they could find it – often in support of far-flung military campaigns. Flying beaten-up old propeller-engined airliners long after jets had replaced them on passenger routes, small charter outfits – sometimes little more than one man and a plane – took risks that bigger operators wouldn't dream of. There's no better example of this than the church-sponsored airlift that supplied Nigeria's breakaway state of Biafra in the late 1970s.

Taking off at night to avoid Nigerian MiGs, the propliners flew north from the island of São Tomé into a bush landing strip scraped out where a road had been. Perhaps a million lives were saved by the three-year airlift.

Since the Second World War, alongside charter operators like those in

A single Douglas C-74 Globemaster was used during the Berlin Airlift, but it made its presence felt. Shuttling back and forth for 20 hours, the giant airlifter once flew in 125 tons of coal in a single day.

Biafra providing air transport as and when customers require it, there's been an exponential growth in scheduled international express air freight. This accounts for 90 per cent of a global total that's grown from less than 100,000 tons in 1939 to around 40 million tons a year, a figure expected to double over the next twenty years. The numbers are mind-boggling. Six billion flowers are transported each year. Nine million bottles of Beaujolais Nouveau fly out of France over five days annually. Over 50,000 tons of salmon from producers in Scotland and Norway is flown all around the world.

And, for BOAC at least, it all started with Indian monkeys. In the 1950s American medical researchers had an almost insatiable demand for monkeys to use in medical experiments as they searched for a cure for polio. The British airline supplying them was unable to get rid of the stench left by the terrified animals before once more loading passengers, so they decided to invest in dedicated cargo aircraft. Carrying live freight remains big business. In 2011 the German airline Lufthansa, continuing what Moore-Brabazon and his pig started in 1909, transported 80 million tropical fish and 300 tons of worms. As a result of the latter, they can claim to have flown more creatures than people.

But while the day-in, day-out delivery of, for instance, the 1 million tons of fruit and vegetables flown into the UK every year continues to soar, it remains the one-offs that capture the imagination: the 1087-plus Ethiopian Jews evacuated to Israel aboard a single Boeing 747 in 1991; the 330 passengers squeezed aboard a World Airways 727 on the last flight out of Da Nang, Vietnam, in 1975 – including sixty in the cargo holds and eight in the undercarriage bays; the mattresses lining the floor of Air Foyle's Antonov An-124 to evacuate refugees from Kuwait after the 1991 Iraqi invasion; a killer whale, Shamu, flown by the Flying Tiger Line; a giraffe aboard a HeavyLift CL-44 Conroy Guppy; or the 189-ton generator heaved into the air by the world's biggest aircraft, the Antonov An-225.

It's impressive stuff for sure, but the appeal for me remains with the real Freight Dogs. Like characters from a Graham Greene novel, these tough operators who, provided the price is right, will fly their patched-up, past-it jets to any Third World hellhole you like are where the romance lies.

If *Star Wars*, as the opening credits would have us believe, took place 'a long time ago', it makes Han Solo, in his beaten-up old transport ship the *Millennium Falcon*, the original Freight Dog. As one pilot put it more recently: 'You can fly light or heavy, early or late, just get your money up front.'

Han and Chewy would, I'm sure, agree.

Pigs in Space

Flying Animals

While the sheep, duck and cockerel sent aloft in a hot-air balloon by the Montgolfier brothers enjoyed a relatively sedate ride, animals' subsequent experience of aviation was to be rather more explosive, unpleasant and dangerous – like that of the unsuspecting pigs who were yanked from the ground and winched into the back of passing aircraft to test the Fulton air hook. Other creatures were even less fortunate.

In 1962, to test the ejection capsule of the B-58 Hustler nuclear bomber at supersonic speeds, Himalayan and American black bears were fired out of B-58 cockpits at velocities approaching twice the speed of sound and at altitudes of up to 45,000 feet. While one or two were unscathed, others suffered fractures and whiplash. Beyond that, it's reported that they were treated well after their ordeal. Right up until the moment they were put down before an autopsy was performed, that is.

These pigs and bears are the forgotten pioneers of aviation history, though. Just like their human counterparts, it was the animal astronauts at the time that bagged the headlines and hogged the limelight. And while you might have known that Laika, a dog, and Ham, a chimpanzee, were sent into space, I'm guessing that the monkeys launched by Argentina are less familiar.

Here are some of the animals that have earned their astronaut wings:

Brine shrimp
Bullfrog
Cai monkey
Carp
Carpenter bees
Cats
   (*Sent into space by France in 1963.*)
Chimpanzees
   (*Ham, in 1961, was first.*)
Crickets

Dogs
(*Two Soviet dogs, Tsygan and Dezik, were first in 1951. Laika, the first dog in orbit, was launched in 1957.*)
Flat rock scorpions
Flour beetles
Frogs
Fruit flies
   (*In 1947 they became the*

first living things in space – unless there's something out there already ...)
Garden orb spiders
Golden orb spiders
Guinea pigs
Harvester ants
Horsfield's tortoise
   (*The first animal to visit deep space during a 1968 Soviet mission to the moon.*)

House spiders
Japanese killifish
Japanese tree frogs
Jellyfish
Macaque monkey
Madagascar hissing
  cockroaches
Meal worms
Mice
Monarch butterfly
Mummichog
  *(The first fish in space,
  in 1972.)*
Newts
  *(Launched in 1985 by the
  USSR, their forearms had
  been amputated in order
  to study the effect of space
  on regeneration.)*
Oyster toadfish
Painted lady butterfly
Rats
Rhesus monkeys
Roundworms
  *(*Caenorhabditis elegans
  *worms were the only
  survivors of the 2003
  Space Shuttle* Columbia
  disaster.)
Sand desert beetles
Sea urchins
Seed-harvester ants
Silkworms
Snails
Squirrel monkeys
Stick insects
Swordtail fish
Tardigrades
  *(In 2007 these inhabitants
  of extreme environments
  were subjected to the
  vacuum of space without
  protection for ten days –
  68 per cent survived.)*

Turtles
  *(Sent into space by Iran
  in 2010 to mark the
  thirty-first anniversary
  of the revolution.
  Of course.)*
Wasps
Wine flies
Zebra danio fish

*Named after Holloman
Aerospace Medical Center,
chimpanzee astronaut Ham
was apparently none the
worse for his 16-minute
spaceflight aboard a Mercury-
Redstone rocket in 1961.
But it was all a far cry from
Cameroon in West Africa,
where he was born in 1956.*

Putting Out Fire
The World of Aerial Firefighting

You think you're having a bad day? Then consider the man who, clad in a full wetsuit, fins, diving mask and scuba tanks, was found in a burnt-out area of woodland following a forest fire. A post-mortem established that he had died, not of burns or smoke inhalation, but of massive internal injuries. On further investigation, it was discovered that he had been diving 20 miles away from the fire on the day he died.

Investigators soon realized that the unfortunate diver had been minding his own business when he was scooped up by a firefighting aircraft that was filling its tanks with water before returning to the blaze. Man and water were then dropped on to the fire. He was reckoned to have been alive when he hit the ground, and, it was estimated, put out the flames over an area of only 12 square feet.

It's a great story, but it doesn't stand up to scrutiny. For over seventy years, though, firefighters have been dropped from planes to tackle forest fires, and, just possibly, it was a memory of what happened to a team dropped into a blaze in 1949 that provided the kernel from which the urban legend grew. Their story ends no more happily.

Getting to the fire was usually the easy bit, but it had been a rough flight for the sixteen smokejumpers of the United States Forest Service (USFS). Turbulent air had bounced their twin-engined C-47 transport plane around the sky for 40 minutes, and one of the men was so airsick that he was told not to jump. It was a decision that probably saved his life.

The smokejumpers were an elite – shock troops in the battle against wildfires. Since 1940, teams of these young men – often students doing the job for a couple of seasons – had been parachuted in to fight forest fires. In nine years, none had ever been killed by fire. But on 5 August 1949 at Mann Gulch, Montana, that statistic would be terribly undone. Just after the smokejumpers tumbled into the wilderness, the fire blew up, roaring so loud that the men couldn't make themselves heard, and consuming 3000 acres of woodland in just 10 minutes. Only three men would survive the devastation.

OPPOSITE: *Six thousand litres lighter. Designed from the outset as an aerial firefighter, the Canadair CL-415 SuperScooper is used throughout the world. The planes' distinctive yellow paint job makes them a familiar feature of any Mediterranean summer holiday.*

Parachuting men in to fight wildfire was not the USFS's first attempt to intervene from the air. After using aircraft to patrol remote areas of woodland as early as 1919, in 1930 aircraft were used to drop water on fires. But it was pretty unsophisticated stuff.

It wasn't until 1955 that an ex-military pilot called Floyd Nolta, who had built a successful crop-dusting company in California after the war, produced the first airtanker. While filming the flying scenes in the 1944 movie *Thirty Seconds Over Tokyo*, Nolta had flown a B-25 bomber under the San Francisco Bay Bridge. He therefore didn't take much persuading to cut a hole in the bottom of a Boeing Stearman biplane and try bombing a grassfire that had been lit next to the runway.

Less than a month later his brother Vance used one of the company Stearmans to put out a real Californian wildfire. His success would provide a new lease of life for a whole rag-tag fleet of redundant Second World

War aircraft. Converted B-17 Flying Fortress bombers, PBY Catalina amphibians, US Navy TBM Avenger torpedo bombers and PBY4-2 Privateer long-range maritime patrol bombers were all back in business. This time, though, their only weapon was water, and the target of their attack runs was fire. It offered exhilarating flying for pilots who were not, perhaps, temperamentally suited to the mundanity of ferrying passengers around.

In Canada, design work began on a purpose-built waterbomber. The Canadair CL-215 Scooper first flew in 1967, and it's this rugged little amphibian and its successor, the CL-415 SuperScooper, that the public most closely associates with aerial firefighting. Being painted bright yellow helps with that. So too does their ubiquity. Used in ten different countries, over 200 have been built, and it doesn't even have to land to refill its water tanks. Or not quite, at least. By skimming along the surface of a lake for a quarter of a mile, the Scooper can fill its tanks with 6 tons of water and return quickly to the fire. It's not the only one that can perform this trick, however.

Russia, with some of the largest areas of woodland in the world, suffers from more forest fires than any other country. A government-run aerial firefighting agency, in operation since the mid-1930s, employs an army of 4500 smokejumpers. Alongside them are 600 pilots flying a variety of firefighting aircraft and helicopters, including the Il-76 TP, for many years the largest, fastest and most capable waterbomber in the world. But Russia has also developed its own, rather different firefighting amphibian – the Beriev Be-200 Altair. Powered by a pair of turbofan jet engines and using the latest, digital fly-by-wire controls, it can cruise at twice the speed and carry twice as much water as even the newest SuperScoopers.

The big Beriev really is a fabulous and unique aircraft, a genuinely modern, mature jet flying boat design that has also been pressed into service in Italy, Greece, Indonesia, Israel and Portugal, where, in 2006, one was nearly lost after clipping the treetops. It was just the most recent reminder of how hazardous the job of flying airtankers can be. Since 1967, fifty-six lives have been lost in thirty-five accidents involving CL-215s and CL-415s. During the same period, at least six firefighting PBY Catalinas, four C-54s, three C-119 Flying Boxcars, two P-3 Orions and another two C-130 Hercules airtankers were destroyed. On the same day in 2012 two P3V Neptunes crashed. The

OPPOSITE: *The Martin JRM Mars. Over 65 years since it was first delivered to the US Navy one of these giants, Hawaii Mars, is still flying, ready to dump over 7000 gallons of water on any fire that's asking for it. There's nothing else like it in the sky.*

two-man crew of one of them was lost. The statistics alone make it clear that the aircrews flying airtankers are no less committed and courageous than those twelve young smokejumpers who died in 1949.

I want to finish with a story that, sadly, has to begin with the death of another waterbomber crew. In 1961 the four men were killed when their aircraft hit a hillside while fighting a fire in British Columbia. To date, thankfully, this remains the only crash suffered by the type of aircraft they were flying, at that time the freshest recruit to the ranks of the aerial firefighters. It was also, by quite a long chalk, the most impressive aircraft to have done so. And, over fifty years later, that remains the case. If elsewhere in this book I've given you the impression that the days of the big flying boats, such as Pan Am's Boeing Clippers, or Imperial Airways' Empire Class are gone, I'm very happy to report that that's not quite the case. *Nearly*, but not quite. Reader, I give you the magnificent Martin Mars.

This giant flying boat first flew in 1942, but entered service with the US Navy only three years later. The end of the Second World War meant the twenty on order weren't needed, so only the handful already built joined the navy. For a decade the aircraft provided a useful transport link between California and Hawaii until the four still in service with the Navy were sold to a Canadian company in 1959. Since then, the two remaining flying boats – another was destroyed on the ground by a typhoon in 1962 – have been fighting fires. In 2012, one Mars was retired to a museum, but one of the two huge red-and-white birds is still on duty, ready to fight wildfires more impressively and elegantly than anything else in the sky – and keep intact the last remaining thread of a link with the golden age of the flying boat. Long may that continue.

PROJECT CANCELLED

BAC TSR2
Supersonic low-level strike bomber

After completing the maiden flight of Britain's dramatic-looking new supersonic strike jet in 1964, the test pilot Roland 'Bee' Beamont stated that the TSR2 'looks like being a real winner'. After what had been a difficult gestation, perhaps the aircraft, needle-nosed and beautiful in an all-over white paint scheme, had turned a corner. As the test programme advanced, Beamont's initial assessment was only reinforced. 'One of the most remarkable designs in aviation history,' he said. 'In a class of its own.'

What could possibly go wrong? As it happened, nearly everything.

TSR2 was conceived in 1957, the same year Britain's Defence Secretary announced that the RAF was 'unlikely to require' another generation of manned fighters or bombers and would instead use missiles. Somehow the nascent TSR2 programme slipped through the net. The price extracted by a government desperate to rationalize the aviation industry was that any company hoping to build the new jet had to do so in partnership with another. The British Aircraft Corporation had not existed the year before it won the contract. Somehow BAC, a forced marriage between Vickers-Armstrong and English Electric, forged ahead with what appeared to be a promising design. But such a technically ambitious project was, almost inevitably, subject to delays, complications and rising costs. That made it a target.

For those with an axe to grind, TSR2 became a byword for waste and hubris. Against this backdrop, BAC continued to develop its aircraft and, in 1963, released a photograph of a very sleek and purposeful-looking machine approaching completion. It was too little too late to turn the tide, though. Early supporters in both the government and RAF were losing faith. Worse, there was an election coming and the opposition's views were clear: TSR2 was a scandal. Then, in June 1964, they won the election.

Three months later, the fuselage of the second prototype was badly damaged when it fell off the back of a lorry. It was a cruel humiliation for the men trying to bring TSR2 to life. But it wasn't to be. 'This inherited monster has gone on long enough,' said the new government, and cancelled the programme.

Roland Beamont thought TSR2 was 'potentially one of the most effective military aircraft of all time'. It would most likely have been in RAF service well into the 1990s. Instead, of the airframes in various stages of construction at the time of cancellation, a couple were used for target practice, and ten found themselves in the hands of R. J. Coley & Son Limited of Hounslow. The claim made on the Middlesex company's advertisement ends our story:

**BUYERS OF ALL CLASSES OF SURPLUS AIRCRAFT MATERIAL
FOR REDUCTION TO SCRAP**

The once-great British aviation industry would never again build on its own an aircraft even remotely as ambitious as TSR2. The tragedy of it all was that it had shown that it could.

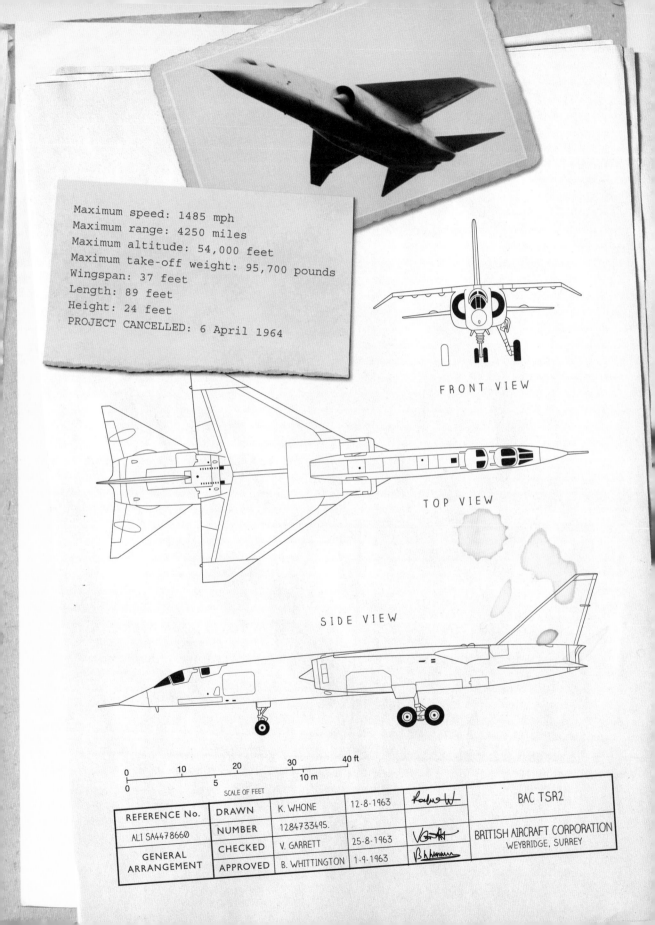

Maximum speed: 1485 mph
Maximum range: 4250 miles
Maximum altitude: 54,000 feet
Maximum take-off weight: 95,700 pounds
Wingspan: 37 feet
Length: 89 feet
Height: 24 feet
PROJECT CANCELLED: 6 April 1964

FRONT VIEW

TOP VIEW

SIDE VIEW

SCALE OF FEET

REFERENCE No.	DRAWN	K. WHONE	12-8-1963	Rodno W	BAC TSR2
ALI SA4478660	NUMBER	1284733495.			BRITISH AIRCRAFT CORPORATION
GENERAL ARRANGEMENT	CHECKED	V. GARRETT	25-8-1963		WEYBRIDGE, SURREY
	APPROVED	B. WHITTINGTON	1-9-1963		

English Electric Canberra

Simplicity, versatility, record-breaking performance, combat-proven capability, longevity and export success, the Canberra's CV is overflowing. In fact, it's so good that the USA decided to build over 400 of her own, two of which are still in service with NASA today. While flying the Canberra during the Vietnam War in the late 1960s, Chuck Yeager described the jet as 'damned effective'.

First flight: 13 May 1949
Principal operator: Royal Air Force
Last operational flight: Retired by the RAF in 2006

How Many?
A Few Notable Production Runs

I learned to fly in the Cessna 172, and it's clear that there's absolutely nothing remarkable about that. Purely in terms of the number built, it's the most successful aircraft in history. Given the level of aircraft production during the Second World War, when US factories alone produced over 300,000 planes, that's a remarkable production. Unlike those Second World War record-breakers, though, the 172's still being built today. That total is still rising and so, it's safe to say, it will remain the all-time champ. Alongside the untouchable Cessna, though, there are other surprises. The US aircraft built in the greatest numbers during the Second World War wasn't a fighter, or even the famous Flying Fortress: it was the B-24 Liberator. The most numerous British bomber wasn't the Lancaster or the Mosquito, but the two-engined Wellington. Then there's the Avro Anson, which, at the beginning of the Second World War, was outdated in its role as a maritime reconnaissance aircraft, but turned out to be the perfect machine for training raw pilots to fly multi-engined bombers. Consequently, over 11,000 were built.

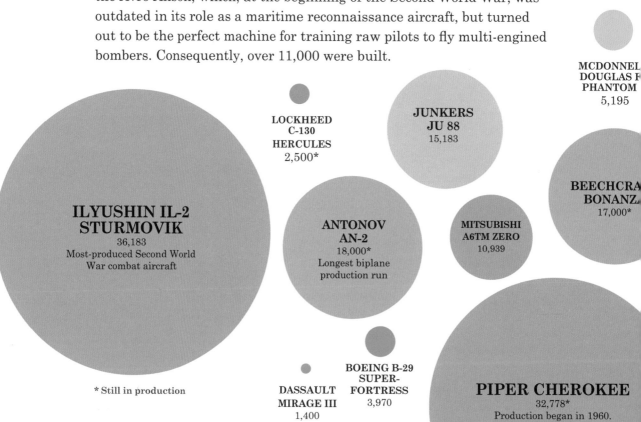

MCDONNEL
DOUGLAS F
PHANTOM
5,195

LOCKHEED
C-130
HERCULES
2,500*

JUNKERS
JU 88
15,183

BEECHCRA
BONANZ.
17,000*

ILYUSHIN IL-2
STURMOVIK
36,183
Most-produced Second World
War combat aircraft

ANTONOV
AN-2
18,000*
Longest biplane
production run

MITSUBISHI
A6TM ZERO
10,939

BOEING B-29
SUPER-
FORTRESS
3,970

PIPER CHEROKEE
32,778*
Production began in 1960.
Still being built.

DASSAULT
MIRAGE III
1,400

* Still in production

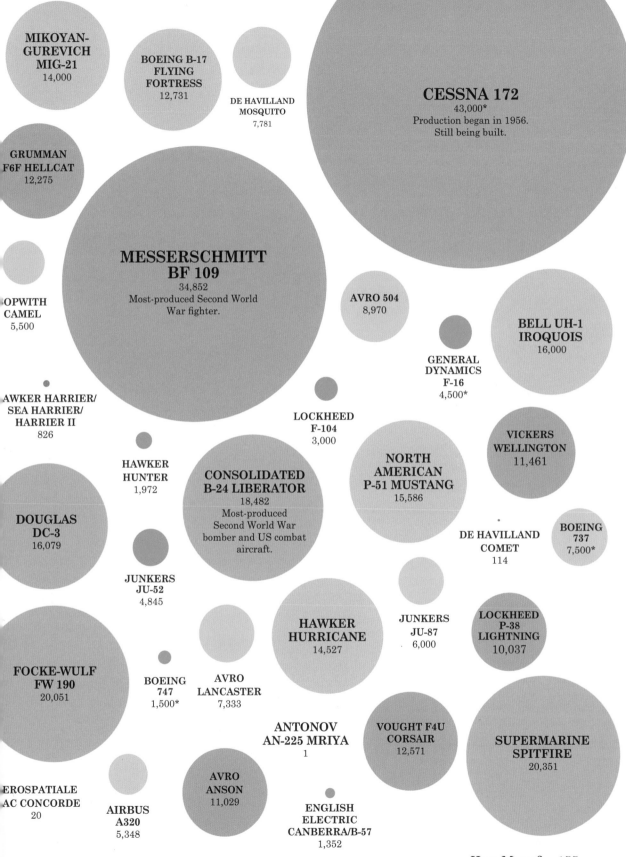

MIKOYAN-
GUREVICH
MIG-21
14,000

BOEING B-17
FLYING
FORTRESS
12,731

DE HAVILLAND
MOSQUITO
7,781

CESSNA 172
43,000*
Production began in 1956.
Still being built.

GRUMMAN
F6F HELLCAT
12,275

MESSERSCHMITT
BF 109
34,852
Most-produced Second World
War fighter.

AVRO 504
8,970

BELL UH-1
IROQUOIS
16,000

OPWITH
CAMEL
5,500

GENERAL
DYNAMICS
F-16
4,500*

AWKER HARRIER/
SEA HARRIER/
HARRIER II
826

LOCKHEED
F-104
3,000

VICKERS
WELLINGTON
11,461

HAWKER
HUNTER
1,972

CONSOLIDATED
B-24 LIBERATOR
18,482
Most-produced
Second World War
bomber and US combat
aircraft.

NORTH
AMERICAN
P-51 MUSTANG
15,586

DE HAVILLAND
COMET
114

BOEING
737
7,500*

DOUGLAS
DC-3
16,079

JUNKERS
JU-52
4,845

JUNKERS
JU-87
6,000

LOCKHEED
P-38
LIGHTNING
10,037

HAWKER
HURRICANE
14,527

FOCKE-WULF
FW 190
20,051

BOEING
747
1,500*

AVRO
LANCASTER
7,333

ANTONOV
AN-225 MRIYA
1

VOUGHT F4U
CORSAIR
12,571

SUPERMARINE
SPITFIRE
20,351

EROSPATIALE
AC CONCORDE
20

AIRBUS
A320
5,348

AVRO
ANSON
11,029

ENGLISH
ELECTRIC
CANBERRA/B-57
1,352

How Many?   155

Great Planes

Lockheed C-130 Hercules

Still in production nearly years after it first flew, the C-130 Hercules is impressive because of its sheer ubiquity. At the first sign of trouble, conflict or disaster you can be sure that a Hercules will be involved. No other aircraft being built today has enjoyed as varied or as exciting a career as the Herc. Always in the thick of it – unlike most pointy-nosed, slick-winged fighter jets – the C-130 gets . And, it seems, for pretty much everything. If you want interesting aviation stories, wherever the Hercules is flying is the place to look.

First flight: 23 August 1954
Principal operators: US Air Force, US Marine Corps, Royal Air Force
Last operational flight: Not for some time . . .

Flying in a Milk Bottle

The Story of Polar Aviation

There are at least seven South Poles, including the magnetic pole, the pole of rotation, the geographic pole and the pole of inaccessibility, the last being the point on Antarctica that is furthest in all directions from the sea. Dr Leonid Rogozov was a physician at Vostok Station, the Soviet base established in 1957 at the southern pole of cold – the coldest place on Earth – where temperatures as low as minus 89°C have been recorded. In April 1961 Rogozov began suffering from acute stomach pain, which he recognized as appendicitis. Without an operation, he would die.

Unfortunately, April falls at the beginning of the polar winter, and the pole of cold, which is high and remote, is hit especially hard. Nothing can fly, so no help could reach Rogozov. The only physician at the Soviet polar station was Rogozov himself, so he would have to remove his own appendix in order to survive. 'It's almost impossible,' he wrote in his diary, 'but I can't just fold my arms and give up.'

Taking on supplies at McMurdo Station. The Douglas R4D – a version of the ubiquitous DC-3 – was the backbone of the US Navy's development squadron, VXE-6, until the introduction of the LC-130 Hercules in 1962.

Helped by a mirror, but working without gloves and largely by feel, Rogozov fought off faintness throughout the operation. When he cut out his appendix, he felt his heart seize in response, but an hour and three-quarters later he'd successfully completed the operation. He was back on duty two weeks later.

Clearly, flying in Antarctica is not a year-round activity, even for VXE-6, the squadron set up by the US Navy in support of their country's Antarctic programme. Over a period of 45 years, until the squadron was disestablished in 1999, 20 personnel gave their lives, and the remains of crashed and abandoned aircraft and helicopters were left dotted around the continent in a grim echo of the early days of polar aviation.

Following Salomon Andrée's fatal expedition to reach the North Pole by balloon in 1897, other pioneers met with mixed results. In 1907 and 1909 American journalist Walter Wellman failed in his attempts to fly to the North Pole by airship. In 1926 legendary polar explorer Roald Amundsen, the man who beat Captain Scott in the race to reach the South Pole on foot, made an attempt on the North Pole (90°N) in a pair of German Dornier Wal flying boats. The team got within 120 miles of their target before being

forced to land. It was three weeks before they were able to escape the ice in a single aircraft and return to the safety of Spitsbergen in Norway.

Later that year, the US Navy's Richard Byrd, along with pilot Floyd Bennett, claimed to have made a round trip from Spitsbergen to the North Pole in a Fokker Trimotor. Although airborne for over 15 hours, the duration of the flight was believed by some to have been implausibly quick. Two days after their return, Amundsen left Spitsbergen in the airship *Norge*, flown by Italian aviator Umberto Nobile. Also aboard was the expedition's American sponsor, Lincoln Ellsworth. Three days later, after dropping Norwegian, Italian and American flags as they overflew the pole, they arrived in Alaska.

Two years after that success, Nobile mounted a second expedition to the North Pole, which was to end in disaster. His airship *Italia* crashed into the pack ice, tipping out nine survivors, before climbing away, never to be seen again. On 18 June 1928, over three weeks into a massive international search and rescue effort, a plane carrying Roald Amundsen to Spitsbergen to lend his expertise was also lost without trace. Meanwhile, the survivors, living off polar-bear meat, were found by a Swedish pilot five days after Amundsen's death, but it was another three weeks before the last of them would be rescued by a Russian icebreaker.

And it was the Russians who, throughout the 1930s, began to dominate Arctic aviation, landing near the North Pole for the first time in 1937 to establish a polar ice station. After the Second World War, their ability to operate aircraft in such conditions began to worry the US military as new Cold War battle lines were established. Ironically, it was an American pilot flying a US fighter plane who did much to alert US Air Defenses to the danger. On 29 May 1951 Charles F. Blair, Jr., an experienced naval test pilot and airline captain, flew a modified P-51C Mustang he'd named *Excalibur III* from Norway to Fairbanks, Alaska. Using a $10 astrocompass to navigate, he completed the 3260-mile journey across the North Pole in 10 hours and 27 minutes. And if *he* could do it, USAF planners decided, so too could Soviet bombers.

Although no more than a frozen sea, the North Pole was, in aviation terms, always going to be a waypoint rather than a destination in itself. From 1945, the RAF's Empire Air Navigation School, flying modified Avro Lancaster and Lincoln bombers, staged a series of much-publicized 'Aries' flights in search of the north magnetic pole. Today airliners travelling between North America and South-East Asia routinely fly over the North Pole because, at 30,000 feet, it's simply the shortest distance between two

A bearded Sir Hubert Wilkins poses alongside one of the two Lockheed Vega floatplanes he took to Antarctica in 1928. On his historic 1300-mile survey flight over the Antarctic peninsula, he and his co-pilot carried with them supplies of biscuits, chocolate, malted milk tablets, nuts, pemmican – a high-calorie mixture of fat and meat – and raisins in case of emergency.

points. Cruising at that height also carries none of the risks that the Arctic pioneers took. In Antarctica, though, the story has always been different.

Although he missed out on being first to the South Pole, Captain Robert Falcon Scott became the first man ever to fly over Antarctica, when, in 1902, he rose above McMurdo Sound in a gas balloon. During the next ascent, his third lieutenant, Ernest Shackleton, took photographs of the landscape before a rip in the balloon's envelope brought him back down to Earth. It was a further 26 years before anyone attempted to fly an aeroplane over the ice.

Australian explorer Sir Hubert Wilkins had been knighted after a daring flight across the Arctic in 1928. Forced down by a storm, he and his co-pilot were lucky to survive. Later that year the same Lockheed Vega monoplane crashed through thin ice following an initial 20-minute flight in Antarctica, forcing Wilkins to use her sister plane, another Vega, for an 11-hour survey of the Antarctic peninsula. The glory, however, would be reserved for whoever made the first flight over the South Pole.

Although doubts have lingered about the veracity of Richard Byrd's claim to be the first to fly over the North Pole, there's no argument about his place in Antarctic aviation. During the austral summer of 1929, Byrd unequivocally became the first man to overfly the South Pole.

In 1946, and now an admiral, Byrd led a task group participating in
Operation Highjump, an armada of US Navy ships and aircraft sent south
to conduct surveys and consolidate America's presence in Antarctica.
He returned in 1955 commanding Operation Deep Freeze I, part of an
international initiative to improve understanding of the region. The US
Navy's VXE-6 Antarctic development squadron (originally VX-6) was
established the same year. They conducted nine flights during that first
season, but the Deep Freeze deployment became an annual one and the
squadron, which dubbed itself the 'Puckered Penguins', became the most
expert and experienced polar aviation unit in history.

In 1962 they acquired the first of the ski-equipped Lockheed LC-130
Hercules transports that became synonymous with US Antarctic flying.
Alongside these, C-130s of New Zealand, Australia, Italy, Uruguay,
Argentina and Chile also ferried in and out of the ice runway at McMurdo
Sound in support of the scientists. And in 1972, after the loss of two US Navy
Hercs, a pair of RAF C-130s were deployed to McMurdo to help plug the gap.
On 8 December one of the crews managed an overflight of the pole itself.

The first concerted British aviation effort in Antarctica had been 17 years
earlier, between 1955 and 1957, when a pair of Canso flying boats surveyed
60,000 miles of previously unmapped territory. Their successors, the red

ABOVE: *A ski-equipped de Havilland Canada Twin Otter of the British
Antarctic Survey takes off from Burns Bluff, Antarctica. BAS operates
four of the rugged twin turboprops.*

de Havilland Canada Twin Otters and DHC-7 Dash 7 of the British Antarctic Survey, still operate today, but the US operation remains pre-eminent.

Before its replacement by an Air National Guard unit at the end of the 1999 season, the VXE-6 had transported nearly 200,000 passengers and 10 million gallons of fuel in support of the Antarctic research programme. During the southern hemisphere summer (November–March), the frequency of flights to and from Antarctica gave the impression of being almost routine. The 237 passengers boarding Air New Zealand Flight 901 on 28 November 1979 would certainly have believed that.

Since 1977, Air New Zealand and the Australian airline Qantas had flown commercial sightseeing flights over Antarctica, often in the company of an eminent guide. In fact, the explorer Sir Edmund Hillary was supposed to have been on board Flight 901 until a diary clash forced him to back out.

Four hours after taking off from Auckland, the big Air New Zealand McDonnell-Douglas DC-10 was given clearance to descend to 10,000 feet and continue visually. The decision regarding altitude now rested with the pilots. It was a bright, clear day and they informed air traffic control that they were descending to 2000 feet. Ahead of them, a blanket of cloud masking its outline against the sky, lay Mount Erebus, rising 12,500 feet above the sea. Unfortunately, navigational errors before their departure meant the crew were not where they thought. Even worse, Captain Jim Collins had to cope with 'whiteout', where the snow merges seamlessly with the white sky to obliterate the horizon. It looked from the cockpit as if they were maintaining height over the flat McMurdo ice shelf. In reality, Erebus was rising to meet them with every yard of forward flight. At 12.49 p.m. an electronic alarm sounded to warn the crew they were dangerously close to the ground.

Collins ordered full power in order to climb to safety, but it was too late. Six seconds later, the airliner smashed into the mountainside. About an hour later, the US Navy reported that it had lost radio contact with the jet.

Just a year earlier, VXE-6 crews had evacuated the survivors of a Soviet air crash on Antarctica. This time round, there was no one left to save.

The tragic loss of Flight 901 brought an end to commercial sightseeing flights over Antarctica. Today only a route between South Africa and New Zealand would carry commercial passengers across Antarctica, but there is no direct flight.

'Flying in a milk bottle', the expression used by one of the air accident investigators to describe the whiteout conditions experienced by the crew of Flight 901, is once more the sole preserve of specialists.

Meatbox, Buff and Shagbat
101 Aircraft Nicknames

As fighter pilots attract callsigns, so aircraft are given nicknames. Sometimes they display no more imagination than is on offer in your average sports autobiography. The Mosquito becomes the 'Mossie', the Hurricane the 'Hurry', the Spitfire the 'Spit' and the Lancaster the 'Lanc'. On other occasions an official designation gets adapted. The B-1 Lancer (or B-ONE Lancer) has become the 'Bone', the Grumman S2F Tracker the 'Stoof', and, cleverly, in the case of the F-106 Delta Dart the 'Six'. Sometimes it's the appearance or a physical feature that is the inspiration, as in the case of the F4U Corsair's 'Bent-Wing Bird' or the A-6 Intruder's 'Drumstick'. Then there are the names that are prompted by a characteristic of the aircraft's performance or safety record and these can be biting. The Skywarrior's lack of ejection seats meant its A3D designation led to 'All Three Dead'. Problems with contaminated cabin air inevitably led to the BAe 146 airliner being saddled with 'Gas Chamber'. And, just occasionally, nicknames can become so widely used that they end up more or less displacing the given name, as in the case of the Huey (né Iroquois) helicopter, or actually being formally adopted. For years, the long-snouted F-111 swing-wing strike jet was known to its crews as the 'Aardvark'. In 1996, at a ceremony marking its retirement from the US Air Force after nearly thirty years on the frontline, Aardvark became its official name.

NICKNAME	MANUFACTURER/MODEL	NICKNAME	MANUFACTURER/MODEL
Aardvark	General Dynamics F-111	Canuck	Avro CF-100
Acemaker	Grumman F6F Hellcat	Concordski	Tupolev Tu-144 Charger
Aerosplat	Cessna 152 Aerobat	Cranberry	Martin B-57 Canberra
All Three Dead	Douglas A3D Skywarrior	Crocodile	Mil Mi-24 Hind
Aluminum Overcast	Convair B-36 Peacemaker	Crouze, Le	Vought F-8FN Crusader (in France)
Banana Jet	Blackburn Buccaneer		
Barney	Boeing C-17 Globemaster III	Daffy	Boulton-Paul Defiant
Beast, The	Supermarine Scimitar	Dave	Lockheed Martin F-35 Lightning II
Bent-Wing Bird	Vought F4U Corsair		
Bone	Rockwell B-1 Lancer	Deuce, The	Convair F-102 Delta Dagger
Black Jet, The	Lockheed F-117 Nighthawk	Doodlebug	V-1 flying bomb
		Double Ugly	McDonnell Douglas F-4 Phantom II
Bubble	Bell 47		
BUFF	Boeing B-52	Dragon Lady	Lockheed U2
(Big Ugly Fat Fella)	Stratofortress	Drumstick	Grumman A-6 Intruder
Bug	McDonnell-Douglas F/A-18 Hornet	Dumbo	Consolidated PBY Catalina

NICKNAME	MANUFACTURER/MODEL	NICKNAME	MANUFACTURER/MODEL
Dutch Oven	Fokker 100	Pig, The	General Dynamics F-111 Aardvark (in Australia)
Eierlegende Wollmilchsau, Die *(The Egg-Laying Wool Milk Pig)*	Panavia Tornado (in Germany)	Pisser	Sikorsky H-53 Sea Stallion
		Puff the Magic Dragon	Douglas AC-47
Fat Albert	Lockheed C-130 Hercules	Rhino	McDonnell Douglas F-4 Phantom II
Fliegender Ziegelstein *(Flying Brick)*	McDonnell Douglas F-4 Phantom II	Scooter	Douglas A-4 Skyhawk
		Shagbat	Supermarine Walrus
Flying Flat Iron	Gloster Javelin	SHAR	BAe Sea Harrier
Flying Longhouse	Bristol Beverley	Sled	Lockheed SR-71 Blackbird
Flying Porcupine	Short Sunderland	SLUF *(Short Little Ugly Fella)*	LTV A-7 Corvair II
Flying Potato	Martin-Marietta X-24A		
Flying Shithouse	Kaman HH043 Huskie	Slug	Short Belfast
Flying Suitcase	Handley-Page Hampden	Snake	Bell AH-1 Cobra
Fork-Tailed Devil	Lockheed P-38 Lightning	Spad	Douglas A-1 Skyraider
FRED *(F**king Ridiculous Economic Disaster)*	Lockheed C-5 Galaxy	Sparkvark	General Dynamics EF-111 Raven
		Spooky	Lockheed AC-130 Spectre
		Spruce Goose	Hughes H-4 Hercules
Frightening	English Electric Lightning	Stoof	Grumman S2F Tracker
Gas Chamber, The	BAe 146	Stratobladder	KC-135 Stratotanker
Gooney Bird	Douglas C-47 Skytrain	Stringbag	Fairey Swordfish
Gravel Truck, The	De Havilland DHC-4 Caribou	Super Scooper	Canadair C-415
		T-Bird	Lockheed T-33
Grizzly	Airbus A400M Atlas	Thud	F-105 Thunderbolt
Ground Gripper	Hawker Siddeley Trident	Tiffy	Hawker Typhoon
Habu	Lockheed SR-71 Blackbird	Tin Triangle	Avro Vulcan
		Tonka	Panavia Tornado
Halibag	Handley-Page Halifax	Toom	McDonnell Douglas F-4 Phantom II
Hoover	Lockheed S-6 Viking	Tweety Bird	Cessna T-37
Huey	Bell UH-1 Iroquois	Vickers Knickers	Vickers VC-10
Hun	North American F-100 Super Sabre	Viper	General Dynamics F-16 Fighting Falcon
Iron Tadpole	Grumman A-6 Intruder		
JP	Hunting Jet Provost	Warthog	Fairchild A-10 Thunderbolt II
Jug, The	Republic P-47 Thunderbolt	Whale	Douglas A-3 Skywarrior
		Whiskey	Bell AH-1W Cobra
Jumbo	Boeing 747	Whispering Death	Bristol Beaufighter
Jump Jet	Harrier	Whispering Giant	Bristol Britannia
Little Bird	Hughes OH-6 Cayuse	Whispering Nissen Hut	Short Skyvan
Lizzie	Westland Lysander		
Meatbox	Gloster Meteor	Whistling Tit	Armstrong Whitworth Argosy
MiG Master	Vought F-8 Crusader	Widowmaker	Lockheed F-104 Starfighter
Missile with a Man in It	Lockheed F-104 Starfighter	Wimpy	Vickers Wellington
		Wooden Wonder	de Havilland Mosquito
Muerte Negra, La *(The Black Death)*	BAe Sea Harrier (by Argentine fighter pilots)	Wokka	Chinook
One-Oh-Wonder	McDonnell F-101 Voodoo		

A Lot Less Bovver
with a Hover
The Hovercraft Story

In the early 1950s, Sir Christopher Cockerell, the inventor of the hovercraft, tried to interest Britain's military in his revolutionary new idea. Using a working model of his invention, he conducted demonstrations of the technology to all three branches of the armed forces. And although it was enough to get his work classified, no funding was forthcoming. 'The navy,' he reported later, 'said it was a plane, not a boat; the air force said it was a boat, not a plane.' The army, meanwhile, displayed no interest at all.

We'll ignore all three of them. For our purposes – and thus justifying its inclusion in this book – the hovercraft is a flying machine (albeit not one that flies very high).

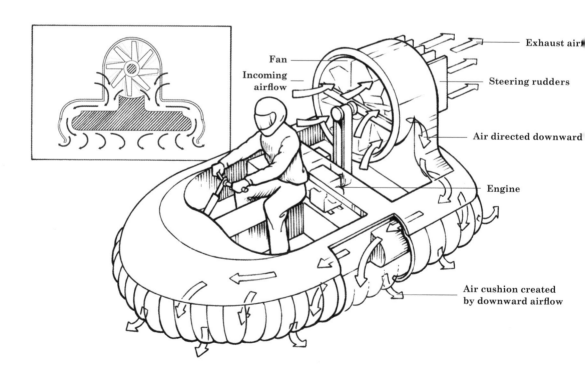

Fan

Incoming airflow

Exhaust air

Steering rudders

Air directed downward

Engine

Air cushion created by downward airflow

Cockerell's idea was simple. His vehicle worked by riding a cushion of air generated by fans and was therefore capable of travelling with equal ease over both land and water.

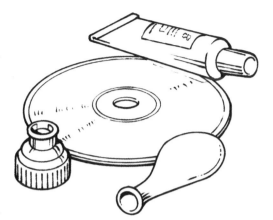

The principle that Cockerell first explored using a hairdryer and two tin cans is so simple that it's easy to make a working model at home from a CD, a water bottle nozzle, a balloon and some strong glue.

HOW TO DO IT

1. Unscrew the nozzle from a sports water bottle. If necessary, sand the bottom of the nozzle a little so that it's flat.

2. Glue the water bottle nozzle over the hole in the middle of the CD and leave it long enough to set.

3. Blow up a balloon, pinch the end, then stretch it over the nozzle glued to the CD – be careful to keep pinching while doing this so that the air doesn't escape. It's a bit fiddly, but no more than it is trying to tie a knot in the end.

4. Put the CD on a flat, smooth surface – a glass table is perfect – gently release the neck of the balloon and give it a nudge. Your hovercraft will now go blowing across the table like a flatulent ice hockey puck.

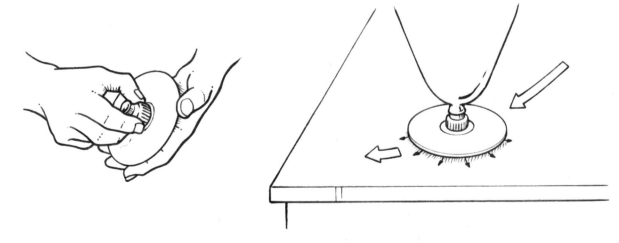

ELEVEN HOVERCRAFT FACTS

1. The world's first practical people-carrying hovercraft was the SR.N1, which first hovered on 11 June 1959.
2. SR.N1 made the first hovercraft crossing of the English Channel on 25 July 1959, the fiftieth anniversary of Louis Blériot's first aerial crossing.
3. SR.N1's chief test pilot, Commander Peter 'Sleepy' Lamb, was at the time of the crossing also the holder of the British records for height and airspeed, which he set while flying the rocket-powered SR.53 fighter prototype.
4. The world's first car-carrying hovercraft, the 'Mountbatten' Class SR.N4, entered service in 1968. It was, at the time, the largest hovercraft in the world.
5. Both the US Navy and Army trialled the use of combat hovercraft in Vietnam, using the Bell SK-5, a licence-built version of the British SR.N5. Typically enough, they looked a lot more rock 'n' roll than their British counterparts.
6. In 1969–70 the Trans-Africa Hovercraft Expedition travelled 5000 miles through Western and Equatorial Africa. Although they met President Mobutu of Zaire and discovered that a hovercraft could pass over an egg without damaging it, deputy leader Robin Hanbury-Tenison said later that the effort had taught him 'a lot about how expeditions should not be run'.

Although the world's first practical hovercraft set records and attracted huge interest from the public, the Saunders-Roe SR.N1 was not a machine fêted for her good looks.

The first passenger-carrying SR.N4 was christened Princess Margaret. *I'm not sure whether she would have been pleased or not. Especially when* Princess Anne *set the record for the fastest Channel crossing.*

7. The British Hovercraft Corporation created the world's largest Union flag when, to celebrate the Queen's Silver Jubilee in 1977, it painted one on the doors of its hangar at East Cowes, Isle of Wight.

8. Capable of 70 knots, the SR.N4 Mk III set the record for the fastest Channel crossing on 14 September 1995 when it travelled between Dover and Boulogne in just 22 minutes.

9. The RTV-31, an experimental hovercraft train, was developed in Britain throughout the 1960s and early 1970s. It was hoped it would provide 250 mph trains, but it was cancelled in 1973.

10. The world's largest hovercraft is now the Russian 'Zubr' Class Air-Cushioned Landing Craft. Capable of carrying up to 500 troops, it also became the first Russian-built ship to be used by a NATO member when four were acquired by the Greek Navy.

11. After weathering the opening of the Channel Tunnel, the cross-Channel hovercraft service ended in 2000, after thirty-two years, when the abolition of duty-free sales within the European Union in 1999 made it commercially unviable.

Rocket Man

The Story of John Stapp

In 1955, a 45-year-old doctor who had once hoped to become a paediatrician made the cover of *Time* magazine. John Stapp was one of the most famous people in America. Today, few people know his name, but some of you reading this will owe him your life.

Stapp joined the US Army Air Corps in 1944. In 1946, after a posting to the Aeromedical Laboratory, he flew a series of flights in a stripped-down B-17 Flying Fortress bomber to study the effects of high altitude on the human body. For over 65 hours at 45,000 feet inside the stratosphere, Stapp had used himself as the test subject. It was an approach he persevered with on his next assignment: exploring the ability of the human body to withstand sudden deceleration, using a rocket-powered sled on rails known as Gee Whiz. It was a job you'd think twice about giving to a guinea pig.

It was widely held that 18G – that is, eighteen times the force of gravity – was the limit of human endurance, but anecdotal evidence from crash survivors suggested otherwise. In December 1947, after months of tests using a crash-test dummy named Oscar Eightball, Stapp, facing backwards, strapped himself into Gee Whiz. A single rocket accelerated the sled to 90 mph before coming to an abrupt stop in a water trap. At the end of the first run Stapp had momentarily experienced 10G. The next day he added two more rockets. Nine months later – during which time he broke his wrist (twice), his collarbone and ribs, and lost fillings – he'd added forward-facing runs to his repertoire and survived a deceleration of 35G.

But as Stapp pushed the envelope, pilots in experimental rocketplanes and new jet fighter prototypes were doing the same. As supersonic flight became routine, so too did the requirement to escape from an aircraft flying faster than the speed of sound. But was that survivable?

Using a new sled, Sonic Wind, powered by up to twelve rockets capable of generating the same thrust used to launch a V-2 ballistic missile, Stapp planned to find out. In March 1954, before his first run aboard the 750 mph sled, he told a waiting reporter: 'I assure you I'm not looking forward to this.'

At the end, a still adrenalin-charged Stapp said he felt fine, 'ready to do it again this afternoon'. But he would ride the sled on only two more occasions. In November that year he knocked off a 12G run, claiming it as his 'easiest', but it was his next encounter with Sonic Wind in which he planned to tackle the speed of sound, then decelerate to a stop in just 1.4 seconds. It would be like strapping himself to a bullet.

As nine rockets fired together, Stapp roared off down the rails. Clamped in his mouth was a rubber bite block containing an accelerometer. As he passed 600 mph, he overtook a T-33 jet that was supposed to be following his progress. Then he hit the water brake, sending an explosive white plume of spray into the air. From the cockpit of the T-33, pilot Joe Kittinger feared the worst. 'Inconceivable,' he thought, 'that anybody could go that fast and then just stop, and survive.'

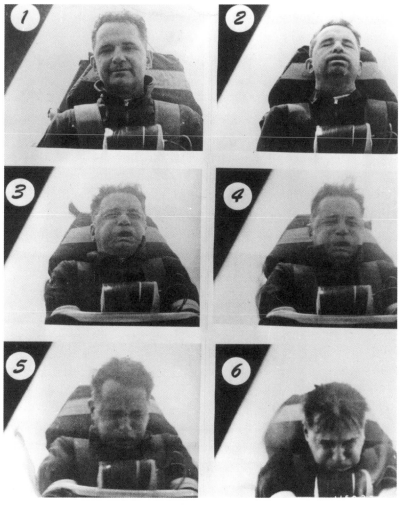

The effect of the massive acceleration and deceleration John Stapp experienced during one of his rocket sled runs is painfully apparent.

During the early years of the space programme, NASA scientists referred to 'eyeballs-in' and 'eyeballs-out' phases of flight. Powerful acceleration would force blood to the back of the head, draining the eyes and causing tunnel vision and grey-out. Deceleration was worse, forcing blood forward, and bursting capillaries like the popped juice sacs of an orange. When Stapp was helped out of Sonic Wind, his eyes were completely filled with blood.

Momentarily, he had experienced over 46G – forty-six times the force of gravity. And for over a second he'd endured 25G. It was calculated to be equivalent to an ejection at over 1½ times the speed of sound at an altitude of over 7½ miles. Unable to see, Stapp said: 'This time I get the white cane and the seeing-eye dog.' Fortunately, he didn't need them. A day later, despite his eyes' bloodshot appearance, his vision had all but come back. And he was now famous. Newspapers dubbed him 'the fastest man on Earth'. None of the hoopla was of much interest to Stapp, but he did recognize that it provided him with an opportunity.

During the rocket-sled tests, 'the bravest man in the Air Force' had realized that alongside saving the lives of pilots, his research was equally relevant to the car industry. The year after his final ride aboard Sonic Wind, Stapp announced: 'I'm leading a crusade for the prevention of needless deaths.' And when, in 1966, President Lyndon Johnson made it compulsory for all new cars in America to be fitted with seatbelts (actually being required to wear them took a little longer to legislate), John Stapp stood beside him. Stapp died in 1999 but his contribution to road safety is in no danger of being forgotten. The 57th annual Stapp Car Crash Conference will be held in Orlando, Florida in November 2013.

THE INCREDIBLE 7-TON MAN

For all his lasting legacy, it wasn't actually JoÚ Stapp who posted the highest G-load ever recorded. That honour goes to a US Air Force captain called Eli Beeding. In 1958, during a series of tests overseen by Stapp, Beeding was, for just under half a second, subjected to a whopping 82.6G.

Assuming Beeding was of fairly average build, his body in that fraction of a second weighed over *7 tons*. By comparison, an African elephant usually tops out around 5 tons. Beeding's head alone weighed nearly half a ton.

Beeding himself compared the experience to being hit in the small of the back with a baseball bat. He reckoned that 83G was probably the limit of human endurance. No one has yet felt the urge to prove otherwise . . .

Don't Touch That Button!
The Aircraft Cockpit

To the untutored eye the array of switches and dials in an aircraft appears almost comic in its complexity. It is, in fact, less daunting than first impressions suggest, and much the same whether you're in a little piston-engined puddle-jumper or Concorde. The pilot's three priorities are to aviate, navigate and communicate, and just six of the dials are required for these tasks. Only if there is no autopilot and you're absolutely in control of flying the plane should you worry about anything else.

Airspeed indicator
If flying straight and level with the needle in the green, you're OK. In smooth air, if not manoeuvring, it's safe to fly with the needle in the yellow. Never exceed the red line.

Attitude indicator
The AI indicates pitch and roll and, if you're flying blind – in cloud, for instance – is the most important instrument.

Altimeter
This indicates height by measuring air pressure above a point of your choosing. You can therefore calibrate it for height above high ground as opposed to height above sea level.

Turn coordinator
As you'd expect, this measures your rate of turn. It's generally calibrated to indicate a 2-minute turn, i.e. the bank angle you'd need to complete a 360-degree turn in 2 minutes.

Heading indicator
Also known as a direction indicator, this gives the same information as a compass, but rather than using magnetism, it uses a gyroscope and needs to be set by the pilot.

Vertical speed indicator
This give an instantaneous indication of your rate of climb or descent and is a crucial indicator of whether or not you're flying straight and level.

In Search of Dan Dare
British Rocketplanes

Colonel Dan Dare of the Interplanetary Space Fleet first flew out of the pages of *Eagle* comic in 1950. While America and Russia competed to be the first to put a man into outer space, it seemed Britain would have to make do with Colonel Dare and his rocket ship *Anastasia*. And yet, for the best part of a decade, the possibility of a British manned space programme was more than just science fiction.

The RAF, it was decided, needed to be in the business of 'Near Space Control' and 'Far Space Control'. The pre-transistor, pre-microchip technology of the day meant it was thought that, at the very least, there would be a need for astronauts to change satellites' faulty vacuum tube valves.

Companies such as de Havilland, English Electric, Rolls-Royce, Saunders-Roe and Armstrong-Whitworth drew up plans for space hardware, and rocket test facilities were built in Cumbria and the Isle of Wight. In Manchester a textiles company called P. Frankenstein & Sons developed spacesuits, which were tested at facilities in Canada because this was to be an effort shared by the British Empire. At Woomera in the South Australian desert, a massive man-rated launch pad was built. Transport aircraft were designed to carry rockets to facilities as far afield as Libya, Borneo and British Somaliland. And in Stevenage, Hertfordshire, a factory capable of building fifty rockets a year was set up. The rocket, planned as both a ballistic nuclear missile and satellite launch vehicle, was to be called Blue Streak.

In 1959 a disagreement with *Eagle* comic's new owners forced Frank Hampson, Dan Dare's creator, to leave. Their objection was to the cost and complexity involved in bringing the Pilot of the Future to life. It proved to be a hint of what was to come. A year later, in July 1960, the government told the country that the RAF's Manned Space Programme had been cancelled. Cost and complexity were again to blame.

Blue Streak stumbled on as a civilian programme, and even flew a number of successful trial flights in the mid-1960s, but we're still waiting for the real Dan Dare.

Since those heady days in the 1950s, there's been no shortage of *designs* for British rocketplanes. A few of them are described opposite.

Armstrong-Whitworth 'Pyramid'

Declassified and described at the 1959 Commonwealth Spaceflight Symposium – before the cancellation of Britain's military space programme – the Pyramid was a credible solution to the challenge of re-entry, designed to be launched with an uprated Blue Streak rocket. Sharp-edged, wedge-shaped and flat-bottomed, the two-man Pyramid was a lifting-body design in all but name.

Saunders-Roe SR.53

Uniquely among the designs on this page, the Saunders-Roe SR.53 was built and flew an extensive test programme in the late 1950s. Powered by both a rocket and jet engine, the SR.53 set British speed and altitude records but ambitious plans to launch it to the edge of space from the back of a V-bomber never progressed beyond blueprints for fitting spaceship-style reaction controls in the wingtips and nose.

Avro Z.101

The Avro Z.101 was an intriguing 1961 proposal to create a British X-15-style hypersonic research aircraft by adding an undercarriage and a cockpit to a Blue Steel nuclear cruise missile. Launched from a V-bomber mothership and expected to be capable of speeds up to Mach 5 and altitudes of 300,000 feet, the combination of Blue Steel's unreliability with the lack of an ejection seat would have made the pilot's task an unenviable one.

BAC MUSTARD

The Multi-Unit Space Transport and Recovery Device gave a great acronym (you can't help but wonder if perhaps that came first and the design second). It was a 1966 plan from the British Aircraft Corporation for a trio of reusable machines, using two as fuel-carrying boosters and a third as an orbiter. Very similar concepts were explored and abandoned in the US during the same period.

British Aerospace HOTOL

Built around a revolutionary air-breathing rocket engine, for a while during the 1980s

ABOVE: *The Saunders-Roe SR.53. A British rocketplane that flew.*
BELOW: *The BAC MUSTARD. A British rocketplane that didn't.*

HOTOL (Horizontal Take-Off and Landing) felt as if it had a chance of making it off the drawing board. Its designers struggled to overcome stability problems caused by the location of the engines at the rear. Then, with the project's cancellation, found the engine technology they'd invented was classified top secret by the government.

Reaction Engines Skylon

Son of HOTOL. Skylon is a private initiative run by the engineers behind the 1980s BAe spaceplane design. Designed to deliver satellites to low Earth orbit while taking off and landing from a runway, Skylon would be a game-changer. The team has got around government obstruction, addressed aerodynamic challenges and had European Space Agency confirmation that their SABRE air-breathing rocket engine technology works. Now they need money. Good luck.

'Talk to me, Goose ...'
Some Fictional Pilots

Steve Austin
The Six Million Dollar Man, rebuilt to be better, faster, stronger after suffering severe injuries in a crash during flight testing over the Mojave Desert.

Pete 'Maverick' Mitchell (above)
Feels the need for speed. Loves beach volleyball, being dangerous and singing 'You've Lost That Lovin' Feelin''. Hates Iceman ... until invited to be his wingman 'anytime'.

Luke Skywalker
Star Wars hero who, in a sequence inspired by *The Dam Busters* and *633 Squadron* films, destroys the Death Star.

Nick 'Goose' Bradshaw
Sent to Top Gun with Maverick, but Goose *shouldn't* be on this list as he wasn't a pilot at all, but an RIO, or Radar Intercept Officer.

Dan Dare
Eagle comic's quintessentially British Interplanetary Space Fleet hero and Mekon botherer.

James 'Biggles' Bigglesworth
The most famous fictional pilot of all? Captain W. E. Johns's legendary First World War ace.

Buck Danny
Since 1947, this fictional US military aviator has been the star of over fifty French *bandes-dessinées* – or graphic novels.

Stringfellow Hawke
Vietnam veteran Hawke is the pilot entrusted with the supersonic attack helicopter prototype *Airwolf*.

Major Tom
Astronaut hero of David Bowie's 'Space Oddity'. Lost in space. And, we learned later, a junkie.

Hal Jordan
Test pilot Jordan was given a power ring by a dying alien and was transformed into a superhero – the Green Lantern. Or something.

H. M. Murdock

A-Team member 'Howling Mad' Murdock was supposedly the best chopper pilot in Vietnam. On the flipside, he was officially declared insane, of course.

Starbuck

Forget the original series, hard-living aviator Kara Thrace, callsign 'Starbuck', from the 2004 remake of *Battlestar Galactica* is the only Starbuck.

Pussy Galore (above)

The seductive leader of Pussy Galore's Flying Circus in the James Bond classic *Goldfinger*. In Ian Fleming's original novel she was an acrobat, not a pilot.

Squadron Commander the Lord Flashheart

Royal Flying Corps ace, sex machine and Blackadder's nemesis in *Blackadder Goes Forth.*

Mitchell Gant

Doesn't say much, and even then it's a whisper or a snarl. Clint Eastwood, of course, playing the only man who can steal the Soviet's top secret Firefox.

Ben Grimm

Better known as Fantastic Four member 'The Thing'. This military test pilot joined NASA, only for cosmic rays to give him super-strength and bad skin.

Virgil Tracy

Supermarionated pilot of the best Thunderbird of all: half-transport jet, half-tortoise, *Thunderbird 2.*

Buck Rogers

In the 1979 movie and TV series Buck Rogers was an astronaut who awakes after 500 years in suspended animation to find himself in the twenty-fifth century.

(The Great) Waldo Pepper

Billed as 'The Second Greatest Flyer in the World', Robert Redford's Second World War veteran turned barnstormer is determined to be the first aviator to fly an outside loop.

Sir Percy Ware-Armitage

Played by the great Terry-Thomas in the 1965 film *Those Magnificent Men in Their Flying Machines.*

Han Solo

Obviously you can't have Luke Skywalker in here without also including the infinitely cooler pilot of the *Millennium Falcon* freighter.

Ted Striker

Traumatized, heartbroken and near blinded by tsunamis of sweat, ex-combat pilot Striker overcomes his fear of flying to land comedy classic *Airplane!* safely.

Who Are You?
Insignia of Today's Air Forces

During a 1910 bombing competition in Vienna, Bohemia (whatever happened to them?), France, Italy, Poland, Romania and Russia all painted identifying stripes on the wings of their aircraft. But this was little more than an aerial jousting tournament. The French started the modern style of national insignia in 1912, three years after the creation of their air service. Copying the style of the country's national cockade – the identifying ribbon design used on military hats – the familiar tricolour roundel appeared on French military aircraft.

Worried that the Union flag might be mistaken for a German Cross, the British Royal Flying Corps soon followed suit, reversing the colours of the French design (both designs survive to this day, albeit more often in their low-visibility guise). Romania was the first to follow the French lead. Then everybody else piled in . . .

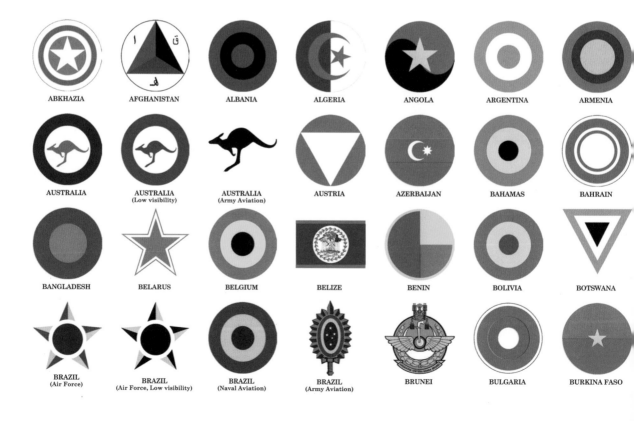

BURUNDI	CAMBODIA	CAMEROON	CANADA	CANADA (Low visibility)	CENTRAL AFRICAN REPUBLIC	CHAD
CHILE	CHILE (Low visibility)	REP. OF CHINA (TAIWAN)	REP. OF CHINA (TAIWAN) (Low visibility)	PEOPLE'S REP. OF CHINA	COLOMBIA	COLOMBIA (Low visibility)
COLOMBIA (Naval Aviation)	COMOROS	DEMOCRATIC REPUBLIC OF CONGO	REPUBLIC OF CONGO	CÔTE D'IVOIRE	CROATIA	CROATIA (Low visibility)
CUBA	CZECH REPUBLIC	CZECH REPUBLIC (Low visibility)	DENMARK	DJIBOUTI	DOMINICAN REPUBLIC	DOMINICAN REPUBLIC (Low visibility)
ECUADOR	ECUADOR (Naval Aviation)	EGYPT	EL SALVADOR	EQUATORIAL GUINEA	ERITREA	ESTONIA
ETHIOPIA	FINLAND	FRANCE	FRANCE (Naval Aviation)	FRANCE (Naval Aviation, Low visibility)	GABON	GEORGIA
GERMANY	GHANA	GREECE	GREECE (Low visibility)	GUATEMALA	GUINEA	GUINEA-BISSAU
HONDURAS	HUNGARY	HUNGARY (Low visibility)	ICELAND	INDIA	INDONESIA	INDONESIA (Army Aviation)
INDONESIA (Naval Aviation)	IRAN	IRAQ	REPUBLIC OF IRELAND	ISRAEL	ITALY	JAMAICA

JAPAN

JORDAN

KAZAKHSTAN

KENYA

KOREA, NORTH (DPRK)

KOREA, SOUTH (ROK)

KOREA, SOUTH (ROK)
(Low visibility)

KUWAIT

KYRGYZSTAN

LAOS

LATVIA

LEBANON

LESOTHO

FREE LIBYAN AIR FORC

LITHUANIA

LUXEMBOURG

MACEDONIA

MALAWI

MALAYSIA

MALAYSIA
(Naval Aviation)

MALDIVES

MALI

MALTA

MAURITANIA

MAURITIUS

MEXICO

MEXICO
(Low visibility)

MEXICO
(Naval Aviation)

MOLDOVA

MONGOLIA

MONTENEGRO

MOROCCO
(Combat Aircraft)

MOROCCO
(Non-combat Aircraft)

MOZAMBIQUE

MYANMAR

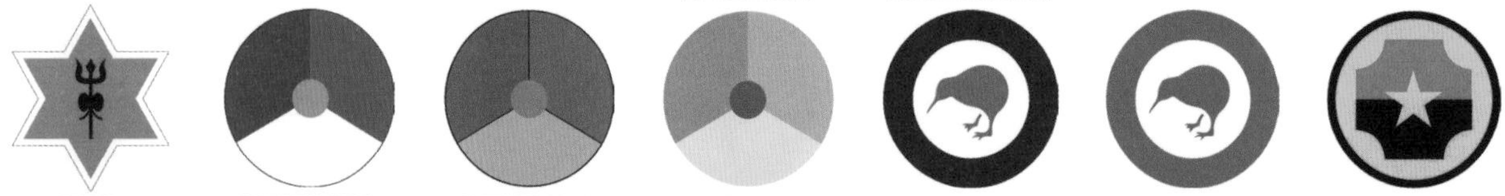

NEPAL

NETHERLANDS

NETHERLANDS
(Low visibility)

NETHERLANDS
(Alternative low visibility)

NEW ZEALAND

NEW ZEALAND
(Low visibility)

NICARAGUA

NIGER

NIGERIA

NIGERIA
(Naval Aviation)

NORWAY

NORWAY
(Low visibility)

PAKISTAN

PANAMA

PAPUA NEW GUINEA

PARAGUAY

PERU

PERU
(Naval Aviation)

PHILIPPINES

PHILIPPINES
(Low visibility)

POLAND

PORTUGAL

PORTUGAL
(Low visibility)

QATAR

ROMANIA

RUSSIA

RWANDA

SAUDI ARABIA

SAUDI ARABIA (Low visibility)	SENEGAL	SERBIA	SERBIA (Low visibility)	SIERRA LEONE	SINGAPORE	SINGAPORE (Low visibility)
SLOVAKIA	SLOVAKIA (Low visibility)	SLOVENIA	SOMALIA	SOUTH AFRICA	SOUTH AFRICA (Low visibility)	SOVEREIGN MILITARY ORDER OF MALTA
SPAIN	SRI LANKA	SUDAN	SURINAME	SWEDEN	SWEDEN (Low visibility)	SWITZERLAND
SYRIA	TANZANIA	THAILAND	TOGO	TRANSNISTRIA	TRINIDAD AND TOBAGO	TUNISIA
TURKEY	TURKMENISTAN	UGANDA	UKRAINE	UKRAINE (Naval Aviation)	UNITED ARAB EMIRATES	UNITED ARAB EMIRATES (Low visibility)
UNITED KINGDOM	UNITED KINGDOM (Low visibility)	UNITED KINGDOM (Low visibility, light)	UNITED STATES	UNITED STATES (Low visibility)	UNITED STATES (Alternative low visibility)	URUGUAY
URUGUAY (Naval Aviation)	UZBEKISTAN	VENEZUELA	VENEZUELA (Naval Aviation)	VIETNAM	YEMEN	ZAMBIA
ZIMBABWE	INTERNATIONAL SYMBOL OF CIVIL DEFENCE	HONG KONG FLYING SERVICE	NATO	POLAND (Border Guard)	UNITED NATIONS	US COAST GUARD

'The first time I ever saw a jet I shot it down'*

Fighter Combat during the Jet Age

Although both German Messerschmitt Me-262 and British Gloster Meteor jet fighters saw frontline service during the Second World War, they never met in combat. The first dogfight between two jet fighters would have to wait for a war that caught Western military planners by surprise.

When, at 0400 hours on 25 June 1950, North Korea attacked her neighbour to the south, it marked the beginning of three years of fighting. South Korea lacked an air force capable of offering any resistance. Two days later the United Nations passed a resolution authorizing whatever assistance South Korea needed to repel the attack. US Air Force units based in Japan might have been caught by surprise by the invasion, but its fighter squadrons were soon able to establish complete superiority over North Korea's collection of Second World War-vintage Soviet propeller aircraft. Their advantage wouldn't last long.

North American F-86 Sabres of the USAF's 51st Fighter Interceptor Group prepare for a mission at their base in South Korea. No. 2 Squadron of the South African Air Force also distinguished themselves by flying Sabres during the Korean War.

* Chuck Yeager, as ever, cuts to the chase.

With the North Koreans pushed back towards the Chinese border, the Chinese themselves joined the fight in November. And they sent MiG-15s, the very latest Soviet fighter design.

On 8 November, six MiGs climbed out of their bases in North Korea. South of the border, the pilots of two flights of patrolling USAF F-80 Shooting Stars, forbidden from crossing the border to go after them, could only watch – until, in pairs, the MiGs began diving towards them. The American pilots turned to meet them, but the old straight-winged F-80 was outclassed by the powerful, heavily armed MiG. It was also heavier. So as five of the MiGs climbed away to safety, the sixth, still in a shallow dive, found it had a Shooting Star which, using gravity to its advantage, was closing the gap. Unable to shake off his pursuer, the MiG was shot down with a five-second burst from the American's machine guns.

The next day, a similarly disadvantaged US Navy Grumman F9F Panther scored a kill against a MiG-15.

In the first two dogfights between opposing jet fighters – in a war that military planners had not expected – victory had gone, on both occasions, to the inferior aircraft. It was a good illustration of how much more there is to winning an air war than who's got the best jet. It's a point that's been underlined in every conflict since.

A USAF McDonnell-Douglas F-4C Phantom rolls in towards a target in Vietnam. The multi-role Phantom was equally capable as a fighter and as an attack aircraft.

In Korea, in an effort to even things out, the USAF deployed its latest fighter, the F-86 Sabre. Similar in many ways to the MiG-15, it was underpowered by comparison and therefore slower to accelerate, and unable to reach the same high altitude. It was also less heavily armed. In order to protect the vulnerable attack aircraft supporting the troops on the ground, the Sabres had to place themselves in harm's way near the Chinese border and wait to be attacked by the MiGs. On the face of it, this gave the Communist jets an advantage, but the Sabres won a decisive victory over the MiGs. All the same, US fighter pilots – the really decisive factor determining the result – never wanted to find themselves at a disadvantage again. What they needed was fighters that could fly faster and higher than anything else in the sky.

There were just a couple of problems with that conclusion.

Much of the high-altitude fighting between the MiGs and Sabres was contained in a relatively small patch of sky near the Chinese border. Discrete from the battle on the ground further south, it was something of a last hurrah for the notion of gladiatorial fighter combat carving white lines in the sky. The MiGs were largely prevented from interfering with the land battle. But in wars to come, with fewer aircraft having to cover a greater area, this kind of stratospheric isolation wasn't possible. As US fighter pilots were calling for more pure performance, their battlefield was moving closer to the ground, where, in denser air, that high-altitude advantage was pretty irrelevant. And there was something else.

When Taiwanese Sabres met Chinese MiG-15s in combat in 1958, the MiG's ability to climb above the US fighter to safety or accelerate away counted for nothing. It didn't take long to put yourself beyond the range of a machine gun. As the MiG pilots discovered, though, it wasn't nearly so easy to escape a heat-seeking Sidewinder missile with a 2-mile range travelling at three times your speed.

If war between India and Pakistan in 1965 showed that fighting at lower altitudes negated the advantage of higher-performance jets, two years later the Israeli Air Force took it to extremes. Outnumbered by over three to one by their Arab counterparts, Israel's 170-strong fighter force evened the odds with a surprise attack that destroyed over 300 enemy aircraft on the ground. The raids, led by French-built Dassault Mirage IIIs and Super Mystères, gave a graphic demonstration of what a well-organized, well-trained air force could achieve if it was allowed to take the gloves off. News of their success must have been pretty galling for American fighter crews at war in Vietnam.

As well as geographical disadvantages meaning that they were often reliant on in-flight refuelling to complete their missions, US aircrews had their hands tied by complicated rules of engagement. For much of the war, attacking enemy aircraft on the ground wasn't an option open to them. Nor were they allowed to make the most of superior missile technology that might have kept North Vietnamese MiGs at arm's length. Instead, big, high-performance jets, such as the Republic F-105 Thunderchief and the superb McDonnell-Douglas F-4 Phantom II, were forced into fights at lower altitudes with more agile MiGs, including the fast MiG-21. Sometimes it took a little lateral thinking to wrest an advantage.

Colonel Robin Olds was the commanding officer of the 'Wolf Pack', the USAF's 8th Tactical Fighter Wing based in Thailand. A decorated Second World War fighter ace with twelve Luftwaffe kills to his name, Olds thought if he could just create the appearance that his F-4 fighters were bombers, he might tempt the MiGs into combat. As Olds, leading the first wave, approached Hanoi, he was passed news over the radio that the MiGs were being scrambled. Half an hour later, seven of them had been shot down without the loss of a single Phantom. Olds himself had barrel-rolled round one of them before knocking it out of the sky with a Sidewinder missile.

Over the year that followed, the Wolf Pack claimed another twenty-three MiGs. The North Vietnamese defenders couldn't ignore a US bombing raid against their capital, but it was impossible to tell whether or not they were hunter or hunted until they were airborne.

Unlike Korea, in Vietnam, American fighter pilots had gone to war in a machine that the record books made clear was the hottest ship in the sky. It could fly faster and higher than anything else, but none of this gave them the kind of decisive advantage they perhaps had hoped for. Slower, less-sophisticated MiG-17s and MiG-19s continued to give them a running until the end of the war. Again, it was largely up to the men themselves to overcome the disadvantages of geography, circumstance and politics to emerge on top.

When an unlikely war broke out in the South Atlantic, the conclusions drawn by Sabre pilots in Korea were dealt another blow. Since the entry into service of jets such as the Lockheed F-104 Starfighter (a direct response to appeals from Korean veterans for performance above all else) and the English Electric Lightning alongside the Phantom, Mirage and MiG-21, it seemed almost ridiculous to imagine that anyone would want to go to war in a fighter that was subsonic. That was until the Royal Navy, facing the retirement of its last aircraft carrier, looked at the vertical-take-off Harrier again and decided it was better than nothing. So when Argentina invaded the Falkland Islands in 1982, British pilots went to war in the slowest frontline fighter aircraft operated by any NATO country at the time. What's more, 'With just fifteen or twenty carrier-based planes,' said one Argentine fighter pilot before the war, 'it would be very difficult for the British.' But over the six weeks of fighting that followed, the small Fleet Air Arm Sea Harrier force shot down over twenty enemy aircraft without suffering a single loss in air-to-air combat.

Their success encapsulated all that had been learned since Korea. Operating at low-to-medium altitudes negated the performance advantage of the supersonic Mirages and Daggers (as did the extreme range at which they were forced to operate). The accurate and reliable AIM-9L Sidewinder missiles illustrated that weapons technology had become as important as the raw performance of the aircraft carrying it. And, as had been demonstrated in Korea, Vietnam and Israel, superior tactics and training were more important than marginal differences in the quality of the machinery.

During the 1950s and 1960s it seemed that every new fighter design turned out by American and Soviet factories could fly faster and higher than what had come before. That came to an end in the 1970s. The last new fighter plane to establish any significant new performance records first flew in 1977. When, nine years after that debut, a stripped-down Sukhoi Su-27 (dubbed the P.42) seized a clutch of time-to-height records from the slightly older and similarly impressive American McDonnell-Douglas F-15, it marked the end of an era. More recent designs, such as the F-22 Raptor or F-35 Lightning II Joint Strike Fighter, are slower than those mighty twentieth-century speedsters. And it doesn't matter.

Modern air-to-air missiles make the 2-mile range of the first Sidewinders look about as useful as a bow and arrow. Today's medium-range missiles can cover 50 miles-plus at over four times the speed of sound. Perhaps technology has finally delivered on its promise of no more dogfights. Maybe there's no longer a need to manoeuvre yourself into your opponent's six o'clock than there is to get up and change the TV channel rather than reach for the remote.

It's probably no bad thing. It's always been too easy to regard the fighter pilot as somehow separate from the grimy, bloody business of war; too easy to forget that the job of the fighter plane has *always* been, ultimately, to influence and enable what's happening at ground level. As one US Air Force ground attack pilot so eloquently put it: 'You can shoot down every MiG the Soviets employ, but if you return to base and the lead Soviet tank commander is eating breakfast in your snack bar, Jack, you've lost the war.'

A BAe Sea Harrier FRS1 of 800 Naval Air Squadron takes off from HMS Hermes *to mount a combat air patrol in defence of British ships and ground forces. Such was their reputation that Argentine pilots christened them* La Muerte Negra – *the Black Death.*

It Seemed Like a Good Idea at the Time

A Different Sort of Nuclear Bomber

In 1957, US car giant Ford unveiled a scale model of a new concept car. Nothing unusual about that. Sleek and finned, it looked like a Batmobile in white, chrome and primary colour. Nor was it odd that the design had no engine – it was a scale model after all. What *was* revolutionary was that there were no plans to include an internal combustion engine should the car go into production. The car was also expected to be able to travel over 5000 miles without needing to fill up. The clue was in the new car's name: Ford's Nucleon was designed to be powered by a small atomic reactor.

In retrospect, it was a daft idea, but no more so than a nuclear-powered aircraft. And as Ford had been working on the Nucleon, the USAF, lured by the prospect of a bomber force with almost unlimited range, funded the Aircraft Nuclear Propulsion (ANP) project. And, unlike Ford, it did more than build a model.

After being damaged in a storm, a Convair B-36 Peacemaker bomber, instead of being repaired and returned to the frontline, was modified to carry a nuclear reactor in its bomb bay. Then, protected by a 12-ton lead-and-rubber radiation shield, a tank of water and 6-inch-thick acrylic-glass cockpit windows, test pilots flew the reactor around the skies of Texas and New Mexico and hoped for the best.

Although operational, the reactor didn't actually power the engines, but that was the eventual goal. Consequently, alongside the test flight programme, General Electric built two prototype nuclear-powered jet engines.

The American programme might have come to an end in 1957, but a similar effort was gathering momentum in the Soviet Union, and throughout the 1960s a Tupolev Tu-95 'Bear' carrying a nuclear reactor conducted a series of test flights. The aircraft's crews, however, were inadequately shielded from the effects of the radiation.

'We'd all been irradiated,' one of the test pilots later explained, 'but we ignored it. Of the two test crews, only three men survived: a young navigator, a military navigator and me. The first to go – a young technician – took only three years to die …'

During the NB-36 test programme, every single flight was escorted by a cargo plane carrying armed paratroopers. In the event of an NB-36 crash the soldiers were to parachute in to secure the area.

Disaster struck not only the crews. Between 1949 and 1954, eleven B-36 bombers – the aircraft used in the American ANP programme – crashed. They went down in Texas, Oklahoma, Washington and South Dakota in the USA, in Canada, and in Wiltshire in the UK. Had they been nuclear-powered, the results don't bear thinking about.

Thankfully, although the 1950s and 1960s produced a welter of exotic, speculative nuclear-powered designs – in Britain the possibility of a nuclear-powered version of the giant Saunders-Roe Princess flying boat was even mooted – they went nowhere, kicked into touch by ballistic missiles, more efficient jet engines and common sense.

It Seemed Like a Good Idea at the Time   189

MARTIN P6M SEAMASTER
Jet-flying boat bomber

In the early 1950s, concerned about losing influence to the air force over control of America's nuclear arsenal, the US Navy pursued the idea of a 'Seaplane Striking Force'. It was a radical decision at the time, and one that now seems as if it belongs firmly in a retro vision of the future. But the SeaMaster was real. What's more, this magnificent result of the navy's rivalry with the air force came very close to entering squadron service by the end of the decade.

The navy described the aircraft as 'unusually promising', but it hadn't been an easy journey. The first prototype was destroyed in a crash, as was the second. And problems with vibration at high speeds plagued the project. Then the successful development of the Polaris ballistic missile removed the big flying boat's *raison d'être*. Despite this, in 1959 the first aircrews began training to fly the SeaMaster. It wasn't to be, though, and that summer the programme was cancelled.

However, none of this takes away from the technical achievements of the SeaMaster. She was the first and only flying boat to break the sound barrier; she could lift nearly one and a half times the bombload of Britain's new Vulcan jet bomber; and because of the strength needed to operate off water, the SeaMaster was also robust in the air and capable of flying exceptionally fast at low altitude. She looked great too. Unfortunately, none of these attributes were enough to save a single one. As is all too often the case with cancellations, every remaining SeaMaster was destroyed.

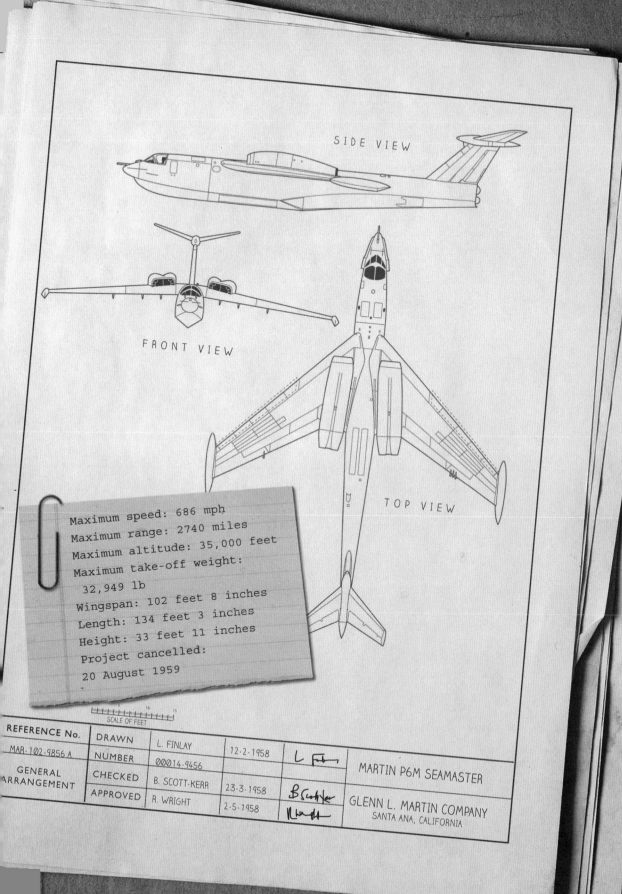

SIDE VIEW

FRONT VIEW

TOP VIEW

Maximum speed: 686 mph
Maximum range: 2740 miles
Maximum altitude: 35,000 feet
Maximum take-off weight:
  32,949 lb
Wingspan: 102 feet 8 inches
Length: 134 feet 3 inches
Height: 33 feet 11 inches
Project cancelled:
20 August 1959

SCALE OF FEET

REFERENCE No.	DRAWN	L. FINLAY	12-2-1958		MARTIN P6M SEAMASTER
MAR-102-9856 A	NUMBER	00014-9456			
GENERAL	CHECKED	B. SCOTT-KERR	23-3-1958		GLENN L. MARTIN COMPANY
ARRANGEMENT	APPROVED	R. WRIGHT	2-5-1958		SANTA ANA, CALIFORNIA

Simon W. Atack

Great Planes

Bell UH-1 Iroquois

It's not the prettiest, fastest, biggest, most glamorous, exotic or advanced, but the UH-1, or Huey as it became known, was the first modern battlefield helicopter and definitely represented a step-change in helicopter design. With over 16,000 built, the Huey was a machine that became an icon. Think of the Vietnam War and you think of the Huey. Think of the Huey and you think of *Apocalypse Now* and Wagner's 'Ride of the Valkyries'. Bell's masterpiece was, is and always will be army helicopter 101.

First flight: 20 October 1956
Principal operator: US Army
Last operational flight: Still in service

Whirlybirds

The Brief History of Helicopters

Rising up in the middle of the South Pacific, over 3500 miles from New Zealand to the south-west and Chile to the east, Henderson Island is one of a small group known collectively as the Pitcairns, named after the island on which the HMS *Bounty* mutineers made their home. One of the most remote places in the world, Henderson, a 14-square-mile coral plateau fringed with golden sand beaches, is home to a bird population that's unique. Like the Galapagos, the island's isolation has meant its wildlife took an evolutionary route all its own, so in 2011 a mission was launched to eradicate the rats, introduced from early ships, that threatened to destroy it. The plan was simple: to distribute baited poison across the whole island, but the dense jungle cover meant that it could only be scattered from the air. This job, beyond the range of any land-based aircraft, meant the scientific expedition had to take along their own aircraft and operate them from a ship modified for the purpose with sea containers and planking.

Another day, another job that could only have been done by helicopter. It's the sort of everyday, minor miracle we all now take for granted. The really extraordinary thing, though, is not so much the breadth of the helicopter's utility, but that it was made to work at all. On the face of it, the idea seems fairly straightforward. Leonardo da Vinci sketched helicopter-like designs. But for a flying machine that works on the same basic principles as a Chinese toy that was around before the birth of Christ, it took a lot of getting right. The helicopter was, as one writer put it, 'one of the most difficult of man's inventions to develop to an acceptable degree of efficiency and safety'.

The helicopter pioneer Igor Sikorsky did more than anyone else to ensure that helicopters enjoy the ubiquity they do today. He was in no doubt about their value. 'If a man is in need of rescue,' he said, 'an airplane can come in and throw flowers on him, and that's just about all. But a direct lift aircraft could come in and save his life.'

Sikorsky was right, of course. The problem, though, wasn't in designing a machine that could go up and down – that just needed enough power – but in building one that could do that *and* get from A to B. An aircraft that could successfully do both of these things would have to be a compromise. And as Sikorsky, at the time better known for building flying boats, laboured on his first helicopter prototype, his colleagues referred to it as 'Igor's Nightmare'.

Throughout the 1930s, European designers, such as Juan de la Cierva, Louis Breguet and René Dorand refined their own helicopter designs. Each contributed his significant breakthroughs but it was the German Heinrich Focke who, in 1936, was first to demonstrate a really successful flying machine with the twin rotor Focke-Achgelis Fa-61. Two years later, the Fa-61 was flown *inside* in front of audiences of 20,000 people at the Berlin Motor Show. It was Sikorsky's VS-300 design, though, which first flew in 1940, that established the template for the vast majority of helicopters that followed.

Even Sikorsky's successful layout was a compromise. Like bad management, a helicopter generates a whir of activity which, at the end of it all, seems to produce something less than you feel it all should. There's a lack of elegance, an inefficiency about the movement and complexity necessary to keep a helicopter in the air. They're slower, shorter-ranged, thirstier, more difficult to fly and generally more fragile than their fixed-wing equivalents, but it's a price worth paying. For all their inherent limitations, no other flying machine can do what they do, a fact the military was quick to recognize.

Igor Sikorsky built his first helicopter, the H-1, in Russia in 1909. It was, he said, a failure in that it could not fly. Thirty years later, in America, the VS-300 pictured here became the template for all modern helicopters.

The US Army, Navy and Coast Guard all placed orders for Sikorsky's new XR-4 helicopter. Nor were the British slow in seeing the potential. Of the first eight XR-4s built, two were dispatched to Britain and, during the transatlantic voyage, successfully flown from the ship. The Admiralty ordered 250. In December 1943 the US Coast Guard set up a new international helicopter training school in New York. A month later the unit's commanding officer was asked if he could fly in ice and blizzards that had grounded fixed-wing aircraft and closed the roads. A massive explosion aboard a US Navy destroyer anchored off New Jersey meant supplies of blood plasma were urgently needed for badly burned survivors. The Sikorsky delivered its life-saving cargo from Manhattan to the front door of the hospital in a journey lasting minutes, not hours. By the end of the year a US Army Sikorsky had picked up the survivors of a downed liaison plane in Burma. Another first.

By the time war broke out in Korea in 1950, a new design from rival firm Bell was well on its way to becoming almost synonymous with the word 'helicopter'. The Bell 47's combination of bubble cockpit and bare scaffold tail boom remains, even today, many people's idea of what a helicopter should look like. As featured in the opening credits of the long-running television series *M*A*S*H*, the Bell 47 served with distinction during the Korean War, flying to safety injured soldiers who would otherwise have died, but it was perhaps its popularity with civilian users – and an earlier hit TV show – that established it in the minds of the public. Nearly 6000 were built during a thirty-year production run, but it was when *Whirlybirds* turned the Bell 47 into a kind of rotary-winged Lassie that its place in the popular imagination was sealed.

Helicopters have always offered film-makers more options than fixed-wing flying machines, which, by their nature, can't hang around. A helicopter can participate in a scene rather than simply streak across it. And that's what

The classic Bell 47 is the archetypal helicopter design, even used by NASA to help train astronauts to land on the moon.

ensured that the Whirlybirds weren't the only iconic helicopters to appear on our screens. It wasn't long before another Bell 47 had been dressed up as a Batcopter, then *Blue Thunder*, *Magnum, P.I.* and *Airwolf* all followed (so too, of course, did *Wings of the Apache*, but that's best left well alone).

Helicopters have been even more important to film-makers on the other side of the camera, though, making it possible to get shots that earlier generations of directors could only have dreamt of. The helicopter has also transformed sports coverage, news-gathering and even traffic reporting. The endless, extraordinary list of jobs taken on by helicopters runs from herding cattle to pouring concrete on the out-of-control Chernobyl nuclear reactor, and includes oil rig support, astronaut recovery, air-ambulance work, polar support, firefighting, mountain rescue and even flying the intact, frozen body of a woolly mammoth out of Siberia.

If there's a helicopter involved, it seems, there's often a story to tell. Everything on the helicopter's CV is dictated by its unique range of abilities and limitations, as much by what it can't do as by what it can. *Blue Thunder* had its whisper mode. In *Airwolf*, much is made of the top-secret machine's supersonic speed and stealth. In reality, helicopters are still slow, low and noisy: for any conventional helicopter, the laws of physics dictate that around 200 mph remains an absolute speed limit. There have been high-altitude spectaculars, such as landing and taking off from the summit of Mount Everest, but even then, at 29,029 feet, we're talking about an altitude substantially lower than that at which a normal airliner cruises. Helicopter pilots spend so much time at low to medium level that flying at height can actually be disorientating. The *wokka-wokka* thump of the big Chinook helicopter's twin rotors is so loud that RAF pilots simply call their aircraft a 'Wokka'.

Nevertheless, none of the drawbacks have stopped the military from trying to push the boundaries of both the way it uses helicopters and the capabilities of the machines themselves. While the Korean War saw the first extensive use of helicopters in combat, it was the disastrous Anglo-French Suez campaign in 1956 that saw the first helicopter air assault, when 500 Royal Marines were flown ashore from commando carriers sitting off the Egyptian coast. During the Indonesian confrontation in the early 1960s, British helicopters played a crucial role in supporting jungle operations that were out of reach by any other means, but it was during America's long war in Vietnam that the helicopter really came of age as a weapon of war.

A US Army Boeing Vertol Chinook over Vietnam. A single RAF Chinook, 'Bravo November', flew over 1500 troops, 650 POWs and 550 tons of cargo during the Falklands War. The same aircraft fought in Iraq and Afghanistan and remains in service today.

The Bell UH-1 Iroquois, known to all simply as the Huey, became perhaps the most iconic aircraft of the Vietnam War. The image of Hueys flying in formation to Wagner's 'Ride of the Valkyries' in the 1979 movie *Apocalypse Now* is indelibly marked on the memory of all who've seen it. When it first flew in 1956, the turbine-powered Huey represented a dramatic step forward in helicopter design. During the Vietnam conflict, around 7000 Hueys flew over *36 million* sorties.

Then there was the HueyCobra. When, in 1965, the army issued an urgent requirement for a dedicated attack helicopter, the result was a design that married the tail and mechanicals of the Huey with a two-seat fighter-style cockpit to create an entirely new breed: the helicopter gunship. Armed with missiles on stub wings and guns in a turret under the nose, the AH-1 brought an entirely new capability to the ground war.

Alongside it, a new tandem rotor design from Boeing Vertol also made its debut. Called the CH-47 Chinook, the new heavy-lift helicopter could carry over forty fully equipped troops ... and almost anything else. On one occasion a Chinook carried 147 refugees. In Vietnam it distinguished itself by recovering thousands of downed aircraft.

Helicopters have been no less important to the world's navies. With the advent of the helicopter, every frigate or destroyer could become a mini aircraft carrier able to make its presence felt beyond the horizon for the first time.

But while low and slow might be exactly what's needed for catching pirates or spotting submarines, the military is still trying to give its helicopters *Airwolf*-type superpowers, and in doing so has added capabilities to its helicopter fleet that would have seemed unthinkable to those early pioneers. In 1967 two Sikorsky HH-3 'Jolly Green Giants' became the first helicopters to fly non-stop across the Atlantic. During the 30-hour journey, each was refuelled in flight nine times by a C-130 tanker plane.

A year later, with the giant Mil Mi-12, the Soviet Union built what remains the largest helicopter ever to fly. In the quest for speed, jets, wings and propellers have all been tested. And in 2011, during the special forces raid that killed Osama bin Laden, US Army Blackhawk helicopters had been fitted with stealth kits that reduced their noise and radar signature.

That mission exemplifies the changing role of the helicopter in modern war. It used to be that in comparison to fast jets, helicopters were considered a less desirable posting for a military pilot. That's changed in recent years, though, because it's usually helicopters, whether in conflict or humanitarian crisis, that are both first in, then in the thick of it subsequently. The recent campaigns in Iraq and Afghanistan have seen helicopters, such as the evergreen Chinook, Blackhawk and Apache gunship, at the tip of the spear. If a military pilot wants action, helicopters are the thing to fly.

And yet it's a strange kind of weapon that has probably saved more lives than it has ended.

Helicopters are still defined by their limitations. They're no good for anything that requires great speed, altitude, range or carrying capacity. You'll never see them flying 300 people across the Atlantic, or even the English Channel. Everything else, though, and it's a good bet there's a helicopter on the job right now. The helicopter has dramatically expanded the range of things humanity can do. Most of it is good, and we feel safer and more connected because of helicopters – never out of reach. Although imperfect – unlike an aeroplane, a helicopter tries to throw itself apart every time it takes to the air – it's their failings that make them part of our lives. Instead of flying high above us, they're down here, interacting and involved, up close and personal, intimately linked with our story.

Chopper

The Anatomy of a Helicopter

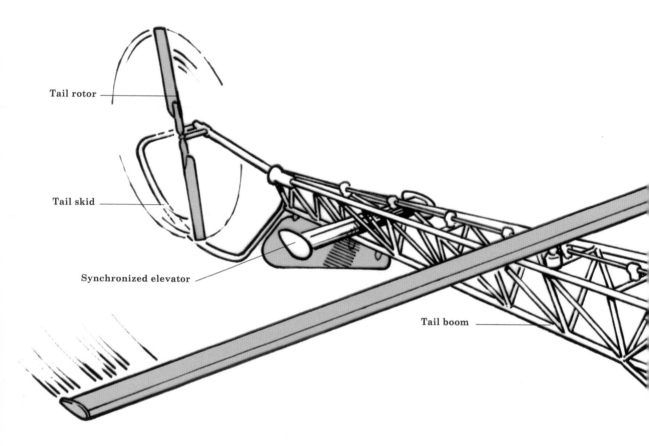

Tail rotor

Tail skid

Synchronized elevator

Tail boom

The illustration here shows the Bell 47 helicopter. While not the most widely built design, it is still, in many people's eyes, the stereotypical helicopter. Certainly, after it first flew in 1945, it went on to become the first really successful helicopter design and, broadly speaking, not a lot's changed since then. Some designs will have a four- or five-bladed main rotor, others might have wheels or floats instead of landing skids, and most will have rather more than a Perspex balloon around the pilot and passengers.

Flight controls are highlighted in green. Lift and forward thrust is provided by the main rotor, while pitch, roll and yaw control come from the main rotor, alongside the elevator and the tail rotor.

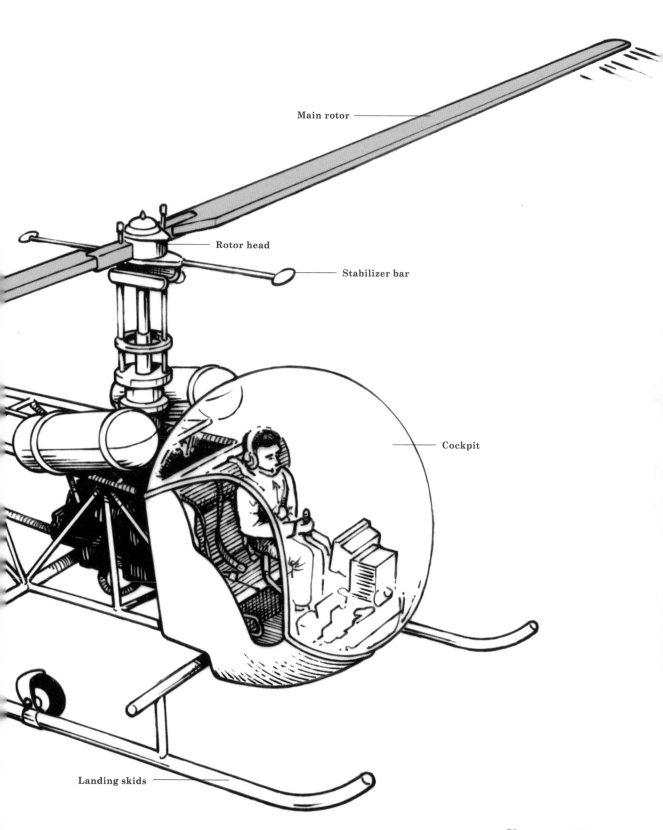

Main rotor

Rotor head

Stabilizer bar

Cockpit

Landing skids

Chopper   201

Beating the Air into Submission

How a Helicopter Flies

The helicopter is the only flying machine I'm aware of in which, during forward flight, part of it – and a crucial one at that – is travelling backwards. It's perhaps one of the reasons why helicopters divide opinion among pilots and enthusiasts. The jokes are well worn:

> – *A helicopter is just a bunch of parts flying in formation. All fine until one of those decides to break formation.*
> – *Helicopters don't fly, they beat the air into submission.*
> – *They don't fly, they're so ugly the ground repels them.*

The jibes are prompted by the compromises inherent in helicopter flight. The same four forces are at work on a helicopter as on a fixed-wing aircraft, but the helicopter deals with them differently, the reason being that the main rotor doesn't provide just lift but also thrust.

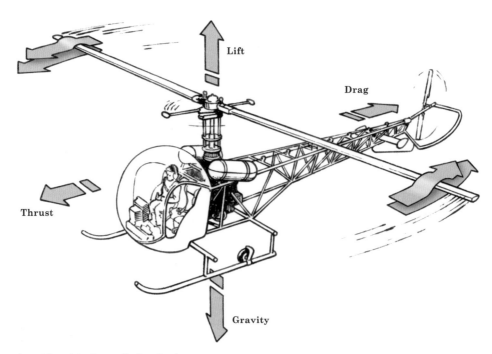

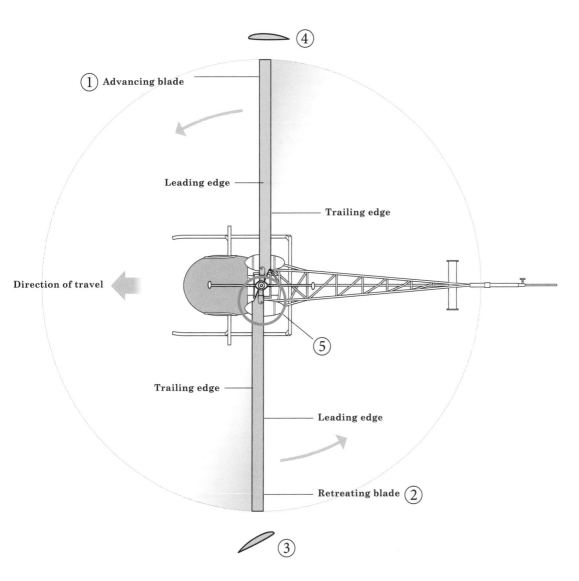

① Advancing blade

Leading edge

Trailing edge

Direction of travel

⑤

Trailing edge

Leading edge

Retreating blade ②

④

③

Here's the science

Each blade of the main rotor is a thin wing. It generates lift as it moves
forward through the air. While hovering, or lifting directly up or down,
the main rotor is nicely balanced as it spins. Wherever each blade is in the
360-degree arc through which it's travelling, its speed relative to the still air
in which it's flying is the same.

The trouble starts when a helicopter starts flying forward. With the addition
of airspeed, different points in that 360-degree arc begin to travel through the
air at different speeds. The helicopter's speed through the air must be added
to that of the blade whose leading edge is travelling in the direction of travel
– (1) the advancing blade – and subtracted from the speed of the blade facing
backward against the direction of travel – (2) the retreating blade.

The lift generated by a wing increases with speed (and decreases as speed decreases). Without a solution, therefore, the retreating blade slicing through the air more slowly than the advancing blade would generate less lift and the helicopter would roll on to its back.

But a wing can be made to generate the same lift at higher and lower speeds if the angle at which it travels through the air – the angle of attack – is changed. As a result, a helicopter's retreating blade travels through the air at a higher angle of attack (3) than the advancing blade (4), so the lift from both sides of the rotor is balanced and the helicopter is able to stay upright.

So, which bit's travelling backwards?

To successfully complete the same 360-degree rotation, the tip of the rotor blade must travel further than the section of the blade nearest the rotor head, but it must do so in the same amount of time. As speed is a function of distance and time, the tip of the blade must travel faster through the air than the inside section. An intriguing consequence of that is that while the outermost section of the retreating blade is the part travelling fastest, as you move in towards the rotor head, the effective airspeed of the blade reduces to zero. Between that point and the rotor head (5) the forward speed of the helicopter is greater than the speed at which the blade is rotating, which means that it's travelling backwards through the air, trailing edge first.

Phew!

Believe me, I've tried to keep this simple, but helicopters are pretty resistant to that. Far, far too much maths involved for my liking. *Budgie the Little Helicopter*, it ain't …

Changing direction

Like a fixed-wing aeroplane, a helicopter has a stick, which is known as the cyclic, and rudder pedals, the anti-torque pedals. There's also one more lever that sits, like the handbrake of a car, at the pilot's left hand. That's the collective lever.

Think of the spinning main rotor as a disc. The cyclic stick controls the angle of that disc. Push the cyclic forward and the disc tilts forward, lower at the front than at the back. This propels the helicopter forwards. Pull it back and you'll slow down or fly backwards. Side to side sends it left and right.

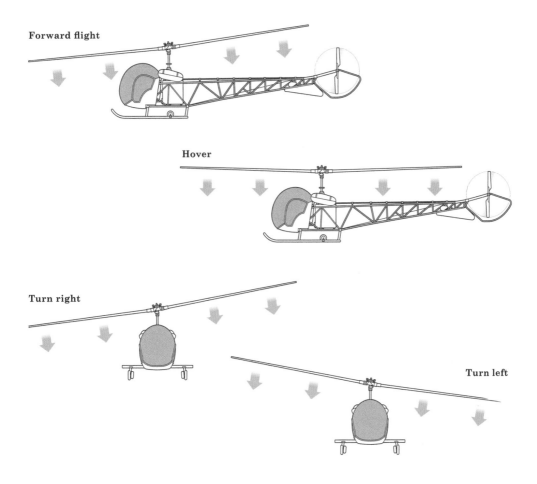

Forward flight

Hover

Turn right

Turn left

The collective lever controls the pitch, or angle of attack, of the blades themselves. Pull up on the collective and you increase the angle of attack, generating more lift, and the helicopter goes up. Lower it and you reduce the angle of attack of the blades, reduce the lift and the helicopter will sink.

The rudder pedals control the tail rotor, and they're called anti-torque pedals for good reason. It's possible to fly a fixed-wing aircraft without using the rudder, but that's not the case in a helicopter. For while the rudder pedals control yaw in the same way as in an aeroplane, they do more than provide directional control. The helicopter's engine and gearbox don't discriminate between the rotor and the fuselage. The tail rotor stops the chopper spinning round and round uncontrollably in the opposite direction to the rotor.

Those Magnificent Men in Their Flying Machines

Fifteen Flying Films

As a genre, the aviation movie isn't one overly blessed with quality. So, as ever, what follows is a *very* subjective list. In choosing what's here, I've tried to focus on movies that took the trouble to film real pilots flying real aircraft rather than rely solely on models and CGI. Everything is open to argument, but the best is easy. *Airplane!* No contest.

Airplane! (1980)
Played deadpan, this comedy classic spawned a glut of imitators. The original and best feels exactly like the disaster movies it so brilliantly spoofed.

Armageddon (1998)
It's completely absurd in every way, but this story of oil drillers turned astronauts saving the world just sweeps you along.

Battle of Britain (1969)
A great cast features in this epic account of the RAF's fight for Britain's survival. Some terrific aerial footage (although quite a lot of models were used too).

The Bridges at Toko-Ri (1954)
Like *Top Gun*, this was made with the full cooperation of the US Navy, and it shows. It features fabulous footage of 1950s US Navy carrier operations and Grace Kelly. What's not to like?

The Dam Busters (1955)
One of the very best. Great story, great flying scenes. Incomparable theme tune. There's talk of a remake. I hope it happens. I hope it's good. And, people, if they do change the name of the dog, it *really* doesn't matter.

The Final Countdown (1980)
A nuclear-powered US aircraft carrier slips back in time to the build-up to the attack on Pearl Harbor. You've got to love any movie that has Kirk Douglas ordering a pair of F-14 Tomcats to 'Splash the Zeros'.

Fire Birds/Wings of the Apache (1990)
This effort to do for helicopters what *Top Gun* did for jet fighters was rightly panned as one of the worst movies ever, but it features some great flying scenes.

Flight of the Phoenix (1965)
'It's not a party, there is no booze,' said the trailer for no particularly good reason. James Stewart, Richard Attenborough and Ernest Borgnine lead an all-star cast, stranded in the desert, trying to build a new aircraft out of the wreckage of their old one.

THE AUTHENTIC...FANTASTIC STORY OF THE WORLD'S FIRST ROCKET SHIP
ACTUALLY FILMED IN SPACE!

The Rocket Ship That Challenged Outer Space!

X-15 starring David McLean · Charles Bronson · James Gregory · Mary Tyler Moore   An Essex Production   PANAVISION® TECHNICOLOR®
Directed by Richard D. Donner   Produced by Henry Sanicola and Tony Lazzarino
Executive Producer Howard W. Koch   Screenplay by Tony Lazzarino and James Warner Bellah   Released thru UNITED UA ARTISTS

The Great Waldo Pepper (1975)

It's clear why this Robert Redford movie is a favourite with pilots. It's about veteran First World War fighter pilots barnstorming their way across America and includes incredible stunt-flying.

The Right Stuff (1983)

An epic film of Tom Wolfe's classic account of the birth of the space race in America. Real care was taken to make sure the flying looked right. And Sam Shepard as Chuck Yeager? Perfect.

633 Squadron (1964)

The perfect Sunday-afternoon war film features fabulous footage of RAF Mosquitos attacking their target through a Norwegian fjord.

The Sound Barrier (1952)

David Lean, director of *Lawrence of Arabia*, turns his attention to the dawn of the jet age – a mouthwatering prospect. Beautifully made, it features great footage of early 1950s British jets.

Those Magnificent Men in Their Flying Machines (1965)

Great fun. The brilliant Terry-Thomas leads a who's-who of British character actors in this fabulous comedy about a pre-First World War air race involving an amazing collection of machines, some of them built specially for the movie.

Top Gun (1986)

With pretty much every line being quotable, this is a pop-culture classic. You know the story: Tom Cruise aims to be best of the best. Made with full US Navy cooperation, the aerial footage of duelling F-14 Tomcats won't be bettered.

X-15 (1961)

'Actually filmed in space!' was a line they couldn't even use for *Apollo 13*. Narrated by James Stewart, this semi-documentary features real footage of the X-15 and stars Charles Bronson. Amazingly, it was directed by Richard Donner, who later made *Lethal Weapon*.

Great Planes

McDonnell-Douglas F-4 Phantom II

'As awkward as a goose with drooping tail feathers and middle-age spread,' said the US Navy. 'So ugly, I wondered if it had been delivered upside down,' said the US Air Force. To look at, then, the Phantom II was something of an acquired taste. But what a machine she turned out to be. World air speed records, altitude records and time-to-climb records all fell to America's new superfighter. And over the next quarter century more than 5000 were built. The Phabulous Phantom was a one-jet air force.

First flight: 27 May 1958
Principal operator: US Navy, US Air Force, US Marine Corps
Last operational flight: Still in service

PHILIP E. WEST
©

'Indian Ocean. Present Day.'*
How Aircraft Carriers Work

The US Navy's F/A-18 Hornet typically requires around 2600 feet of runway to take off. And while regulations dictate that it needs a 7000-foot strip to land, a lightly loaded Hornet can be brought to a halt after a landing run of less than 3000 feet. The 100,000-ton Nimitz Class aircraft carriers that are home to the jets are huge. These floating cities, carrying three squadrons of Hornets, each have a self-contained air force bigger than those operated by most countries.

They are, however, only a little over 1000 feet long – not, according to the numbers, long enough to operate F/A-18 Hornets. Or, indeed, anything much other than helicopters.

Since 1918, when HMS *Argus*, the world's first flat-top aircraft carrier, was commissioned into the Royal Navy, naval aviation has seen the weight and performance of aircraft increase dramatically. The first aircraft to land on HMS *Argus* was a Sopwith Ship Strutter biplane. It weighed a little over 2000 lb and had a maximum speed of 87 knots. Fully loaded, the big F-14 Tomcat flown by Maverick and Goose in *Top Gun*, was thirty-five times as heavy. And forget *top* speed: the Tomcat's landing speed alone was 125 knots. Despite the vast differences – if the *Argus* was steaming into wind, the little Ship Strutter could pretty much touch down at walking pace – naval aviation is a far safer occupation now than at any time previously. Fatal crashes as aircraft flew on and off the deck used to be routine – as high as one in every fifty landings. Now, happily, they're vanishingly rare. A number of crucial innovations have helped make that possible.

OPPOSITE: *The swing-wing Grumman F-14 Tomcat was the US Navy's frontline fighter for over 30 years. 'Anytime, Baby!', a slogan used by her crews, was originally offered as a challenge to Air Force F-15 pilots.*

*Those of you who are as geeky as me might recognize this. For the rest of you, it's the location, we're told, of the carrier that features in the fabulously moody footage during the opening of *Top Gun*.

Angled deck

Until the late 1950s all aircraft flew from the centreline of the flightdeck. They either took off from stern to bow using the full length available, or were launched from the bow with the help of a catapult. When landing, if they failed to catch the arrestor wire, they were caught by a raised crash barrier that stopped them ploughing into aircraft parked on the front half of the flightdeck. As catching a wire was not guaranteed, landing aircraft frequently became tangled in the crash barrier – bad news for the plane and sometimes fatal for the pilot. At the end of the Second World War, a Royal Navy aviator, Captain Dennis Cambell, realized that if the landing strip was placed across the deck at an angle, it wouldn't matter if a pilot missed the wires – he could just keep going and come around again for another go. By the 1960s all conventional aircraft carriers used angled decks.

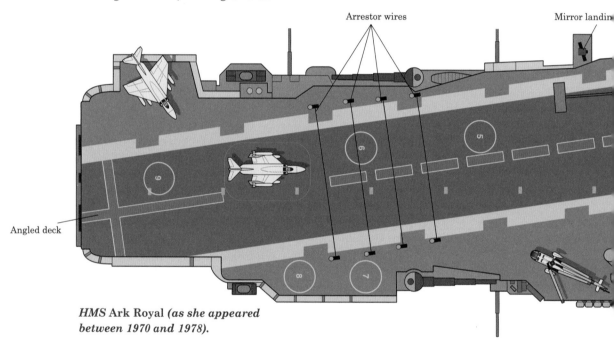

HMS Ark Royal *(as she appeared between 1970 and 1978).*

Arrestor wire

By trailing a hook designed to catch thick raised wires stretched across the deck, a modern jet carrier-borne aircraft can be slowed to a halt over just 250 feet. In the early days of arresting gear, cables ran through pulleys to sandbags that soaked up the kinetic energy of the landing aircraft. Today the wires and pulleys use hydraulic brakes to absorb the much more substantial forces involved in slowing down heavier and faster aircraft. Four parallel wires cross the flightdeck at 50-foot intervals 200 feet ahead of the stern of the ship. Pilots are rated on their ability to consistently hit wire three. Wires two and four are deemed satisfactory, but wire one – the closest to the stern of the ship and therefore considered an accident – earns the pilot a black mark.

Mirror landing sight

Appalled at the fatality rate among pilots landing back on board aircraft carriers, Fleet Air Arm pilot Lieutenant Commander Nick Goodhart devised a simple system that he thought could improve their chances. He demonstrated by placing an open powder compact halfway along the deck of a model aircraft with the mirror facing backwards, and placed a torch pointing forwards and shining into the mirror. His secretary was asked to walk towards the mirror, making sure that the spot of light in it always stayed centred. She had to bend her knees more and more as she approached until eventually her chin was resting on the back of the model. Success! Scaled up and used on real aircraft carriers, it took the guesswork and subjectivity out of the approach to a carrier's flightdeck. If pilots followed the direction of the landing sight, they knew they were on the correct glide path. The drop in accidents was immediate

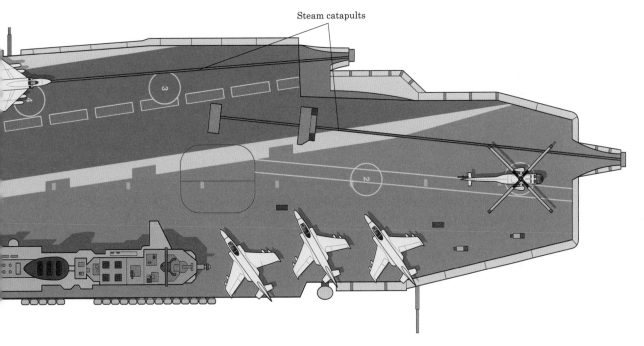

Steam catapults

Steam catapult

Hydraulic catapults used to launch aircraft during the 1950s were notoriously unreliable. In 1954, one on USS *Bennington* exploded, killing 100 crewmen. Fortunately, a British naval engineer, Commander Colin Mitchell, came up with the idea of powering catapults using steam from the ship's boiler. A trial catapult installed in HMS *Perseus* proved an outstanding success, capable of launching aircraft from a ship at anchor, whereas a hydraulic catapult required her to be steaming at 40 knots. The commander of the US Navy's Air Forces in the Atlantic was so impressed that he immediately bought five. Today each of the ten US Navy's nuclear-powered aircraft carriers has four steam catapults. A towbar attached to the aircraft's nosewheel slots into a shuttle protruding from a long groove in the deck. Beneath the deck the shuttle is attached to a piston powered by high-pressure steam from the ship's boilers and can take a heavily loaded F/A-18 Hornet from zero to 165 mph in just 2 seconds.

Batsmen and Paddles
The Art of the Landing Deck Officer

Landing on the pitching deck of an aircraft carrier has never been an easy thing to do. And until the advent of optical landing sights in the mid-1950s, carrier pilots were guided by an experienced naval aviator standing on the deck. The Royal Navy called them 'batsmen'. In the US Navy, the landing signals officers, or LSOs, were nicknamed 'paddles'. Standing out on the flightdeck, exposed to the elements, was never a job any red-blooded fighter pilot yearned for, but all understood that it was one of the most crucial any of them could do. When there was no significant margin for error, the LSO's judgement, making sure pilots were alert to when their approach was too high, too low, too fast or too slow, saved lives. An elaborate system of hand signals, akin to a sort of reactive, adrenalin-charged semaphore, was employed.

After the Second World War, when jets were introduced, approach speeds rose at the same time as throttle response times slowed down, and the job became even tougher. Every so often, when a landing went badly wrong, the LSOs found themselves in as much danger as the pilots.

Opposite are the signals used by the LSOs aboard US carriers.

A Fleet Air Arm batsman guides a Grumman Hellcat fighter on to the deck.

YOUR WHEELS
ARE UP

NO FLAPS

ANGLING
APPROACH

ORBIT

GOOD ROGER

HOOK NOT DOWN

TOO FAST

LOW

PULL UP A BIT/
LOW DIP

DROP IT/
HIGH DIP

SLANT/
TURN IT IN

TOO MUCH
RUDDER

LAND
CUT

GO AROUND
WAVE OFF

HIGH

COME ON/
TOO SLOW

FAIREY ROTODYNE
Vertical take-off and landing transport aircraft

'The Fairey Rotodyne is the aircraft for fast, economical travel offering the advantages of air transport to everyone, everywhere.' So said the narrator of a promotional film made by the manufacturer, Fairey. There seemed to be good reason for confidence. The Rotodyne had claimed a world air-speed record, attracted orders from North America to Japan, and secured an agreement with the Kaman Aircraft Corporation for licensed production in the United States; which meant that an order from the US Army for as many as 200 might be a possibility for what was, at the time of its first flight in 1958, the largest transport helicopter in the world. Except she wasn't a helicopter. Not quite.

The Rotodyne was a unique hybrid. To take off and land vertically, jets on the tips of the rotor were powered by air bled from the two turboprop engines beneath the machine's short wings. After translating to forward flight, the jets were switched off and the rotor was feathered, with forward speed from the two engines. Lift was provided by both the wing and a freewheeling rotor. Unloading the rotor meant the Rotodyne could cruise much faster than contemporary helicopters. British European Airways had its eye on using the Rotodyne to provide a city centre to city centre service between European capitals. There was one important caveat, however. Fairey had to find a way to make its machine quieter.

From over 500 feet away, the banshee scream of the tip jets was louder than a pneumatic drill from less than 50 feet. If the sound of breathing is 10 decibels, then the shriek of the Rotodyne taking off and landing was much closer to 194 decibels, or the loudest sound possible. The trouble was, she was supposed to fly in and out of city centres.

While BEA wavered, the project team were confident they could reduce the noise to acceptable levels. In pursuit of that, over forty different noise suppressors were tested, but in February 1962 government funding was cut off, and by the end of the year the single Rotodyne prototype had been broken up for scrap.

She was a machine that seemed genuinely to be a whisker from changing the way the world flew. That it never happened was nothing at all to do with her remarkable qualities as a flying machine.

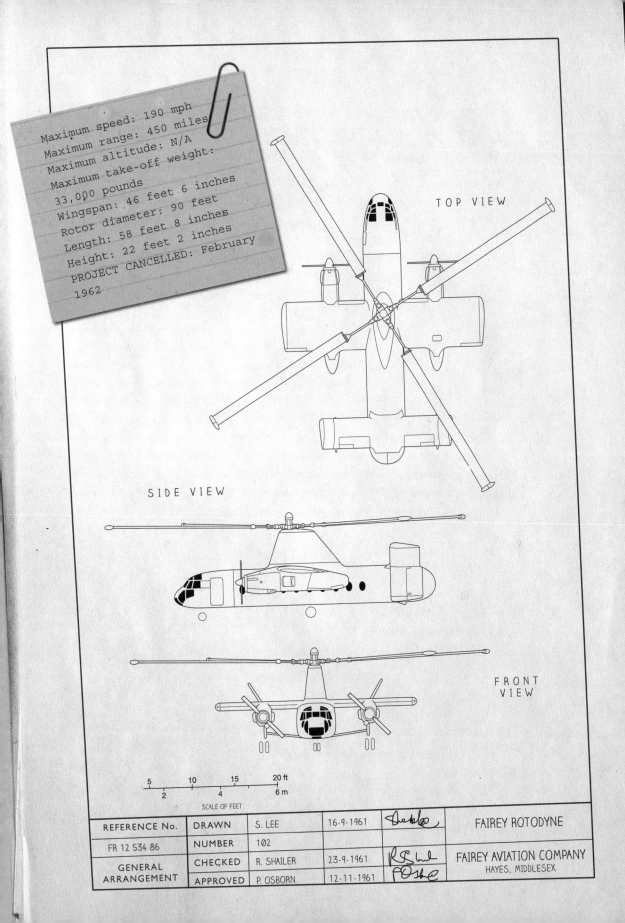

Maximum speed: 190 mph
Maximum range: 450 miles
Maximum altitude: N/A
Maximum take-off weight:
33,000 pounds
Wingspan: 46 feet 6 inches
Rotor diameter: 90 feet
Length: 58 feet 8 inches
Height: 22 feet 2 inches
PROJECT CANCELLED: February
1962

TOP VIEW

SIDE VIEW

FRONT VIEW

SCALE OF FEET
5   10   15   20 ft
2   4   6 m

REFERENCE No.	DRAWN	S. LEE	16-9-1961		FAIREY ROTODYNE
FR 12 534 86	NUMBER	102			FAIREY AVIATION COMPANY
GENERAL ARRANGEMENT	CHECKED	R. SHAILER	23-9-1961		HAYES, MIDDLESEX
	APPROVED	P. OSBORN	12-11-1961		

All Around the World

Which Countries Make Their Own Aircraft?

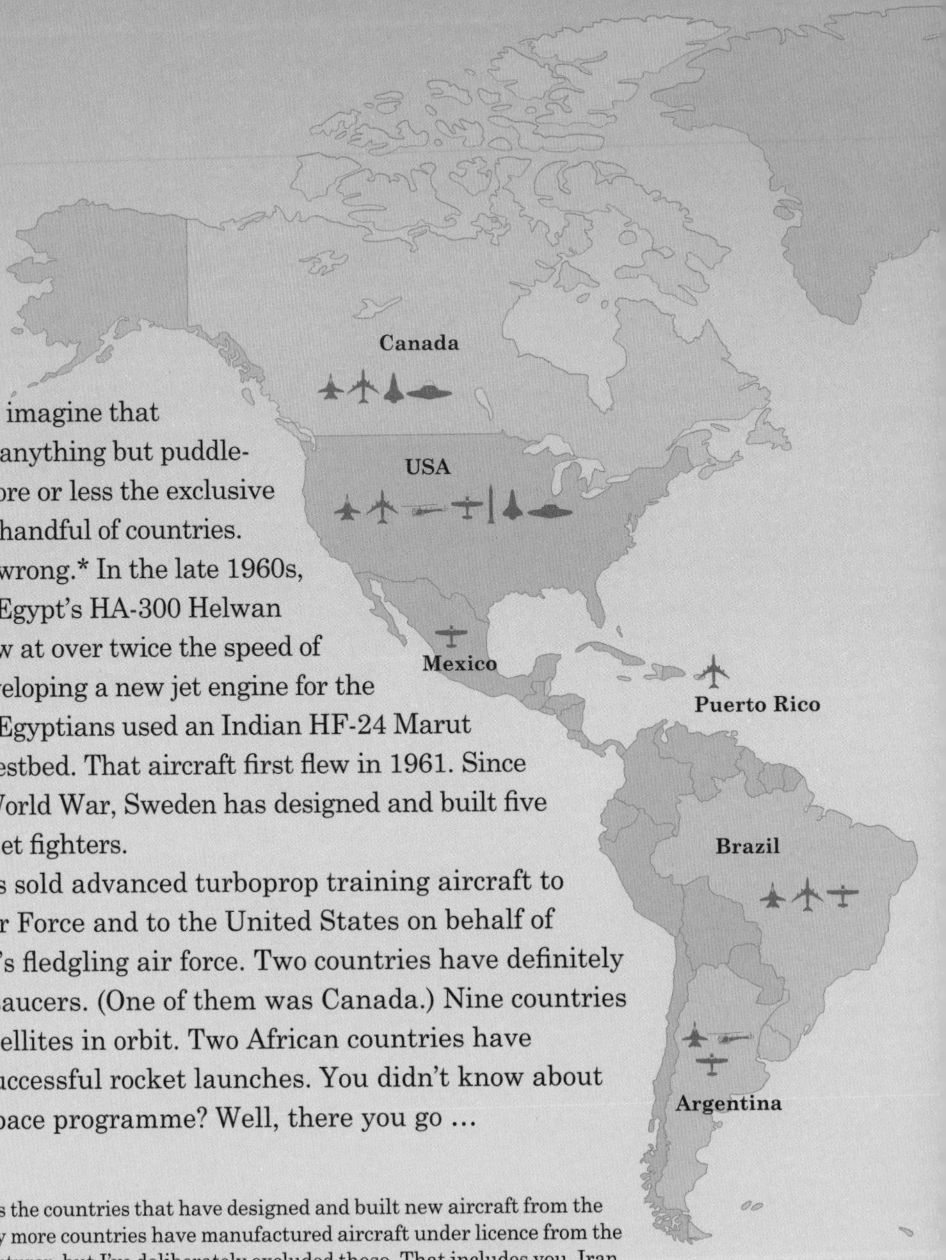

Canada

USA

Mexico

Puerto Rico

Brazil

Argentina

You might imagine that building anything but puddle-jumpers is more or less the exclusive preserve of a handful of countries. But you'd be wrong.* In the late 1960s, for instance, Egypt's HA-300 Helwan jet fighter flew at over twice the speed of sound. In developing a new jet engine for the Helwan, the Egyptians used an Indian HF-24 Marut fighter as a testbed. That aircraft first flew in 1961. Since the Second World War, Sweden has designed and built five outstanding jet fighters.

Brazil has sold advanced turboprop training aircraft to the Royal Air Force and to the United States on behalf of Afghanistan's fledgling air force. Two countries have definitely built flying saucers. (One of them was Canada.) Nine countries have put satellites in orbit. Two African countries have conducted successful rocket launches. You didn't know about the Congo space programme? Well, there you go ...

*This map shows the countries that have designed and built new aircraft from the ground up. Many more countries have manufactured aircraft under licence from the original manufacturer, but I've deliberately excluded these. That includes you, Iran, because lopping the tail fin off an American F-5 Freedom Fighter and attaching two new fins in its place doesn't mean you've designed a super-duper, all-conquering new jet fighter, I'm afraid.

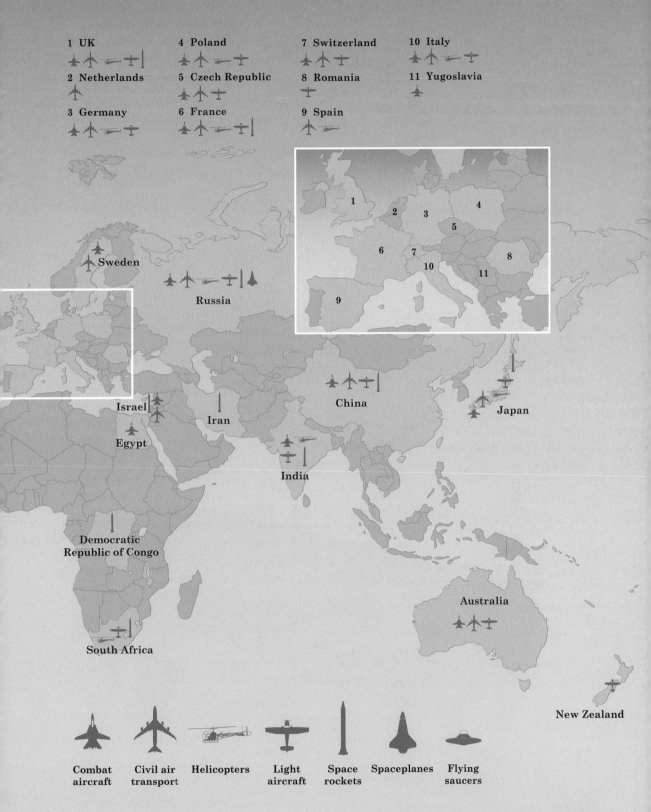

1 UK

2 Netherlands

3 Germany

4 Poland

5 Czech Republic

6 France

7 Switzerland

8 Romania

9 Spain

10 Italy

11 Yugoslavia

Sweden

Russia

Israel

Egypt

Iran

China

Japan

India

Democratic
Republic of Congo

Australia

South Africa

New Zealand

Combat
aircraft

Civil air
transport

Helicopters

Light
aircraft

Space
rockets

Spaceplanes

Flying
saucers

AVRO CANADA CF-105 ARROW
Twin-engined, long-range interceptor

For a country such as Canada to commit, in 1953, to building a machine as advanced as the Avro CF-105 Arrow was bold in the extreme. Announcing the intention to do so, the government minister responsible said, 'We have started on a program of development that gives me the shudders.' But just four years later, Avro's engineers had succeeded in building an awesome-looking delta-winged machine. She first flew in March 1958, and it was clear to all those involved in the test programme that there was record-breaking potential.

A month later, during her first high-speed run, an air-traffic controller exclaimed, 'Look at that son of a bitch go! … WILL … YOU … LOOK … AT THAT SON OF A BITCH GO!' The Arrow was recorded flying at 50,000 feet and Mach 1.98. All involved knew she was capable of much more, but she never had the chance to show it. Less than a year after her triumphant first flight, the Arrow was abruptly cancelled in favour of surface-to-air missiles.

Never again would Canada design a combat aircraft. And it was a decision that still smacks of vandalism.

One member of its parliament, fiercely opposing the cancellation, described the Arrow as 'The greatest single achievement in Canadian aviation history, and the greatest combined effort of design and development ever undertaken in this country.'

The United States certainly thought so, and hired many of the engineers who had been working on the Arrow to work for NASA, where they were to distinguish themselves during the effort to put a man on the moon.

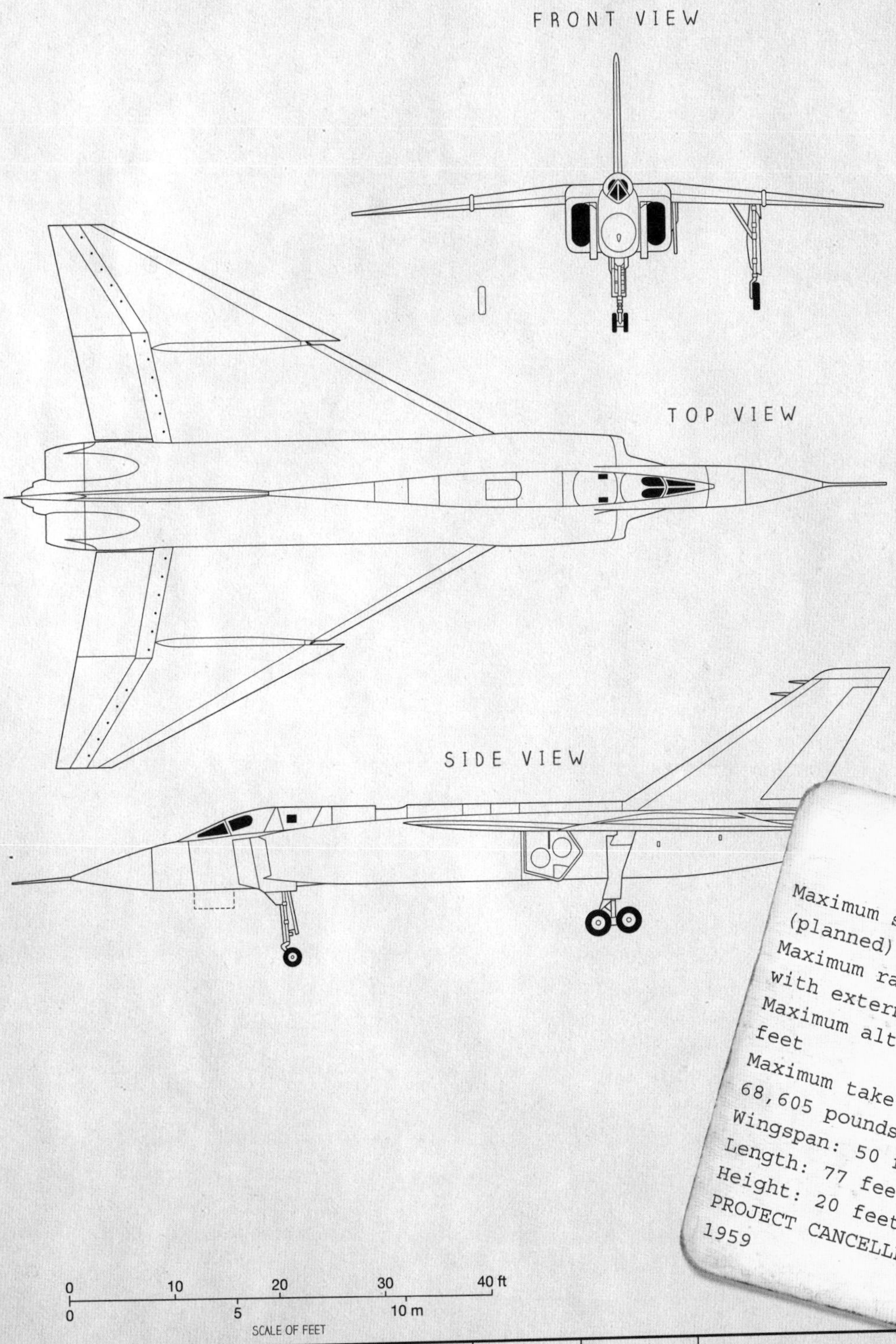

FRONT VIEW

TOP VIEW

SIDE VIEW

Maximum speed: Mach 2+
(planned)
Maximum range: 1500 miles
with external fuel
Maximum altitude: 60,000
feet
Maximum take-off weight:
68,605 pounds
Wingspan: 50 feet
Length: 77 feet 9 inches
Height: 20 feet 6 inches
PROJECT CANCELLED: February
1959

| 0 | 10 | 20 | 30 | 40 ft |
| 0 | 5 | | 10 m | |

SCALE OF FEET

REFERENCE No.	DRAWN	M. LUCAS	13-8-58	*Mlucas*	AVRO CANADA CF-105 ARROW
012847593302-AV	NUMBER	1203330			
GENERAL ARRANGEMENT	CHECKED	J. HOLLAND	29-9-58	*J Holland*	AVRO CANADA TORONTO, ONTARIO
	APPROVED	G. HARLEY	12-10-58	*G Harley*	

Great Planes

Boeing 707

The 707 showed us what a modern jet airliner looks like. After the failure of the British Comet, the world's first jet airliner, it fell to the Boeing aircraft to revolutionize air travel. Capable of crossing the Atlantic in just 6 hours, the 707 was a catalyst for everything that's now familiar about air travel. But in that, it also began the now-complete process of stripping commercial aviation of any last vestige of glamour or style. A flight aboard a Pan Am 707 in the early 1960s was a wonderful, exotic thing. Sadly, it marked the beginning of the end.

First flight: 20 December 1957
Principal operator: Pan Am – then pretty much everyone else
Last operational flight: Still in service

I'm Leaving on a Jet Plane

Air Travel for Everyone

When the world's first jet-powered airliner returned from Paris, she covered the distance in 41 minutes at a speed of 322 mph – remarkably quick at that time. *Flight* magazine hailed the achievement of the machine that climbed like 'an airborne, trackless express train' with none of the noise and vibration that passengers in piston-engined airliners endured. The magazine urged the country to quickly establish a scheduled jet service to and from the Continent. The 'great fillip to national prestige' that it would surely generate would be more than enough to offset any small financial loss.

The journey to Le Bourget and back was made in November 1946 in a civilian version of the Avro Lancaster bomber called the Lancastrian. It was a pretty Heath Robinson affair. Only two of the Lancastrian's four piston engines were replaced with Rolls-Royce Nene jets. The remaining pair of propellers were used during take-off and landing, then shut down in flight. Inside what was essentially a Lancaster bomber fuselage, there wasn't room to seat passengers facing forwards, so they sat in a long row facing sideways.

Britain emerged from the Second World War without any homegrown airliners worthy of the name. But the same month that *Flight* magazine first reported on the Nene-Lancastrian, the Ministry of Supply had placed an order for something rather more special: a brand-new, clean-sheet design for a pure jet airliner.

When, burnished in a natural metal finish, the de Havilland Comet first flew in the summer of 1949, she looked more advanced than anything else in the sky, but it was much more than skin-deep. The beautiful new four-engined jet was literally years ahead of any competition. It entered service with BOAC in the summer of 1952 and passengers loved it. The Comet didn't churn its way through the murk at lower altitudes, but climbed effortlessly above the weather. It was enough, three months later, for the US airline Pan Am to place its first ever order for a foreign-built aircraft.

By the end of the year, the British government had given the green light to an even more advanced jet. The Vickers V.1000 was expected to fly in 1955,

OPPOSITE: *The prototype de Havilland Comet, the world's first jet airliner, represented a revolutionary step forward when she first flew in 1949.*

but eighteen months later, after the sudden, unexplained loss of three BOAC Comets and everyone on board, the dream was dead.

The Royal Navy salvaged the wreckage of the second Comet and experts quickly deduced what had happened. The pressurized fuselage of the Comet had blown apart with such speed and force that the blue and gold paint along its sides had been impressed on the outside of the wings. The cause was traced to metal fatigue.

In July 1954, three months after the third Comet went down and the whole fleet was grounded, Boeing flew a four-engined prototype known as the 367-80. Unlike the Comet, which had its four engines elegantly buried in the wingroots in the style of contemporary British bomber designs, the Dash-80, as Boeing called it, hung its engines on pylons below the wings as they had done with their own bomber design, the B-47 Stratojet. And like the Stratojet, the Dash-80 was agile for a big aircraft, able even to perform barrel-rolls. If the Comet was fragile, it seemed Boeing's new offering was anything but. The company decided to christen the new machine the 707.

The following year France joined the fray, eager to show its mettle after its aviation industry had been forced to sit out the war. The Sud-Aviation Caravelle may have borrowed the design of the nose and cockpit entirely from the Comet, but everything behind that was new, including the idea of placing the two engines on the fuselage near the tail. It made the Caravelle the quietest of all the first-generation jet airliners.

In May, a month after the French design took to the air, the Soviet Union flew her first jet airliner. Clearly based on the design of the Tupolev Tu-16 nuclear bomber, the Tu-104 airliner was successful and pressed into service quickly. With the withdrawal of the Comet, and the new US and French designs not yet ready, it was the world's only operational jet airliner.

Then, in June, Boeing's American rival Douglas, builders of the legendary DC-3, began work on its own jet airliner, the DC-8.

Even though production versions of this and the 707 were still at least two years off, the promise of both was enough for Pan Am to place orders for them in October 1955. In November, with the substantially built prototype just six months away from its first flight, the British cancelled the Vickers V.1000. It was a disastrous decision. Just as the new American jet airliner designs triggered a worldwide buying spree, the British abandoned an aircraft that had the potential to seize a substantial slice of the market. BOAC, whose lack of interest sealed the V.1000's fate, had failed to appreciate how the world was changing.

The clean lines of the Vickers VC-10 reflected its performance. Concorde is the only airliner to have flown the transatlantic crossing between London and New York faster.

Yet by the end of 1955 there was still no direct, non-stop transatlantic airline service, jet or otherwise. Barely 600,000 people a year were flying across the Atlantic, far fewer than those who crossed by sea. Flying remained an exclusive, expensive affair. Passengers were pampered by cabin crew, whom Pan Am specified should ideally be 'blue-eyed with brown hair, poised and self-possessed, slender, 5 feet 3 inches tall, 115 pounds, 23 years old, actively engaged in some participant sport, an expert swimmer, a high-school graduate, with business training – and attractive'. But change was on its way.

In October 1958, by a whisker, BOAC inaugurated the first jet transatlantic service with the Comet IV. (The design flaw of the early aircraft had been fixed.) Although strikingly beautiful, it was too little too late. In the time it had taken to sort out the world's first jet airliner, the bigger American jets had arrived. Just three weeks after BOAC's short-lived victory, Pan Am began its own jet service using the new 707, joined a year later by the DC-8. Not to be outdone by the rival 707's barrel-roll, one DC-8, before being delivered, was flown through the sound barrier in a shallow dive, the only airliner, until Concorde, to fly supersonic.

While speed and glamour were seductive, airlines soon realized that the real advantage of the new jets lay elsewhere – specifically in safety, reliability and ease of maintenance. They were also cheaper to operate.

The year 1958 proved to be a watershed. Alongside the introduction of the jets came economy fares, and for the first time the number of airline

The prototype Airbus A300. The European partnership broke Boeing's stranglehold on the world airliner market and established a template for virtually all subsequent airliner designs.

passengers surpassed the number travelling by sea. By the end of 1960, 1.6 million people were flying, twice as many as were going by ship.

Volume, efficiency and margin came to dominate the airline business, and jets that couldn't compete on these terms, such as the Convair 880, fell by the wayside. As if to emphasize the point, the plane Elvis Presley chose to acquire in 1975 during his Vegas years was a Convair 880.

New jet airliner designs continued to proliferate, and variety was the name of the game. With the 727, Boeing took the same approach as Britain's Hawker Siddeley Trident and clustered three jets around the tail. The Vickers VC10, which first flew in 1962, carried four engines beneath a huge high-mounted tailplane that resembled the fluke of a great whale. Soviet design bureau Ilyushin followed suit a year later with its elegant Il-62, while its rival, Tupolev, again taking a bomber as its starting point, built the world's biggest, longest-range airliner in the extraordinary Tu-114. Although powered by turboprops rather than pure jets, the big swept-wing beast wasn't a great deal slower than its jet rivals and remains the fastest propeller-driven aircraft today.

Then, in 1965, as transatlantic passenger numbers soared towards 4 million, Boeing started designing the world's biggest passenger jet – the 747 – and were so confident of its success that they bet the farm on it. Without a single order, the company privately financed the whole thing itself, and its debt to the banks was greater than any other company's in history. Even a Pan Am order in 1966 worth $525 million covered only half of what Boeing was spending.

The 747 changed everything, though. Capable, in some configurations, of carrying nearly 500 people in eight-abreast seating, the plane saw transatlantic passenger numbers jump sharply after its introduction in 1970. Lockheed and Douglas, with their widebody Tristar and DC-10 respectively were left trailing in the Jumbo's wake. Boeing had needed to sell at least fifty 747s to break even, but to date nearly 1500 have been sold to over eighty different countries. For almost forty years the Jumbo had no rival. Then, in 2005, something even bigger was launched: the Airbus A-380 Super Jumbo.

In 1960, when Boeing bet on size, Britain and France bet on speed. The supersonic Concorde incorporated incredible technological achievements, but it was a sideshow in terms of global air transport. Nevertheless, it paved the way for further collaboration with the creation of the Airbus company. For the last forty years Airbus has successfully challenged Boeing to fly a proportion of the near 3 billion people now flying every year. And while I wish them well, I'm afraid I've got mixed feelings about it.

Early jet airliner design had thrown up a wonderful, exciting variety of shapes, but that came to a halt with the first flight of the Airbus A300 in 1972. From here on airliners would just look like, well, airliners. Tail, two wings, two engines, fat white tube and bluntish nose at the front. Maybe a coloured stripe. That's your lot. Do you want big or small?

For reasons almost entirely to do with cost, planemakers settled on the Airbus A300 and said, from now on this is how things will look. Boeing followed suit, as did the Russians. Airliners became dull. I'm almost embarrassed I can tell the difference between a Boeing 737 and an Airbus A320, but I'm not even sure I *can* tell the difference between an Airbus A330 and a Boeing 767. And I *like* this stuff.

In frontline service with a handful of major airlines, such as American, Delta and SAS, remain a few McDonnell-Douglas MD-80s. These are the last of their breed, Douglas DC-9s in all but name. Designed in the early 1960s, they have high tails, long, graceful fuselages and clean wings unencumbered by engines. They're living fossils, a link to another era. I urge you to catch a glimpse of one while you still can.

A Hell of a Pick-me-up

The Story of the Fulton Skyhook

Just before the credits roll at the end of the James Bond movie *Thunderball*, Sean Connery – wearing a very fetching orange wetsuit – straps himself into a harness and releases a tethered balloon from the dinghy he's sharing with Domino Derval. Seconds later the pair are whipped into the air and winched into the back of a passing B-17 Flying Fortress. As unlikely as it seems, the technique used in the movie was real.

The idea had its roots in 1920s mail pick-up systems and, reportedly, a similar technique was used to extract British SOE agents from occupied Europe during the Second World War, but it was US forces who successfully developed it ... eventually. (First there was a strangled sheep, then an enraged pig got its 125-mph ordeal out of its system by attacking the crew of the aircraft it had been winched onboard.)

Inventor Robert Edison Fulton had been working on a flying car until, running out of funds, he turned his attention to improving an aerial pick-up system he'd first seen demonstrated in London after the Second World War. Instead of trailing a grappling hook from an aircraft to catch a line strung between two poles on the ground, Fulton used two horns, spread at ten-to-two ahead of the pick-up aircraft's nose, to snare a line to the ground held aloft beneath a helium balloon.

The challenge was to remove the violence from the process of being ripped from a stationary position on the ground into the air. Pull that off and it's then just a matter of reeling in the load like a fish that's given up the fight.

By successfully designing a spring-loaded 'sky anchor', Fulton's first human volunteer reported no more than a 'kick in the pants' less forceful than the opening of a parachute. Fulton then went to Alaska with the US Navy's Air Development unit to test his system in the field. Initially at least, it was tried out on inanimate objects, including mail, geological samples and, from an archaeological expedition, massive curved mastodon tusks that were at least 12,500 years old.

OPPOSITE: *Operation Coldfeet. A CIA B-17 Flying Fortress extracts agents from a Soviet Arctic drift station NP-8 four days after they'd been parachuted in. The two men carried with them a 150lb bag of captured film, documents and equipment.*

In 1962 the discovery of an abandoned Soviet ice station beyond the range of helicopters and icebreakers provided a golden opportunity to try the skyhook for real. They called it Operation Coldfeet. Two men were parachuted in, and 72 hours later a modified CIA B-17 Flying Fortress picked them up, using Fulton's system, along with a haul of Soviet equipment.

By 1966 there had been ninety-eight successful live pick-ups, and the USAF, faced with increasing numbers of downed airmen in Vietnam, decided to modify a number of its Special Operations C-130s. Until 1996 the skyhook provided the US military with a method of getting men out from behind enemy lines until long-range helicopters made it redundant.

In thirty years of operations there were just two fatalities. One of them was directly attributable to a failure of the system itself, and on the other occasion a pick-up volunteer suffered from vertigo and became disorientated. The onboard recovery crew failed to secure him, and he stumbled and fell back out of the open hatch to his death. Given the relatively small number of people ever retrieved using the Fulton system, even two deaths mean that, statistically speaking, the odds of killing yourself are rather higher than you'd like.

I've got to say, though, that doesn't stop me in the slightest from wanting to try it.

Read carefully before use. They say men don't read instructions. Before using Fulton's skyhook retrieval system, I think most would force themselves.

The Art of Compromise
Four Different Wing Shapes

Straight

The wing extends at right angles to the fuselage. Straight wings are strong, produce plenty of lift and are relatively easy to manufacture but they can also be aerodynamically inefficient and produce a lot of drag. Ironically, at very high supersonic speeds, a small straight wing produces less drag.

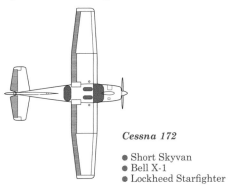

Cessna 172

- Short Skyvan
- Bell X-1
- Lockheed Starfighter

Swept

This configuration angles backwards from the root – where the wing meets the fuselage. At high transonic and supersonic speeds a swept wing produces less drag. They are harder to build and give less strength than a straight wing, produce less lift and usually handle less predictably around stall speed.

North American D-86 Sabre

- Hawker Hunter
- Vought F-8 Crusader
- Dassault Mystère

Delta

The delta wing combines many of the advantages of the straight wing (strength and lift) and swept wing (low transonic and supersonic drag). Disadvantages include high subsonic drag, high landing speeds and, because of the large surface area, a bumpy ride in thick, turbulent air at low altitudes.

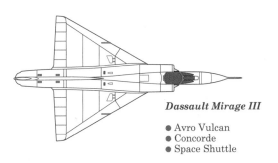

Dassault Mirage III

- Avro Vulcan
- Concorde
- Space Shuttle

Variable Geometry

Hinged at the wing root so they can angle forward and back, swing wings combine the best of both worlds, providing high lift when swept forward and low drag when swept back. A penalty is paid in the weight and complexity of the system, however. Embraced as a solution in the 1970s, they've now fallen out of favour.

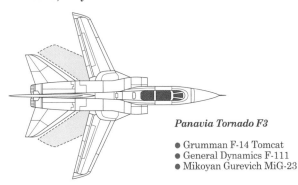

Panavia Tornado F3

- Grumman F-14 Tomcat
- General Dynamics F-111
- Mikoyan Gurevich MiG-23

NORTH AMERICAN XB-70 VALKYRIE
Supersonic strategic bomber

Designed to carry 25 tons of nuclear bombs at three times the speed of sound and at an altitude of 19 miles, everything about the awesome XB-70 Valkyrie was superlative. On its first appearance in 1964, the six-engined XB-70 was at once the heaviest, most powerful and most costly aircraft ever built. It narrowly missed also being the fastest and longest-ranged. Its development resulted in over 700 patents being lodged, and its combination of size and performance remains unmatched today. One test pilot described flying the Valkyrie at three times the speed of sound as like 'driving a Greyhound bus around the racetrack at Indianapolis'. And yet only two prototypes were ever built. As a bomber, the B-70 was stillborn.

Advances in surface-to-air missile technology negated its height and speed as protection and led to its cancellation – hastened by the loss, after a mid-air collision, of one of the prototypes. The challenge of building the B-70 remains arguably the most demanding ever to face a US aircraft manufacturer. The aviation writer Bill Gunston put it well (as he always does):

'In future, when a harassed aircraft engineer feels something is too difficult, he can derive solid comfort from the B-70. Compared with that, his problem – whatever it is – is a pushover.'

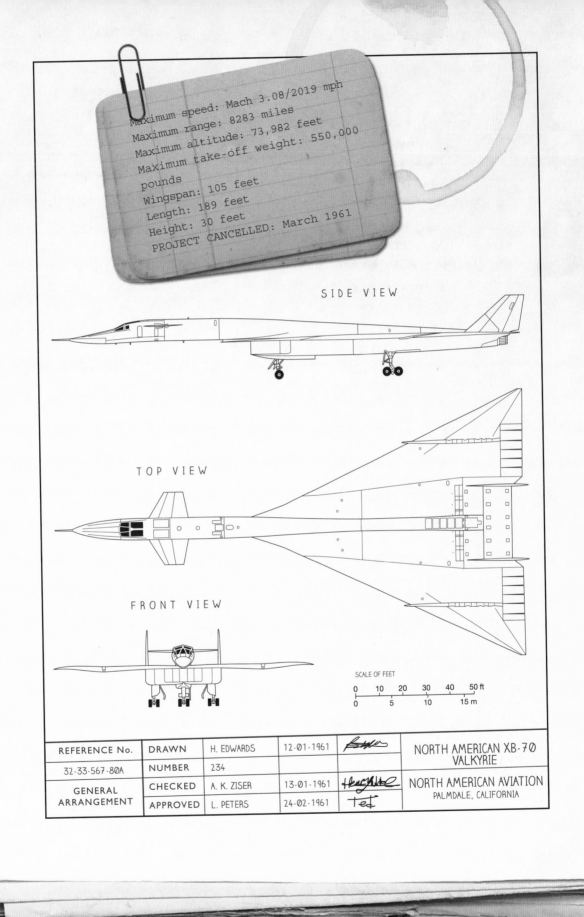

Maximum speed: Mach 3.08/2019 mph
Maximum range: 8283 miles
Maximum altitude: 73,982 feet
Maximum take-off weight: 550,000 pounds
Wingspan: 105 feet
Length: 189 feet
Height: 30 feet
PROJECT CANCELLED: March 1961

SIDE VIEW

TOP VIEW

FRONT VIEW

SCALE OF FEET

| 0 | 10 | 20 | 30 | 40 | 50 ft |
| 0 | | 5 | | 10 | 15 m |

REFERENCE No.	DRAWN	H. EDWARDS	12-01-1961		NORTH AMERICAN XB-70 VALKYRIE
32-33-567-80A	NUMBER	234			
GENERAL ARRANGEMENT	CHECKED	A. K. ZISER	13-01-1961		NORTH AMERICAN AVIATION PALMDALE, CALIFORNIA
	APPROVED	L. PETERS	24-02-1961		

It's All Hot Air (part two)

Felix Baumgartner Raises the Bar

On 14 October 2012 Austrian skydiver Felix Baumgartner claimed Joe Kittinger's record for the highest, fastest freefall with a jump from 128,100 feet (24 miles) high. After stepping from his capsule, he officially became the first person to break the speed of sound in freefall. And yet it wasn't long before one or two sniping voices began to question whether or not it was really as dangerous as we had been led to believe. These cynics had probably not come across the story of Nick Piantanida.

In breaking Joe Kittinger's skydive record, Baumgartner also claimed the official balloon altitude record of 113,740 feet set by Malcolm Ross and Victor Prather in 1961. And yet, strangely enough, Baumgartner wasn't the first man to fly a balloon beyond 120,000 feet. That was Nick Piantanida.

Piantanida was an unlikely record-breaker. After spending much of his childhood off games as a result of a painful bone disease, he later made up for lost time. Fully recovered, he became a pilot, boxer, rock-climber and college basketball star. On graduating in biology, he became a pet-shop owner. Then he discovered skydiving and his life's vocation. He quickly became expert. Acting independently and outside the embrace of NASA or the military, Piantanida decided that he would complete the world's longest freefall and claim the official record for himself. He committed himself completely to studying, saving, fund-raising, preparing and hustling for equipment, and by the summer of 1965 Project Strato Jump was ready.

His first attempt ended in failure. Then, in February 1966, he tried again. The ascent to 120,000 feet, beneath a helium balloon 324 feet long, went as planned and he began the countdown to the jump. At 123,000 feet – higher than any balloonist in history – he reached to disconnect himself from the gondola's oxygen supply. On the ground they heard him over the radio, his voice straining. 'I can't disconnect the oxygen … I don't believe it.' The connection was frozen solid, so he couldn't leave the gondola – couldn't jump. Jettisoning the balloon, he then took over half an hour to descend into an Iowa cornfield beneath the little capsule's reserve parachute. The sight of

OPPOSITE: *A spacesuited Felix Baumgartner plunges towards Earth while training for his record-breaking freefall from 128,100 feet.*

Nick Piantanida. Born 15 August 1932. Died 29 August 1966.

Piantanida, wearing an orange spacesuit and clambering free of his capsule caused a farmer who had come to see what was going on to have a heart attack. And the aeronaut, having neither jumped nor ridden the balloon itself back to Earth, was able to claim neither the freefall record nor the official balloon altitude record. Strike two.

Strato Jump III took place three months later. As the balloon rose through 57,000 feet, ground control heard a sudden blast of air, followed by a scream of 'Emergency!' It's still unclear what went wrong and why, but Piantanida had suffered an explosive decompression at an altitude greater than any other reached by a human being. His blood bubbled in his veins. Although the young aeronaut was alive when he reached the ground, he never recovered consciousness and died in hospital on 29 August 1966.

Felix Baumgartner was born three years later. However off-putting some may have found the carefully orchestrated media and sponsorship campaign that surrounded his jump, there can be no doubting his bravery in making the attempt. In any record attempt every effort is made to improve the odds, but it's impossible to make it risk-free, as another record-breaking balloonist found to his cost thirty-nine years before Piantanida perished and eighty-five years before Baumgartner began his ascent.

On 4 November 1927, Captain Hawthorne C. Gray of the US Army Air Corps was suffocated while attempting to set a new altitude record using a helium balloon. The cause of the failure remains unclear, but the citation for the posthumous Distinguished Flying Cross he was awarded 'for heroism in aerial flight' clearly stated that 'undoubtedly his courage was greater than his oxygen supply'.

Pukin' Dogs and Jolly Rogers
US Navy Fighter Squadrons

You thought that the Dam Busters were as British as roast beef and bad teeth. But when US Navy attack squadron VA-195 destroyed the Hwacheon Dam during the Korean War, they ditched the name 'Tigers' that they'd enjoyed since 1944 and adopted 'Dam Busters' instead.

In US Navy speak 'V' denotes a fixed-wing squadron, 'F' fighter and 'A' attack. Since re-equipping with the multi-role F/A-18 Hornet all the USN's fighter squadrons are now strike fighter units charged with both fleet defence and attack.

SQUADRON NAME	CALLSIGN	SQUADRON NAME	CALLSIGN
VFA-2 – 'Bounty Hunters'	BULLET	VFA-103 – 'Jolly Rogers'	VICTORY
VFA-11 – 'Red Rippers'	RIPPER	VFA-105 – 'Gunslingers'	CANYON
VFA-14 – 'Tophatters'*	CAMELOT	VFA-106 – 'Gladiators'	ROMAN EMPIRE
VFA-15 – 'Valions'	PRIDE	VFA-113 – 'Stingers'	STINGER
VFA-22 – 'Fighting Redcocks'	BEEF/BEEFEATER	VFA-115 – 'Eagles'	TALON
VFA-25 – 'Fist of the Fleet'	FIST	VFA-122 – 'Flying Eagles'	EXPERT
VFA-27 – 'Royal Maces'	CHARGER	VFA-131 – 'Wildcats'	CAT
VFA-31 – 'Tomcatters'	BANDWAGON	VFA-136 – 'Knighthawks'	HAWK
VFA-32 – 'Swordsmen'	GYPSY	VFA-137 – 'Kestrels'	FALCON
VFA-34 – 'Blue Blasters'	JOKER	VFA-143 – 'Pukin' Dogs'	TAPROOM
VFA-37 – 'Ragin' Bulls'	RAGIN'	VFA-146 – 'Blue Diamonds'	DIAMOND
VFA-41 – 'Black Aces'	FAST EAGLE	VFA-147 – 'Argonauts'	JASON
VFA-81 – 'Sunliners'	ZAPPER	VFA-151 – 'Vigilantes'	SWITCH
VFA-83 – 'Rampagers'	RAM	VFA-154 – 'Black Knights'	KNIGHT
VFA-86 – 'Sidewinders'	WINDER	VFA-192 – 'Golden Dragons'	DRAGON
VFA-87 – 'Golden Warriors'	WAR PARTY/PARTY	VFA-195 – 'Dam Busters'	CHIPPY
VFA-94 – 'Mighty Shrikes'	HOBO	VFA-211 – 'Checkmates'	NICKEL
VFA-97 – 'Warhawks'	WARHAWK	VFA-213 – 'Black Lions'	LION
VFA-102 – 'Diamondbacks'	DIAMONDBACK		

* VFA-14 is the oldest squadron in the US Navy, its roots stretching back to 1919. It was for this reason that director Peter Jackson chose the Tophatters to attack King Kong on the Empire State Building in his 2005 movie.

Flying without Wings
The Lifting Body Story

In January 1974, the first of ninety-nine episodes of a new TV series aired in the USA for the first time. The show opened with footage of the test flight of an experimental plane going awry. The pilot, Colonel Steve Austin, struggles to regain control of the machine without success. 'I can't hold her,' he says, 'she's breaking up.' Austin barely survives the subsequent crash and is critically injured. No matter, announces the voice-over. 'We can rebuild him. We have the technology.' Fitted with an atomic-powered bionic arm, eye and legs, Austin is turned into a superman, The Six Million Dollar Man.

Sadly, the technology wasn't available to save the right eye of the test pilot flying the MF-F2 plane, whose real crash featured in the TV show. Instead, after suffering a fractured skull, severe facial injuries and a broken hand when his aircraft tumbled like a rolling log across a dry lake bed, NASA pilot Bruce Peterson lost the sight in his eye to infection.

Peterson had been part of a test programme researching the flying characteristics of what were called 'lifting bodies', wingless aircraft that relied on the shape of the fuselage alone to generate lift.

Throughout the 1960s and 1970s, a series of eight different lifting-body designs were tested in the hope that they might provide the basis of a tough, controllable and reusable re-entry vehicle from space.

At the beginning of the space programme, NASA opted for the simplicity, safety and relatively low cost of a heat-shielded blunt capsule that splashed down in the ocean beneath a parachute. The lifting bodies, machines that shared some of the characteristics of both capsules and winged aircraft, looked to offer an alternative. And they did. Over twelve years, the programme progressed from wooden gliders towed behind a Pontiac to rocket-powered flights at altitudes of up to 90,000 feet. Peterson's crash was the only serious accident in what was an enormously successful research programme that paved the way towards the design of the Space Shuttle.

In the end, the requirements of the US Air Force meant that the final Shuttle design had to have wings (so that it had the gliding range to avoid the possibility of having to land anywhere the US didn't want it to). However, the lifting body concept didn't die with the end of the original programme in 1975.

In 1982, an Australian Navy P-3 patrol plane took photographs of the Soviet Union recovering its own sub-scale lifting-body design from the Indian Ocean after a sub-orbital test flight. NASA was so impressed that it copied it for a new lifting-body design called the HL-20. A mock-up was built and studies conducted, but like its Soviet progenitor, the HL-20 project was strangled by a lack of funds. Nonetheless, the story doesn't end in 1991. Intriguingly, that Soviet design, via the HL-20, has since re-emerged as the blueprint for the privately developed Dream Chaser shuttle. Awarded development funds by NASA in 2012, the updated spaceplane has begun preliminary flight testing.

Like Steve Austin, it seems that the lifting-body concept is going to emerge 'Better ... stronger ... faster.' Although at a cost, it has to be said, of rather more than $6 million.

Look, no wings. The Northrop HL-10 lifting body on the dry lake bed at Edwards Air Force Base after landing. Test pilot Bill Dana watches as Balls 8, *the NASA NB-52 mothership that carried him to altitude before release, flies overhead.*

Great Planes

North American X-15

The incredible X-15 first flew barely a decade after Chuck Yeager broke the sound barrier in 1947. Carried to its release height by a B-52 bomber out of Edwards Air Force Base, the black rocketplane then shattered every major height and speed record in aviation, earning a handful of pilots who flew it their astronaut wings. It would be forty years before anything else came close. An extraordinary step forward.

First flight: 8 June 1959
Principal operators: NASA/US Air Force
Last operational flight: 24 October 1968

Fast, Faster, Fastest
Rise, Fall and Rise of the Rocketplane

I blame Flash Gordon, Dan Dare and Buck Rogers for the rocketplane's allure. It's a 1950s promise of the future. We believed we'd be zooming round in jetpacks and flying cars by now, and flying spaceships to planets around the solar system. Those fictional heroes captured the imagination at a time when only the rocket engine offered any hope of great speed and when, during a brief couple of decades, a series of experimental rocketplanes looked as if they were making the dream a reality.

It's claimed that in AD 1500 a Chinese official called Wan Hu tried to launch himself into the sky in a chair strapped to forty-seven gunpowder rockets. Supposedly, he left the ground before being blown up, and he now has a crater on the moon named after him. History records a handful of similarly disastrous attempts before the first successful rocket-powered flight took place in Germany in 1928.

The Lippisch Ente was a wood-and-fabric tailless glider fitted with a pair of black powder rockets. It would appear to have little in common with the sleek rocketplanes that were to come, but in October 1941 the Messerschmitt Me-163, a machine designed by the same man, flew 150 mph faster than any other aircraft had ever done. Given its severely limited endurance, the little rocket-powered plane, named the *Komet*, was

Over Mojave. In September 1956, the Bell X-2, flown by Captain Mel Apt, became the first aircraft to fly three times faster than the speed of sound.

not a success as a fighter, but it did show the path that, until jet engine technology matured, very high-performance flight would take.

In 1947 Chuck Yeager broke the sound barrier in the rocket-powered Bell X-1. The following year the navy-sponsored Douglas D-558-2 Skyrocket took to the skies and went on to become the first aircraft to fly at twice the speed of sound. Two months later, Yeager, determined to claim the record back for the air force, took a developed Bell X-1, the 'A', to Mach 2.44. Then, in 1956, the swept-wing Bell X-2 raised the bar to over three times the speed of sound. Three weeks later, flying the same aircraft, Iven Kincheloe became the first pilot to roar beyond 100,000 feet and found himself labelled by the press as 'America's first spaceman'.

At the same time, Britain and France, with the Saunders-Roe SR.53 and SNCASO Trident, were testing aircraft that mixed jet and rocket power in search of greater performance, an approach adopted by Lockheed when it added a rocket to its already record-breaking Starfighter to create the NF-104, a machine built to train astronauts ... and pilots of the North American X-15.

It seemed every other rocketplane was really just an hors d'oeuvre for the all-black X-15. Over a ten-year test programme beginning in 1959, the dart-shaped X-15 obliterated every speed and altitude mark set by anything else with wings. In 1963, after being dropped from beneath the wing of NASA's B-52 bomber, pilot Joe Walker flew to an altitude of over 353,000 feet – that's 67 miles high. In doing so, he passed every recognized threshold for space and earned his astronaut wings. Four years later another X-15 pilot, William 'Pete'

Knight, raced to Mach 6.7, still over twice as fast as any other contender for the crown. Only a returning Space Shuttle has ever flown faster.

Yet somehow we forgot to love the Shuttle. When *Columbia* first flew in 1981, and after a five-year absence from space for American astronauts, it was regarded as a triumph. That feeling didn't last. Too often during its lifetime it was characterized as a crushingly expensive delivery truck or defined by tragedy. *Columbia* was the culmination of a programme of test-flying rocketplanes that began with the X-1, but it was a last gasp.

When, in 1969, the X-15 was grounded, it seemed for the next forty years that her achievements would remain untouched. Putative rocketplane programmes, from the USAF's Dyna Soar spaceplane in the early 1960s to the British Aerospace HOTOL project, came and went. The Shuttle *Challenger* was lost, and somehow, because we no longer saw the Shuttle as part of the same story Chuck Yeager began, we were more shocked. Then even more so when *Columbia* was lost to a broken wing in 2003. These rocketplanes are just too risky, we thought, as we never had during the 1950s and 1960s, when the sacrifice made by test pilots felt like a price worth paying for progress.

But just a year later the privately designed SpaceShipOne – another one-man rocketplane – flew into sub-orbital space three times. On her final flight, test pilot Brian Binnie exceeded the altitude reached by Joe Walker in the X-15. In doing so he opened the door on the rocketplane's second coming.

A generation of entrepreneurs and multimillionaires, seemingly inspired by fictional heroes like Buck Rogers, Dan Dare and the real test pilots, astronauts and rocketships that captured their imaginations growing up, now want to build their own.

Scaled Composites, the builder of SpaceShipOne, is working with Virgin Galactic on the larger SpaceShipTwo, designed to carry six passengers into space and back. It's taking bookings at a starting price of $200,000. Based alongside Scaled Composites at its Mojave Desert spaceport, another company, XCOR, is promising spaceflights aboard its Lynx rocketplane from 2014 onwards. Both promise to be utterly exhilarating rides into weightlessness.

Best start saving.

OPPOSITE: *Fitted with a rocket engine in the tail, the Lockheed NF-104A was used by the USAF's Aerospace Research Pilot School to help train astronauts. The school's commandant, Chuck Yeager, nearly died when he lost control of one of the jets while attempting to set a new world altitude record.*

You're a Record Breaker!
The World Air-speed Record

As a boy, I was the proud owner of a little book about air-speed record holders. From the Schneider Trophy races to the awe-inspiring Russian and American supersonic jets of the 1960s and 1970s, the colour illustrations captured my imagination. I turned back again and again to the picture of Neville Duke's modified, red-painted Hawker Hunter seizing the record in 1953, during a period when it seemed the record changed hands every few weeks. For an all-too-brief period it was a duel between Britain and America but it was a contest that, ultimately, America was bound to win.

Back then I hadn't realized just how varied the world of air-speed record-breaking was. Or that one of those Schneider Trophy racers from the 1930s was still the holder of a world air-speed record. It all depends on which category you're looking at.

But here are a few of the best in breed.

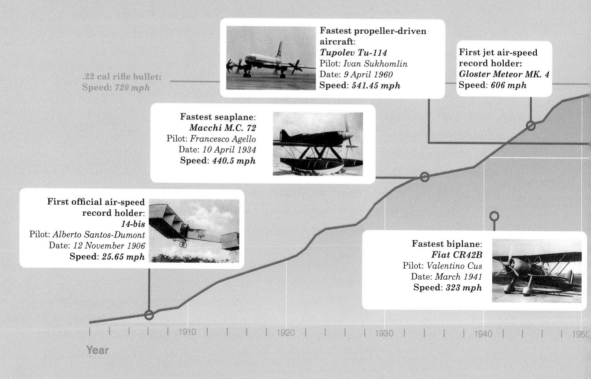

.22 cal rifle bullet:
Speed: *720 mph*

Fastest propeller-driven aircraft:
Tupolev Tu-114
Pilot: *Ivan Sukhomlin*
Date: *9 April 1960*
Speed: *541.45 mph*

First jet air-speed record holder:
Gloster Meteor MK. 4
Speed: *606 mph*

Fastest seaplane:
Macchi M.C. 72
Pilot: *Francesco Agello*
Date: *10 April 1934*
Speed: *440.5 mph*

First official air-speed record holder:
14-bis
Pilot: *Alberto Santos-Dumont*
Date: *12 November 1906*
Speed: *25.65 mph*

Fastest biplane:
Fiat CR42B
Pilot: *Valentino Cus*
Date: *March 1941*
Speed: *323 mph*

Year

1910   1920   1930   1940   1950

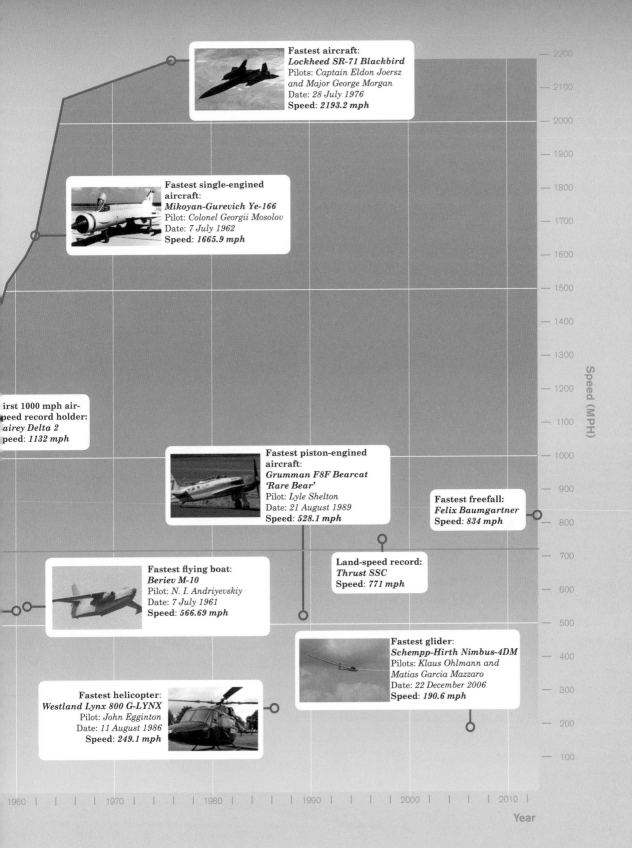

Fastest aircraft:
Lockheed SR-71 Blackbird
Pilots: *Captain Eldon Joersz and Major George Morgan*
Date: *28 July 1976*
Speed: *2193.2 mph*

Fastest single-engined aircraft:
Mikoyan-Gurevich Ye-166
Pilot: *Colonel Georgii Mosolov*
Date: *7 July 1962*
Speed: *1665.9 mph*

First 1000 mph air-speed record holder:
Fairey Delta 2
Speed: *1132 mph*

Fastest piston-engined aircraft:
Grumman F8F Bearcat 'Rare Bear'
Pilot: *Lyle Shelton*
Date: *21 August 1989*
Speed: *528.1 mph*

Fastest freefall:
Felix Baumgartner
Speed: *834 mph*

Land-speed record:
Thrust SSC
Speed: *771 mph*

Fastest flying boat:
Beriev M-10
Pilot: *N. I. Andriyevskiy*
Date: *7 July 1961*
Speed: *566.69 mph*

Fastest glider:
Schempp-Hirth Nimbus-4DM
Pilots: *Klaus Ohlmann and Matias Garcia Mazzaro*
Date: *22 December 2006*
Speed: *190.6 mph*

Fastest helicopter:
Westland Lynx 800 G-LYNX
Pilot: *John Egginton*
Date: *11 August 1986*
Speed: *249.1 mph*

Speed (MPH)

— 2200
— 2100
— 2000
— 1900
— 1800
— 1700
— 1600
— 1500
— 1400
— 1300
— 1200
— 1100
— 1000
— 900
— 800
— 700
— 600
— 500
— 400
— 300
— 200
— 100

1960   1970   1980   1990   2000   2010

Year

But there's a catch ...

Of course, just because an aircraft holds the official world record as recorded and ratified by the FAI – Fédération Aéronautique Internationale – doesn't mean, necessarily, that they are the fastest. And rules change too, so we're not always comparing like with like. Rules and ratification have thrown up a few interesting anomalies ...

Chuck Yeager became the world's most famous pilot when he broke the sound barrier for the first time in the Bell X-1 rocketplane. And in doing so he became the world air-speed record holder, right? Not quite. Before Yeager's totemic flight the record was held by Major Marion Carl of the US Marine Corps, flying a Douglas Skystreak. Because Yeager's X-1 was carried to height beneath the wing of another aircraft, rather than taking off under its own power, it failed to qualify.

That technicality didn't disqualify another rocketplane, the Messerschmitt Me-163. In 1941, the revolutionary little *Komet* should have raised the record from 469.22 mph to 623.65 mph. A huge leap forward. But in wartime the record flight wasn't ratified by the FAI so the old pre-war speed stood until broken by a British Gloster Meteor jet in 1945. At a speed of 606.4 mph ...

Similarly the flying boat record shouldn't belong to the Beriev's barge-like M-10, but to the magnificent Martin P-6M Seamaster, the only flying boat to have broken the sound barrier. But Martin never bothered to put in a call to the FAI in Paris.

However, the most egregious omission has to be that of the rocket-

powered X-15, the fastest winged aircraft of all. In 1967 the X-15, doused in a special ghost-white heat-resistant coating, then dropped from beneath the wing of a B-52 bomber, was flown by test pilot 'Pete' Knight to a speed of Mach 6.7, over 4250 mph. That's nearly seven times the speed of sound and comfortably hypersonic, a term that replaces tired old 'supersonic' at a mere five times the speed of sound.

Still, as athletes who fail to break world records so often point out, it's not about setting records, it's about winning races. And the X-15 certainly did that.

A replica of the radical rocket-powered Messerschmitt Me - 163 Komet. Before the Komet's first combat mission in 1944, ground crew painted the Squadron Commander's aircraft red in homage to the Red Baron's First World War Fokker Dr.1 triplane. Unamused, the CO ordered it to be painted camouflaged again immediately after the flight.

Don't Stop Me Now

Some Songs about Flying

Y ou've got to exercise a little caution when you're picking songs about flying. While some, certainly, draw inspiration from the wonders of aviation, the inspiration of others is less certain. I'd be astonished to discover, for instance, that the Byrds had ever considered for a second using wings, stick and rudder to reach their cruising altitude of 'Eight Miles High'. (That said, their comedown was just as inevitable as anything else 'what goes up'.) There's also a song in the list below that, on the face of it, is an aviation classic. Not so, says the artist who wrote it.* The rest, though, are, in one way or another, connected with aviation. A few of them are actually good songs too …

Five Miles Out – Mike Oldfield

Rocket Man – Elton John

Me-262 – Blue Öyster Cult

Aeroplane – Björk

Spirit of St Louis – British Sea Power

Mighty Wings – Cheap Trick

He's Simple, He's Dumb, He's the Pilot – Grandaddy

747 (Strangers in the Night) – Saxon

Tailgunner – Iron Maiden

Jamaica Mistaica – Jimmy Buffett

Bomber – Motörhead

Enola Gay – Orchestral Manoeuvres in the Dark

Hurricane Fighter Plane – Alien Sex Fiend

Aeroplane – Red Hot Chili Peppers

The Aeroplane Flies High – Smashing Pumpkins

Starfighter Pilot – Snow Patrol

Air Force One – Godley and Creme

Jet – Paul McCartney and Wings

Comin' in on a Wing and a Prayer – Ry Cooder

Supersonic Rocket Ship – The Kinks

Space Oddity – David Bowie

African Night Flight – David Bowie

I Took a Trip on a Gemini Spaceship – The Legendary Stardust Cowboy

Aces High – Iron Maiden

Don't Stop Me Now – Queen

Love Missile F1-11 – Sigue Sigue Sputnik

Leaving on a Jet Plane – John Denver

Jet Airliner – Steve Miller Band

Treetop Flyer – Stephen Stills

Somewhere over China – Jimmy Buffett

Countdown – Rush

A320 – Foo Fighters

Aisle Seat 37-D – Grandaddy

Flight from Ashiya – Kaleidoscope

Amelia – Joni Mitchell

Skylon! – Gruff Rhys

Flying for Me – John Denver

Blast Off Columbia – Roy McCall

Happy Blues for John Glenn – Lightnin' Hopkins

* Although it frequently features in lists of favourite flying songs, Paul McCartney says that 'Jet' was named after a pony he once had.

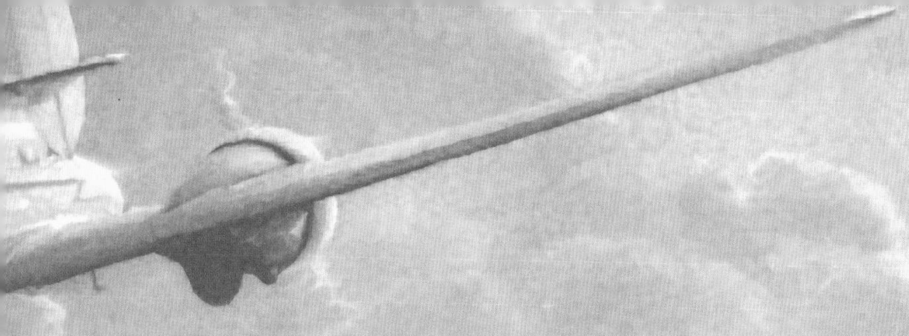

The prize, though, has to go to Robert Calvert, the former frontman of British space rockers Hawkwind (also, of course, responsible for another name on the list opposite, Motörhead, formed by Lemmy Kilmister after he'd been kicked out of Hawkwind). Instead of a song or two alluding to the magic of flying, Calvert went full aviation geek and delivered a whole concept album about the post-war Luftwaffe's experience with the 'missile with a man in it', the Lockheed F-104 Starfighter. Not, it has to be said, the most obvious idea for a concept album. But I suppose a deaf, dumb and blind pinball champion isn't where most of us would have started either.

Anyway, I give you the 1974 album *Captain Lockheed and the Starfighters* by Robert Calvert. Here's the tracklisting in all its glory:

Franz Josef Strauss, Defence Minister, Reviews the Luftwaffe in 1958

The Aerospaceage Inferno

Aircraft Salesman (A Door in the Foot)

The Widow Maker

Two Test Pilots Discuss the Starfighter's Performance

The Right Stuff

Board Meeting (Seen Through a Contract Lens)

The Song of the Gremlin (Part 1)

Ground Crew (Last-minute Reassembly Before Take-off)

Hero with a Wing

Ground Control to Pilot

Ejection

Interview

I Resign

The Song of the Gremlin (Part 2)

Bier Garten

Catch a Falling Starfighter

Great Planes

Lockheed SR-71 Blackbird

This was the one you wanted in Top Trumps. Every schoolboy knew that the legendary SR-71 Blackbird was in an untouchable league of its own. Flying at more than three times the speed of sound and over 15 miles high, nothing else came close. But as important as its dominant performance was the way it looked. An intimidating, seductive, satin-black cocktail of sharp angles and predatory curves showcasing a pair of massive jet engines armed with sharp spikes, it was as if Lockheed had been asked to design a jet for Batman. We'll never see its like again.

First flight: 22 December 1964
Principal operator: US Air Force
Last operational flight: 1998

High as a Kite
How High Do Things Fly?

In 1933, John Buchan, author of *The Thirty-Nine Steps*, approached Douglas Douglas-Hamilton, Marquis of Clydesdale, MP for the Scottish Universities and Commanding Officer of the RAF's 602 City of Glasgow Squadron, and suggested that he lead an expedition to fly over Everest. Buchan was smarting from the American success in flying over the North and South Poles. 'Success,' the writer argued, 'will mean a triumph of British grit and also British materials, besides resulting in an extension of human knowledge of the planet which we inhabit.' Many, not least benefactor Lady Houston who bankrolled the expedition, thought the attempt was suicidal. But Douglas-Hamilton and his team succeeded. And *Wings of Everest*, the film made about the expedition, won an Oscar the following year.

120,000 feet

100,000 feet

90,000 feet

80,000 feet

Tropopause

60,000 feet

Concorde

40,000 feet

Hang-glider

Helicopter

Troposphere

Airliner

20,000 feet

Paraglider

Ballooning Spider

Mont Blanc

Mount Fuji

Burj Khalifa

Empire State Building

Ye-266M
Jet aircraft altitude record

Balloon

Parachute Jump

SR-71 Blackbird

U-2

Caproni Ca.161
Manned piston-engined record (1938)

Glider

Rüppell's Griffon

Bar-headed Goose

Mount Everest

Mount McKinley

Bumblebee

Kilimanjaro

Bat

High as a Kite   257

One of Our Bombers
is Missing

The Birth of the Stealth Fighter

When, in February 1935, Robert Watson-Watt described for the first time how radar might be used to detect enemy aircraft, he noted that it made sense for future bomber designs to include measures that reduced their visibility to radar. That suggestion, though, wasn't passed on to the teams producing new bombers on either side of the Atlantic. In 1941 Watson-Watt tried again. 'A resistive skin,' he concluded, '[provided] a real possibility of camouflaging an aircraft [to radar]', adding, 'How far large scale use of such camouflaging may be feasible or useful is for others to decide.' Whoever they were decided against it, so aircraft manufacturers continued to build machines that telegraphed their presence to the enemy. Reducing the radar return of their bombers was so far from the thoughts of Royal Air Force planners that in 1956 they painted their new fleet of nuclear V-bombers in a white paint scheme that more or less doubled the size of their radar return.

In the USA, however, they were beginning to take the problem more seriously. In August 1956 the CIA expected to be able to fly the U-2 over the Soviet Union with impunity for only another six months. Project Rainbow, an effort to reduce the radar cross-section of the U-2, served only to lower the altitude at which it could fly and therefore made it more vulnerable. When it came to designing a successor, a reduced radar cross-section became an even greater priority. The choice was between two aircraft, the Lockheed A-12 and the Convair Kingfish. The Kingfish generated a smaller radar return, while the Lockheed design had greater speed and range, but also, significantly, promised better programme management. It was the A-12, with some modifications to reduce its radar cross-section, that eventually got the nod. Ultimately, it was to become the high-flying, Mach 3+ SR-71 Blackbird. Yet while some effort had gone into providing it with a degree of stealth, it still, like the U-2, relied on its flight performance to keep it out of trouble.

OPPOSITE: *Not, as appearances suggest, an Imperial Cruiser from* Star Wars, *but the world's first flying stealth prototype, codenamed Have Blue, which first flew in 1977.*

Faced with the conclusions of a study predicting that in a war with the Soviet Union the USAF would be substantially wiped out in less than three weeks, the air force had to find a way to protect its aircraft. And in 1974 DARPA, the Defense Advanced Research Projects Agency, launched Project Harvey (after a 6-foot 3-inch invisible rabbit in a James Stewart movie of the same name) with the aim of building a combat aircraft with the smallest possible radar cross-section.

The man who cracked it was a mathematician called Denys Overholser, whose hobby was reading obscure academic papers with titles such as 'Method of Edge Waves in the Physical Theory of Diffraction'. The equations in the paper, written in 1962 by the chief scientist at the Moscow Institute of Radio Engineering, made the reflection of radar waves off hard surfaces predictable. Overholser, a Lockheed electrical engineer, realized that if you could predict where radar waves would be reflected, then you could design an aircraft to ensure those waves weren't reflected back at the radar transmitter that had sent them.

The design that Overholser's computer modelling came up with was nicknamed Hopeless Diamond because its faceted shape, resembling a cut gem, also looked so woefully unairworthy. However, that was a problem for another day because when the mock-up was mounted on a pole and had a radar pointed at it, there was no sign of it at all. The results were staggering.

Excited Lockheed engineers invited the air force to a test but were unable to replicate their success. On the radar screens was a radar return that, while small, was a great deal bigger than anyone had expected. An inspection of the Hopeless Diamond revealed that a bird perched on top was responsible for the disappointing result. It seemed that Overholser's team had come up with a design that was practically invisible to radar. Now they had to find a way of making the Hopeless Diamond – or at least something pretty similar – fly. To do that they were as reliant on computers as they had been to make her disappear.

The first flying prototype, codenamed Have Blue, was one of the most unstable aircraft ever flown. Without four onboard computers making small corrections over fifty times a second, the weird-looking jet would simply have tumbled through the sky. But it worked. While in the end both aircraft were lost, when it came to radar returns, Lockheed found itself concerned with the effect of merely the odd protruding rivet.

In 1981, just four years after Have Blue first took to the skies, the prototype YF-117 flew for the first time from Groom Lake, Nevada. Although larger, it was recognizably cut from the same cloth as Have Blue.

America's first stealth fighter had been born. The black jet looked like nothing else in the sky, but when, in 1991, it was called on to open the coalition account in Operation Desert Storm, it performed flawlessly.

Who Wanted Concorde?

How the World Nearly Turned Supersonic

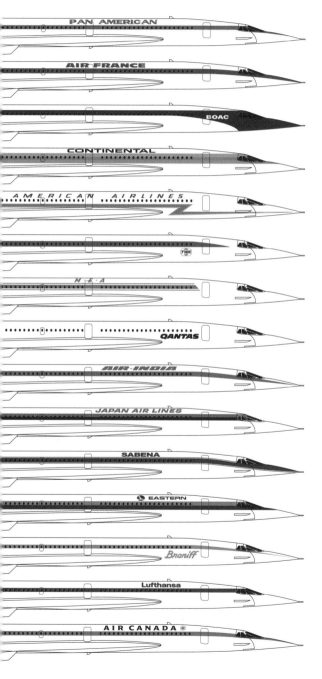

For some time it appeared that the whole world wanted the revolutionary Anglo-French airliner. As excitement built towards the aircraft's first flight, it looked as if Concorde was shaping up to be a supersonic success story. Not to spearhead your airline's fleet with the faster-than-a-speeding-bullet delta seemed as if it would put you at risk of looking a little pedestrian, so the options for orders totted up. By the end of 1967 there were over sixty.

Then it all went wrong. By 1973, when the Soviet Union's Concorde rival, the Tu-144, appeared at the Paris Air Show, Concorde was already facing rejection on the grounds of cost and the noise. When 'Concordski' stalled and fell out of the sky in woods beyond Le Bourget's perimeter, it seemed to seal Concorde's fate.

Of the sixteen countries with delivery positions for Concorde, all but three cancelled. British Airways and Air France, the state-owned airlines of the two countries who'd funded her development and built her, each operated seven Concordes.

The third, Australian airline Qantas, appears never to have got round to cancelling its order, but it seems unlikely that they're still awaiting delivery.

Aurora

The Secret Spyplane. Or Not.

C hris Gibson is a respected aviation writer and researcher with a
reputation for rigour and curiosity. He was also, in the 1980s, a
member of the British Royal Observer Corps (ROC), trained in aircraft
recognition and good at it. So much so that not only was he a member of
an ROC team that won aircraft recognition competitions, but he was also
writing a book on the subject. In simple terms, he was an expert.

For all these reasons, he was one of the last people the US Air Force
would have wanted to catch sight of a unique-looking top-secret spyplane.

But in 1989, while Gibson was working on a North Sea oil platform,
he watched as a formation of four aircraft flew overhead. He recognized
three of them instantly, but the fourth was completely unknown to him. He
considered a number of aircraft it might have been, but dismissed each of
them in turn. He checked the best aircraft recognition manuals in order to
see whether there could have been something he'd missed. None of them
included details of what he saw. He made a sketch of what he'd seen and
reported it to his superiors at the ROC.

Two years later, in June 1991, scientists working for the U.S. Geological
Survey at the California Institute of Technology tracked the progress
of a sonic boom rolling north-east from Los Angeles towards Nevada.
Their array of seismographs extends across California detecting any sign
of earthquake activity, but they'd noticed in the 1980s that they could
accurately identify the speed and track of the returning Space Shuttle. The
boom signature they detected in 1991 was travelling between three and four
times the speed of sound, faster than any aircraft other than the Shuttle.
But there was no Shuttle returning from space that day.

Then, in 2006, the British Ministry of Defence declassified a six-year-
old report giving details of what it called Unexplained Aerial Phenomena.
In trying to explain sightings, it concluded that some 'can be attributed
to covert aircraft programmes'. It gave details of three. One was the well-
known Lockheed SR-71 Blackbird. The other two were redacted – along
with photos – before the report was made public.

Together, these three pieces of information prove nothing. Nor do
multibillion-dollar lines in the US defence budget linked to 'special

An artist's impression of Aurora taking off from RAF Machrihanish on the Mull of Kintyre. Its appearance is based on reports of sightings and informed speculation by aerospace journalists.

programs' or even, on one occasion, something called 'Aurora'. Of course, none of this has stopped people speculating that Aurora is the name of a top-secret hypersonic replacement spyplane brought into service in 1989 to replace the Blackbird. Rumoured to be operating out of both Groom Lake and, on occasion, an expensively refurbished RAF airfield at Macrihanish on the Mull of Kintyre in Scotland, Aurora has been a decades-long obsession for aviation enthusiasts and conspiracy theorists.

The USAF has always denied its existence, but what gives this story a little more credence than aliens at Roswell or faked moon landings is the weight of support there is for its existence among serious journalists from organizations such as *Jane's Defence* or *Aviation Week* – all based on solid investigative reporting.

Does – or did – Aurora exist? Perhaps.

I hope so.

PROJECT CANCELLED

NORTHROP YF-23
Stealth air dominance fighter

Imagine you're the Secretary for the Air Force of the most powerful nation on Earth. You're faced with a choice. After a three-month fly-off between two extraordinarily capable stealth fighter prototypes, you've established that for all the excellence on display from both aircraft, there are clear differences. One of the two designs has better low-speed manoeuvrability. The other is faster, stealthier and has greater operational range. Your original requirement emphasized speed and stealth, but it's worth noting that the jet which is seeming a clear winner, Northrop's YF-23, is also a stunning-looking machine. Its marriage of force and elegance would seem more at home in the hangar deck of *Battlestar Galactica* than on your average USAF flightline. And there's not a fighter pilot alive who wouldn't appreciate that.

This was the early 1990s. The USAF was looking for a new fighter to replace its fleet of F-15s – a big ask – but the new YF-23 was more than up to the task. It was designed by a team that had cut its teeth building the advanced B-2 Spirit stealth bomber, and they knew they had a winner. Its radar cross-section onscreen resembled a spider, so they named their masterpiece the Black Widow II. Its superiority over every other fighter they'd ever encountered was, one engineer said, 'beyond comprehension'. And all the YF-23 had to do was beat the rival Lockheed YF-22 in the fly-off. The Northrop team were confident, though. As one of them said, the Black Widow II 'was really fast – much faster than the YF-22'.

So, of course, in April 1991, the US Air Force Secretary, Donald Rice, announced that Lockheed's YF-22 was the winner.

Like the detail of the YF-23's performance envelope, the reasons for the decision have never been made fully public. It's thought that money, politics and a reluctance to place more eggs in Northrop's basket alongside the difficult B-2 Stealth bomber programme all played their part. Now in frontline service, Lockheed's F-22 Raptor enjoys a clear advantage over all its current rivals, but there's still a nagging feeling that, with the decision to walk away from the YF-23, the US Air Force got second best.

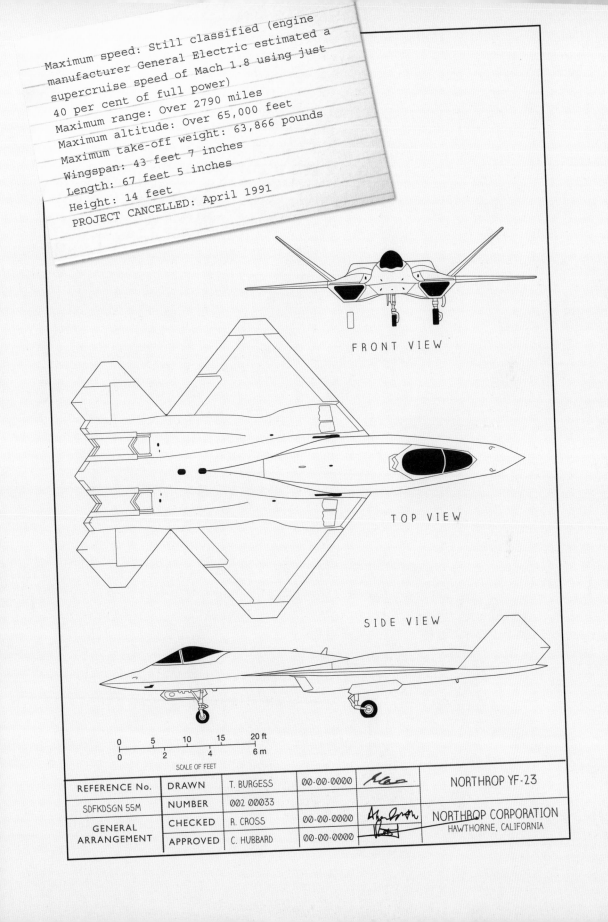

Maximum speed: Still classified (engine
manufacturer General Electric estimated a
supercruise speed of Mach 1.8 using just
40 per cent of full power)
Maximum range: Over 2790 miles
Maximum altitude: Over 65,000 feet
Maximum take-off weight: 63,866 pounds
Wingspan: 43 feet 7 inches
Length: 67 feet 5 inches
Height: 14 feet
PROJECT CANCELLED: April 1991

FRONT VIEW

TOP VIEW

SIDE VIEW

SCALE OF FEET

0	5	10	15	20 ft
0		2	4	6 m

REFERENCE No.	DRAWN	T. BURGESS	00-00-0000		NORTHROP YF-23
SDFKDSGN 55M	NUMBER	002 00033			
GENERAL ARRANGEMENT	CHECKED	R. CROSS	00-00-0000		NORTHROP CORPORATION HAWTHORNE, CALIFORNIA
	APPROVED	C. HUBBARD	00-00-0000		

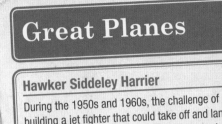

Great Planes

Hawker Siddeley Harrier

During the 1950s and 1960s, the challenge of building a jet fighter that could take off and land vertically like a helicopter became an obsession of aircraft manufacturers around the world. Only the British Harrier pulled it off successfully. Initially derided for being 'unable to carry a matchbox the length of a football field', the robust, versatile Harrier proved all the critics wrong. The little 'jump-jet' that could operate from a forest clearing was a war winner.

First flight: 18 December 1967
Principal operator: Royal Air Force and US Marine Corps
Last operational flight: Still in service

The Caspian Sea Monster

The Rise and Fall of the Ekranoplan

At the end of 1965, the United States Air Force awarded a contract to the aircraft manufacturer Lockheed to build it a new transport aircraft. It was an ambitious project. At nearly 250 feet long and weighing in at almost 200 tons, the C-5 Galaxy would be the largest aircraft in the world.

Less than a year later, and still nearly two years before the C-5 was due to fly, US intelligence made a shocking discovery: the Soviets had something even bigger. A spy satellite overflying the shores of the Caspian Sea took pictures of what looked like a 350-foot-long flying boat. It weighed over 540 tons – around three times the empty weight of a 747. The truncated, almost square wings revealed by the reconnaissance pictures didn't look like they were capable of lifting the machine into the air. Initially it was thought that perhaps it wasn't finished. Subsequent analysis, though, suggested that the machine could fly – just not very well. Uncertain about what they were looking at or what it was for, the Americans christened it the 'Caspian Sea Monster'.

The Soviets themselves called it the Korabl-Maket, or 'Ship-Prototype', and that provides a much clearer indication of the nature of the beast. The

Nearly 300 tons of Lun Ekranoplan at full chat a few feet above the waves. At nearly twice that weight, the biggest Ekranoplan, the KM, was an even more impressive sight.

KM was a machine the Russians called an Ekranoplan – neither aircraft nor ship, but almost a hybrid of the two. It relied on a principle called wing-in-ground-effect. By flying very low, the KM could ride a cushion of air sandwiched between those short, broad wings and the surface of the sea. Powered by ten turbojet engines and designed to fly at just 10 feet above the waves, the KM reached a speed as fast as 460 mph in trials. Not only did flying close to the sea provide as much as 40 per cent more lift, but it also meant the Ekranoplan flew below radar.

While the single, huge KM prototype crashed in fog in 1980 and, because of her great weight, couldn't be salvaged, other smaller designs were developed, including the M-160 Lun cruise missile carrier and the A-90 Orlyonok, a transport version that entered service with the Soviet Navy in 1979.

The navy originally planned to acquire 120 of the A-90s, but in the end just three were ever operational. As the Soviet Union struggled in the final years of the Cold War, support and money for the Ekranoplan programme drained away. For now it remains an intriguing cul-de-sac in the history of aviation, the remains of which are rusting away in a dry dock in the Russian Caspian Sea port of Kaspiysk.

Powered by eight jet engines and carrying six cruise missiles on its back, this near-300-ton Lun class Ekranoplan was capable of skimming along the water's surface at over 340 mph. She's now rusting away at an old naval base on the shores of the Caspian Sea.

'Tactically sound'

The Unrealized Dream of the Airborne Aircraft Carrier

Writing in the USAF's professional journal in 2005, Colonel George D. Kramlinger – a graduate of Naval War College and USAF Fighter Weapons Instructor Course – suggested that the best way for the air force to close its 'global-strike gap' was to build a fleet of airborne aircraft carriers. He proposed sixty to seventy 747 jumbo jet motherships each carrying a stealth fighter on its back, and a similarly stealthy drone beneath its belly. The whole ensemble, capable of being refuelled in the air, would then loiter close to where they were needed, before the drones and stealth fighters were launched to attack at will, returning to the mothership to refuel and rearm. Admitting that his paper could in no way act as a blueprint, he was confident that 'innovation can overcome the technological challenges', and he suggested that the stealth fighters be painted blue, just in case daylight operations were ever necessary.

It's a seductively exciting idea, and on the face of it appears to offer a way of delivering small, lethal, short-ranged warplanes to where they can do most damage. Elsewhere we've touched on the US Navy's operation of biplanes from inside their airships USS *Macon* and *Akron*, but, like Colonel Kramlinger's proposal, there have been plenty of schemes to use fixed-wing aircraft as airborne aircraft carriers too.

The Soviet Union first experimented with launching fighters from Tupolev TB-1 heavy bombers in 1931. It persisted with what it called the Zveno project throughout the 1930s, carrying as many as five aircraft above and below the wings of the big four-engined bombers. Interest in the programme waned until, after witnessing the success of Luftwaffe dive bombers in the opening months of the Second World War, the Soviets wondered if air-launching bomb-carrying Polikarpov I-16s from the backs of Tupolev TB-3 bombers offered them a similar capability. In 1941 the I-16s successfully attacked oil depots and bridges in German-occupied Romania. The little air-launched fighters even managed to shoot down a couple of Luftwaffe Messerschmitt Me-109s. But after thirty missions, the programme was abandoned for good. Both the TB-3s and the I-16s were vulnerable, outclassed by newer, more capable machines.

The Zveno project remains the only time airborne aircraft carriers

A Republic RF-84 Thunderflash launches from its mothership. Clearly we're still some way from building anything like the S.H.I.E.L.D. Helicarrier from the Avengers *movie.*

have gone to war. In doing so, they highlighted some of the problems that plagued similar schemes. Not only is launching and, particularly, recovering from an airborne aircraft carrier difficult and dangerous, but the kind of aircraft that can do so is often at a disadvantage to the conventionally launched aircraft it might meet in combat. This was certainly true of the little McDonnell XF-85 Goblin, a sort of jet-powered egg designed to provide fighter defence for USAF bombers. In seven flights, the Goblin managed to hook up successfully only three times. And twice it smashed into the trapeze and was forced to return to earth for an emergency landing.

Despite the failure of the Goblin, the USAF persevered with the idea. Using a refined trapeze, a bigger GRB-36 bomber and a modified Republic RF-84 Thunderflash, the FICON (Fighter Conveyor) project even saw brief, limited frontline service in the mid-1950s. As a reconnaissance asset, it was said to be 'tactically sound', but the Thunderflash jets were still being damaged attempting to recover to the mothership, and the development of the U-2 at the same time soon meant the whole experiment could be abandoned.

The Soviet Air Force Zveno project doesn't look real but the concept was actually used in combat in the Second World War. The two biplanes on top of the wings had to be hauled up long ramps by ground crew.

It was an idea that refused to die, though. In 1973 the USAF asked Boeing to look at the idea of the airborne aircraft carrier again. This time the company came up with something rather more exciting than a single fighter hanging from a trapeze of an old bomber. Instead it suggested a modified 747 Jumbo carrying up to ten fighters inside the fuselage. And because space was so limited, it couldn't just load the thing with any old fighter. Instead it designed bespoke micro-fighters, tiny little supersonic jets just a quarter of the weight of an F-16, that could be launched, Boeing reckoned, at 80-second intervals. Ten of Boeing's big jets could put an air force of 100 jet fighters into action anywhere in the world within 24 hours. It was a tantalizing prospect, but unbelievably ambitious. Needless to say, it was decided that negotiating the rights to use overseas airbases was a more practical solution to providing the USAF with a global strike capability. It remains the case today.

I'm grateful to Colonel Kramlinger for his spirited 2005 effort to rekindle the idea. I wish his paper had been the spark that led to a fleet of 747 airborne aircraft carriers, but, sadly, being seriously cool wasn't a sufficiently good reason to pursue it.

Turbo Dog and Critter
A Few Notable Airline Callsigns

When an airline pilot radios air-traffic control, he identifies himself with his callsign. This is a combination of the airline's own unique designator and a flight number or aircraft registration, which is specific to a particular aircraft on a specific route. Many of them are dull and obvious: Aeroflot uses Aeroflot, Air Canada uses Air Canada, Lufthansa uses Lufthansa, and so on. But a handful are more interesting or playful. Here are fifty-six telephony designators worth sharing:

Access Air (USA) **CYCLONE**	Lufttaxi Fluggesellschaft (Germany) **GARFIELD**
Aer Lingus (Ireland) **SHAMROCK**	MyTravel (UK) **KESTREL**
African Safari Airways (Kenya) **ZEBRA**	Neos (Italy) **MOONFLOWER**
Air Cargo Carriers (USA) **NIGHT CARGO**	Northwestern Air (Canada) **POLARIS**
Air Cargo Express (USA) **TURBO DOG**	Pacific Southwest Airlines (USA) **SMILEY**
Air Holland (Netherlands) **ORANGE**	Pacific Wings (USA) **TSUNAMI**
Air Mobility Command (US Air Force) **REACH**	Pan American World Airways (USA) **CLIPPER**
America West Airlines (USA) **CACTUS**	Pinnacle Airlines (USA) **FLAGSHIP**
Arrow Air (USA) **BIG A**	Republic Airlines (USA) **BRICKYARD**
Atlas Air (USA) **GIANT**	Royal/VIP Flights (UK) **RAINBOW**
Austin Express (USA) **COWBOY**	Ryan Air Service (USA) **ARCTIC TRANSPORT**
British Airways (UK) **SPEEDBIRD**	San Juan Airlines (USA) **MARINER**
(British Airways Christmas charter flights use the callsign **SANTA**)	SkyEurope (Slovakia) **RELAX**
Brussels Airlines (Belgium) **BEE-LINE**	Sky Trek International Airlines (USA) **PHAZER**
CargoItalia (Italy) **WHITE PELICAN**	South African Airways (S. Africa) **SPRINGBOK**
China Airlines (Taiwan) **DYNASTY**	SwedeJet Airways (Sweden) **BLACKBIRD**
East African Airlines (Uganda) **CRANE**	Swe Fly (Sweden) **FLYING SWEDE**
Eastwind Airlines (USA) **STINGER**	Thunderbird Tours (Canada) **ORCA**
European Air Express (Germany) **STARWING**	Tiger Airways (Singapore) **GO CAT**
Express One International (USA) **LONGHORN**	Titan Airways (UK) **ZAP**
Faroejet (Faroe Islands) **ROCKROSE**	Trans States Airlines (USA) **WATERSKI**
Flight Alaska (USA) **TUNDRA**	Triple O Aviation (Nigeria) **MIGHTY WING**
GoJet Airlines (USA) **LINDBERGH**	Turdus Airways (Netherlands) **HUNTER**
Hahn Air (Germany) **ROOSTER**	ValuJet Airlines (USA) **CRITTER**
Island Express (USA) **SANDY ISLE**	Virgin America (USA) **REDWOOD**
Jetairfly (Belgium) **BEAUTY**	Viva Macau (Macau) **JACKPOT**
Kalitha Air (USA) **CONNIE**	Wright Air Service (USA) **WRIGHT FLYER**
LTE International Airways (Spain) **FUN JET**	Xtra Airways (USA) **CASINO EXPRESS**

The Runway Code
How to Park an Airliner

If you're helping a friend to parallel-park, it's relatively straightforward. You can ask them to wind down the window, stand within earshot and shout helpful things like 'Left hand down a bit', 'You've got about six inches' and 'STOP!' But if you're standing outside an airport terminal with a Jumbo Jet trundling towards you, this plainly is not going to work. Consequently, all pilots and ground handlers use standardized marshalling signals. Whether used with hands, table-tennis bats or fluorescent batons, this aviation sign language removes confusion and chaos. Or certainly most of it.

AIRCRAFT MARSHALLING SIGNALS

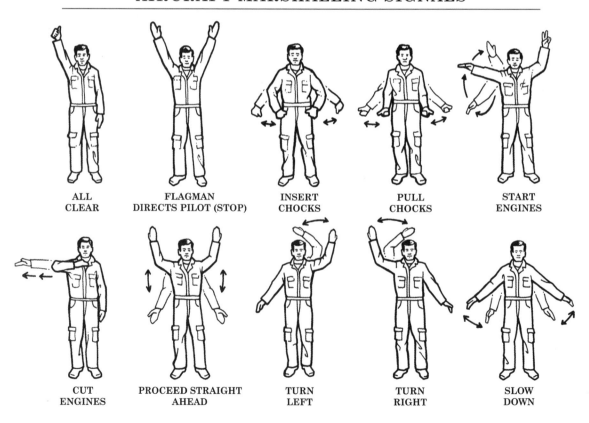

| ALL CLEAR | FLAGMAN DIRECTS PILOT (STOP) | INSERT CHOCKS | PULL CHOCKS | START ENGINES |

| CUT ENGINES | PROCEED STRAIGHT AHEAD | TURN LEFT | TURN RIGHT | SLOW DOWN |

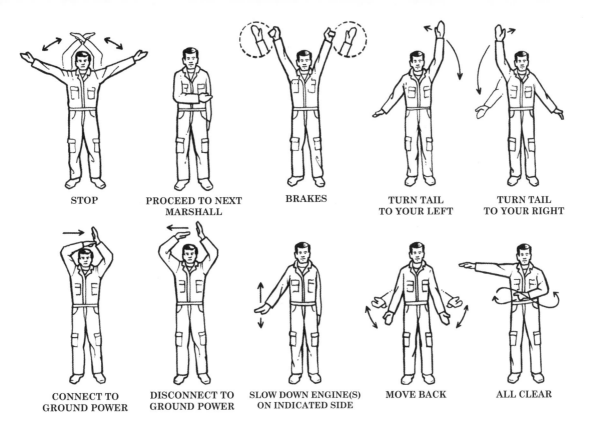

STOP

PROCEED TO NEXT
MARSHALL

BRAKES

TURN TAIL
TO YOUR LEFT

TURN TAIL
TO YOUR RIGHT

CONNECT TO
GROUND POWER

DISCONNECT TO
GROUND POWER

SLOW DOWN ENGINE(S)
ON INDICATED SIDE

MOVE BACK

ALL CLEAR

HELICOPTER MARSHALLING SIGNALS

LIFT
OFF

HOVER

MOVE
UPWARDS

MOVE
DOWNWARDS

(AT THE HOVER)
RELEASE SLING LOAD

ENGAGE
ROTOR

MOVE
HORIZONTALLY

LAND

HOOK-UP

How to Park an Airliner   275

Great Planes

Boeing 747 'Jumbo Jet'

Contemporary reports described it as 'the plane to carry Gulliver'. At 350 tons, it was three times heavier than the Boeing 707. When the first 747 entered service with Pan Am in January 1970, between New York and London, air travel was transformed for ever and no longer the preserve of an elite. The first 361 passengers aboard Pan Am's *Clipper Young America* have since been followed by another 3.5 billion. And the 1500-plus Jumbos built have, between them, flown close to 50 billion miles around the globe.

First flight: 9 February 1969
Principal operator: Pretty much everyone
Last operational flight: Not for some time yet ...

Come and Have a Go If You Think You're Hard Enough

The World's Biggest Air Forces

The countries represented opposite operate the ten biggest fleets of military aircraft in the world. Between them they account for 55 per cent of all the military aircraft on the planet.

Of course, it's not quite as straightforward a picture as the graphic suggests. If you break it down into categories of aircraft, some interesting details emerge. While France sits at number seven on the overall list, she has fewer frontline combat aircraft than North Korea, Pakistan and Egypt. And while the UK scrapes into the top ten on numbers alone, 180 of her total military aircraft fleet – 17 per cent – are propeller-driven training aircraft. In fact, Britain has the fourth-biggest fleet of training aircraft in the world (after the USA, Japan and Egypt). But when it comes to numbers of combat aircraft, she's comfortably outgunned by all the countries who sit above her in the overall top ten. And also by South Korea, Taiwan, Israel, Greece, Saudi Arabia and Germany. The RAF's frontline fast-jet fleet is the same size as that of Turkmenistan.

But if the overall picture is more shaded when subjected to a bit of scrutiny, one thing remains absolutely crystal clear whichever way you cut it: the dominance of the United States. It doesn't matter whether you look at jet fighters, bombers, helicopters, training aircraft, freighters or tankers, the USA is number one in every category by a country mile. She has twice as many fast jets as Russia and China put together (those countries, incidentally, come in second and third). She also has more combat helicopters than the rest of the top ten put together. For now, she remains the world's only superpower.

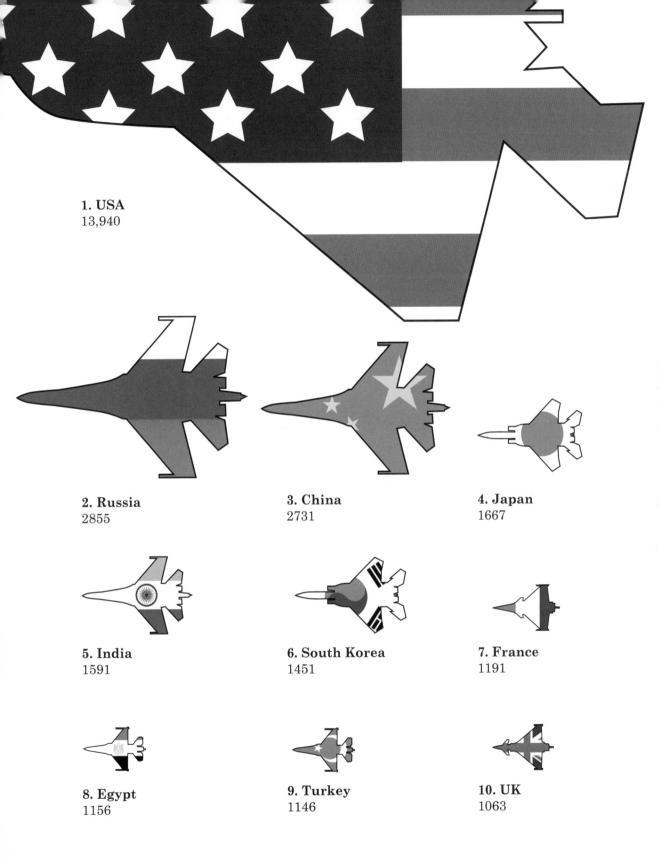

1. USA
13,940

2. Russia
2855

3. China
2731

4. Japan
1667

5. India
1591

6. South Korea
1451

7. France
1191

8. Egypt
1156

9. Turkey
1146

10. UK
1063

The World's Favourite Airline
Who's the Biggest?

The graphic on these pages represents the world's biggest airlines according to the number of aircraft in their fleets. You could measure 'size' in a number of different ways, though, including the number of passengers flown, or the number of passenger miles flown. If you use the former, the Irish budget airline Ryanair breaks into the top ten; if you go for the latter, Emirates makes an appearance. Otherwise, the picture looks pretty familiar using all three methods. The top three remain all–American however you look at it. When it comes to hauling cargo, American airlines are ever more dominant. Whether it's commercial or military, when it comes to aviation, the USA is in a league of its own.

Cargo airlines

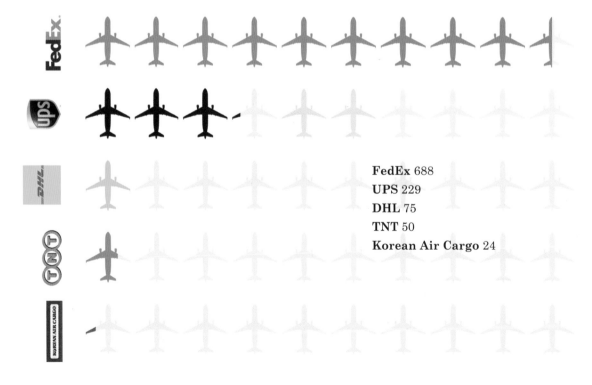

FedEx 688
UPS 229
DHL 75
TNT 50
Korean Air Cargo 24

Commercial airlines

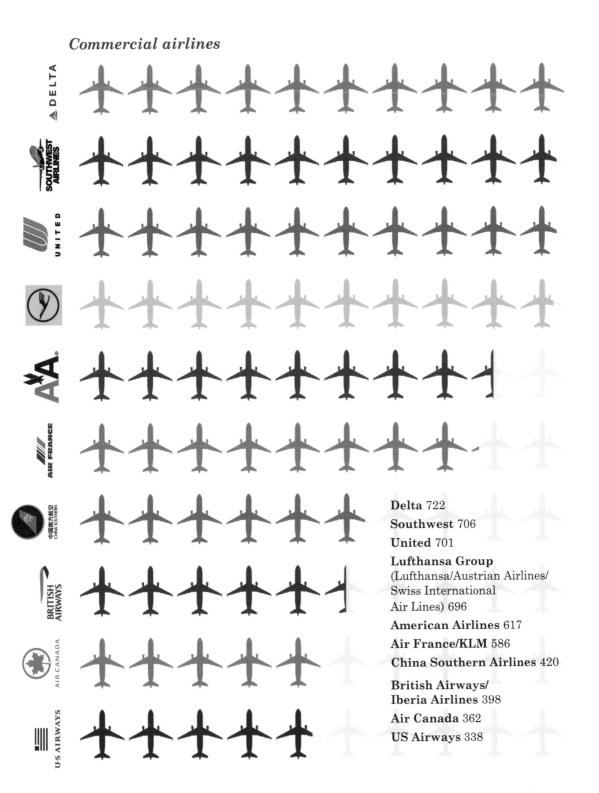

Delta 722
Southwest 706
United 701
Lufthansa Group
(Lufthansa/Austrian Airlines/
Swiss International
Air Lines) 696
American Airlines 617
Air France/KLM 586
China Southern Airlines 420
**British Airways/
Iberia Airlines** 398
Air Canada 362
US Airways 338

Anything, Anywhere, Anytime
A Few Airlines You May Not Have Heard Of

The national flag-carriers and budget airlines might be the first names to spring to mind, but they're not usually the ones who are having the most interesting time of it. For adventure, you need to look a little further afield.

Affretair

As nicknames go, 'Tango Romeo' is a pretty good one, especially when it's been coined by a newspaper based on the callsign of your gun-running cargo plane. Buccaneering Jack 'Tango Romeo' Malloch established an extraordinary succession of aviation companies, including Affretair, Zimbabwe's national cargo airline until 2000. They don't make them like Jack any more.

Born in South Africa, Malloch moved to Rhodesia (present-day Zimbabwe) in 1920 before joining the Royal Air Force in 1943. Following the war, he and his aircraft could be found in the thick of every single hotspot, civil war and conflict that afflicted Africa. Often in the pay of both the CIA and the French secret service, he supported Mad Mike Hoare's mercenaries in the Congo, flew gun-running missions in Biafra (a breakaway Nigerian state) and flew mercenaries into the Comoros for an attempted coup in 1977. But he was best known for his beef-carrying, sanctions-busting flights to Gabon from Rhodesia in the 1970s. From here Affretair's DC-8 jet freighters flew the meat to Europe, earning vital hard currency for Rhodesia's illegal regime. Jack's operations have been credited with keeping Ian Smith's rebel government in power by providing a steady supply of consumer goods, arms and ammunition.

Jack also had a sideline in gun-running during the Yemeni civil war in the 1960s, was jailed in Togo in 1968 after landing with 9 tons of Nigerian banknotes and flew a 65-lb coelacanth 'living fossil' out of the Comoros in 1978. Four years later he was dead, killed when the Spitfire he'd restored crashed near Salisbury (now Harare). I'm sure, as they say, it's how he'd have wanted to go ...

 AIRWORK SERVICES

In 1928, the year it was founded, Airwork's chief pilot, Captain Valentine Baker, had a bullet in his neck. It had been there for over a decade, since the First World War, when he had served with all three services. When warned by doctors that removing the bullet might cause permanent damage, he said 'Leave it alone then', a pragmatism he later brought to his work.

Baker moved on to the Martin-Baker company, which became famous for making the world's best ejection seats, but in 1936 Airwork secured a contract to open an RAF flying school in Scotland. Another seven schools followed, along with a string of maintenance contracts for the RAF and Fleet Air Arm.

After the Second World War, Airwork expanded into civil air transport, launching a passenger service to Nairobi. Flying twin-engined twenty-seat Vickers Vikings on a journey that took three days to complete via Malta, Benghazi, Wadi Halfa, Khartoum, Juba and Entebbe, Airwork was able to compete with the 24-hour BOAC service by offering tickets for just £98 – a third cheaper than their state-owned rival.

Services to Freetown in Sierra Leone, Salisbury in Rhodesia and New York followed, as well as a contract to fly pilgrims to and from Jeddah during the *haj*. Throughout it all, Airwork was busy helping fledgling air forces in places such as Saudi Arabia, Oman, Yemen, Kuwait and Jordan, often supplying pilots as well as maintenance and technical support. This only became a headache when, as happened with Saudi Arabia and Yemen in the late 1960s, Airwork's customers started fighting each other.

AIR AMERICA

With its mantra 'Anything, Anywhere, Anytime, Professionally', Air America was the granddaddy of all the under-the-counter airlines. From 1950, when it first came under the wing of the CIA, Air America, as it became known in 1959, flew cargo throughout South-East Asia, including covert missions into Burma and China. It was during the Vietnam War, however, that this ostensibly civilian airline made its name, conducting operations throughout Burma, Cambodia, Thailand and Laos. Flying an extraordinarily diverse collection of aircraft, from Huey UH-1 helicopters to the big four-engined Lockheed Constellation – and more or less everything else in between – Air America's pilots were the only civilian pilots certified to fly non-civilian-certified aircraft in a combat role.

The distinction was, at best, blurred. Not only did the airline fly diplomats, soldiers, spies, special forces teams and casualty evacuations alongside cargos of food, but they also carried 'hard rice', the code for guns and ammunition.

Air America was disbanded in 1976, only to suffer the indignity of having an 'action comedy' made about it in 1990. Starring Mel Gibson and Robert Downey Jr., the movie based its plot on long-standing rumours that Air America was used to smuggle opium out of Laos on behalf of local rebel leaders. The film was a big hit at the US box office.

AIR FOYLE

Tanks, helicopters, food aid, refugees, fire-fighting equipment for extinguishing oil-head blazes, America's Cup yachts, troops, Richard Branson's hot-air balloon, bulldozers, even a railway locomotive – you name it, Air Foyle has flown it, often to remote and troubled parts of the world.

Launched with a pair of little Piper Aztec light aircraft in 1978, Christopher Foyle's outfit grew quickly until, a little over ten years later, Foyle secured the deal that made him indispensable. In 1989 he took responsibility for a fleet of giant airlifters from the Ukrainian Antonov design bureau. This included the An-124, An-22 and the world's biggest aircraft, a single six-engined An-225, which had been built to carry the Buran, Russia's prototype space shuttle. Perhaps Foyle was always destined to do something a little different.

In 1903 his grandfather founded the famous London bookshop that bears his name, and fond memories of the kind old man at first tempted Christopher into the family business. However, frustration with the aunt who ran the shop like a personal fiefdom, combined with his adventurous spirit and a love of aviation, led him to create the *other* business to carry the family name: Air Foyle.

SOUTHERN AIR TRANSPORT

In 1947 pilot 'Doc' Moor founded Southern Air Transport innocently enough in Florida with a loan from his mother and a leased Douglas C-47. Then, in 1960, the CIA came knocking, bringing Moor's now successful cargo airline under the control of its Pacific Corporation front company. That's when life got really interesting.

Southern Air Transport became the first and biggest civilian operator of the Lockheed C-130 Hercules airlifter. Its aircraft have operated out of 100 countries and seven continents, in support of the US war in Vietnam, in Central America, where in 1986 a SAT C-130 Hercules was shot down, and in numerous African countries. In Papua New Guinea it was solely responsible for sustaining drilling operations in the

central highlands. Completely isolated by impassable terrain, everything had to be flown in.

But it's the list of things it carried that most catches the eye. As well as food aid, military men and material, and heavy industrial equipment, SAT has flown breeding racehorses to Brazil, a cargo of lions from Amsterdam to South Africa, dolphins and killer whales, and the Ramses II collection of antiquities from Egypt.

The SAT story came to a sticky end in 1999 when, on the same day that its former parent, the CIA, alleged that its aircraft had been used for drug trafficking, the company filed for bankruptcy.

It has no website, no published schedule, no in-flight magazine, and passengers don't earn air miles, but Janet Airline, operated by US defence contractor EG&G, has perhaps the most interesting list of destinations of any passenger-carrying airline. If it's your business to visit them, the fleet of Boeing 737s, all white with a distinctive red cheatline running down the fuselage, will fly you to some of the most secret and sensitive locations in the world.

Operating out of McCarran International Airport in Las Vegas since 1972, Janet's jets will take you to Edwards Air Force Base, the Naval Air Station China Lake, Nevada's Tonopah test range and, the most famous destination, Area 51, the top-secret base that's been home to the CIA's U-2 programme, the SR-71 Blackbird, Russian MiGs in US colours, stealth development, and persistent rumours of aliens and UFOs.

They won't sell you a ticket, but who wouldn't want to fly Janet?

CIVIL AIR TRANSPORT

US Lieutenant-General Claire Lee Chennault couldn't have enjoyed a more unusual, interesting or exotic flying career. Born in 1893, he learned to fly during the First World War, and became chief of the Pursuit Section at the Air Corps Tactical School in the 1930s. His outspoken advocacy of pursuit – or fighter interception – brought him into conflict with his superior, and in 1937 he resigned.

Chennault immediately resurfaced in China as air adviser to nationalist leader Chiang Kai-shek during the Chinese war with Japan. It was here that he made his name.

After persuading the US government to provide financial support and aircraft, he turned 300 American mercenary pilots into a fierce underdog air force known as the Flying Tigers, and from 1941 took the fight to Japan.

With the war's end, Chennault remained in China to create Civil Air Transport (CAT), a cargo airline flying surplus Second World War freighters in support of Chiang's war with Mao Zedong's communists. Following Chiang's defeat in 1950, CAT remained at the forefront of the fight against communism in the Far East.

The airline flew thousands of tons of supplies to UN forces during the Korean War in the early 1950s, and airlifted stores and equipment to rebels in Indonesia. In 1959, as America's role in South-East Asia deepened, the CIA, who'd owned Chennault's airline since 1950, re-badged it Air America, an outfit as closely associated with Vietnam as paddy fields and napalm.

BRITISH SOUTH AMERICAN AIRWAYS

During the Second World War, Don Bennett led the RAF's Pathfinder force, the men who flew ahead of the main bomber stream to mark the target. After the war he continued in the same vein when he took control of British South American Airways.

BSAA were pioneers, flying a pot-pourri of old bombers converted for civilian use over new, long-distance routes. (The Lancaster bomber in its guise as the Lancastrian was not, it has to be said, the perfect airliner.) However, the press-on approach that had served Bennett so well during the war was not well suited to running an airline, and BSAA became better known for the mysterious disappearance of a number of its aircraft. The *Stardust* vanished in the Andes, leaving behind only the unexplained radio message 'STENDEC', and two Avro Tudors were lost without trace in what soon became known as the Bermuda Triangle. But whatever the conspiracy theorists might be thinking, the Tudor tragedies can be pretty easily explained. The maker, one aviation writer reported of Avro's design, 'had made the proverbial pig's ear' of it. And by 1949, just three years after it began transatlantic services, BSAA was absorbed back into BOAC.

'Get off my plane!'
The Story of Air Force One

When Harrison Ford throws a terrorist off the hijacked presidential jet in the 1997 movie *Air Force One*, he delivered one of the all-time great movie lines: 'Get off my plane!' But the aircraft he was talking about wasn't Air Force One. In fact there has never been an aircraft that's gone by that name. In reality, it's a callsign given to any aircraft that's carrying POTUS (President of the United States).

When, in 1974, Richard Nixon announced his resignation in the wake of the Watergate scandal, the Boeing VC-137 carrying him to California took off using the callsign Air Force One, but was forced to change its callsign en route because Gerald Ford was sworn in while it was airborne.

First used in 1953 to avoid confusion with commercial air traffic, Air Force One has been most commonly associated with two aircraft: the Boeing VC-137 – a version of the 707 airliner – which entered service during John Kennedy's presidency, and its replacement, the Boeing VC-25, a substantially modified Boeing 747.

In the movie, Harrison Ford's jet features an escape pod and a parachute ramp at the rear. Neither – according to Bill Clinton, at least – features on the real thing. But that distinctive two-tone blue-and-white livery hides a great deal of work under the skin of the two USAF VC-25s that make

up the presidential fleet. It's a good deal more military than appearances would suggest. Capable of being used as an airborne command and control centre in the event of nuclear attack, 238 miles of wiring – twice as much as a standard 747 – has been shielded against the electromagnetic pulse of a nuclear explosion. There's an air-to-air refuelling capacity that will keep the VC-25 aloft long beyond its 7000-mile range. And while the plane is not actually armed, it's packed with countermeasures, including jammers to block enemy radar, chaff dispensers that release clouds of metallic foil to break the lock of a radar-guided missile, and flares that do the same for heat-seekers.

Variations on the callsign include Air Force Two, which is used by the vice-president, most usually aboard a C-32 version of the Boeing 757 airliner, and Marine One when the president's aboard one of the Marine Corps' VH-3D Sea Kings. In 1973, when Richard Nixon travelled aboard a scheduled United Airlines flight, it was given the callsign Executive One. Since then, any civil aircraft carrying the first family becomes Executive One Foxtrot. And in 2003, when a US Navy Lockheed S-3B Viking flew George W. Bush aboard the aircraft carrier USS *Abraham Lincoln*, it did so with the callsign Navy One, the only occasion it's been used.

So far, just the US Coast Guard has missed out on the coveted 'One' callsign. Until called on to rescue POTUS, it will have to make do with Coast Guard Two, used when it flew Vice-President Joe Biden aboard one of its HH-60 Jayhawks over floods in Atlanta in 2009.

Great Planes

Aérospatiale-BAC Concorde

Building Concorde posed one of the most testing engineering challenges in aviation history. The solution offered by British and French engineers blended form and function more beautifully than in any other aeroplane except the Spitfire. The skies have been a much poorer place since the stunning delta's premature retirement. I still miss her.

First flight: 2 March 1969
Principal operators: British Airways and Air France
Last operational flight: November 2003

Wheels with Wings

The Dream of the Flying Car

Harry Potter took to the air in a sky-blue Ford Anglia. There was Chitty Chitty Bang Bang on red and yellow wings that looked like they were made from the awning of a sweet shop. To get airborne, both relied on magic. But in the James Bond adventure *The Man with the Golden Gun*, when the three-nippled villain Scaramanga reaches up to flick switches on a panel on the roof, we know something's up (switches on the roof being a pretty effective way of letting us know we're in a cockpit). His flying car, Q tells Bond, is 'perfectly feasible'. So much so, in fact, that although a model was used in the movie, it was based on a real contraption, built in California, that mated a Ford Pinto with the wings and tail of a Cessna Skymaster. It was called the AVE Mizar. Tragically, the inventors of this intriguing mash-up were killed in 1973 when a wing folded during a test flight and the car fell to the ground.

While the dream of a practical flying car has proved an elusive one, it's been an idea that has certainly sustained a great deal of enthusiasm over the years. It seems that people just always want more. Cars are good.

Convair Model 118 ConvAirCar
USA, 1947

Piasecki VZ-8P (B) Airgeep
USA, 1962

Taylor Aerocar
USA, 1949

Planes are good. It doesn't necessarily follow, however, that combining the two will be even better than either. That, of course, won't stop people dreaming. Included among them is the US military. The Defense Advanced Research Projects Agency, or DARPA, is trying to develop a machine that 'seeks to combine the advantages of ground vehicles and helicopters into a single vehicle'. Of course, they've labelled it the Transformer. The objective being to 'counter … threats while avoiding road obstructions'. And that, when it really boils down to it, is the appeal of the flying car. People don't like being held up.

In pursuit of that dream, there have been cars with detachable wings, like the unfortunate Mizar. One, the Aerocar, towed its wings behind it like a trailer. More modern designs, such as the PAL-V or Transition, change from car to flying machine and back at the touch of a button, while ParaJet's solution is to hang a beach buggy under a parasail – possibly not as mad as it sounds. Anyway, below are just a few of the schemes with which ambitious commuters and imaginative generals have tried to avoid the jams.

ParaJet Skycar
UK, 2009

Chitty Chitty Bang Bang
UK, 1968

AVE Mizar
USA, 1973

Terrafugia Transition
USA, 2012

THERE ONCE WAS AN UGLY DUCKLING
Strange Shapes in the Sky (part two)

There's an old aviation adage that says: 'If it looks right, it is right.' It's a maxim that's based in fact. There was no way that the Spitfire or the P-51 Mustang were going to be dogs. But while it's not a bad place to start, good looks aren't always a cast-iron guarantee of success, any more than a bizarre, unique or inelegant appearance is an assurance of failure.

Bartini Beriev VVA-14
USSR, 1972

Tumenecotrans Bella 1
Russia, 1994

NASA/Ames AD-1
USA, 1979

SNECMA Coléoptère
France, 1959

Hughes XH-17
USA, 1952

Bell X-22
USA, 1966

Dornier Do 31
West Germany, 1967

DINFIA I.A.38
Argentina, 1960

Avro Canada Avrocar VZ-9AV
Canada, 1959

Aero Spacelines Super Guppy
USA, 1965

Scaled Composites Proteus
USA, 1998

Edgley Optica
UK, 1971

Scaled Composites Pond Racer
USA, 1991

Saunders-Roe SR.A/1
UK, 1947

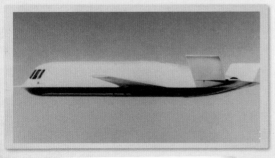

Northrop Tacit Blue
USA, 1982

Transavia Airtruk
Australia, 1965

The Reds
Formations of the Red Arrows

Since their formation in 1964, the Red Arrows have obviously been the best formation acrobatic display team in the world. Unless, of course, you're American. Or French. Or Italian, or Canadian or Australian. You get the picture. The 'Reds' are a symbol of Britain's national pride, the most visible expression of the RAF's professionalism and excellence. But the same is true of the USAF's Thunderbirds and the US Navy's Blue Angels, of the French *Patrouille de France* or Italian *Frecce Tricolori* and other national teams throughout the world. The truth is, they're all outstanding. Who's the best just depends on where you're watching from. This, though, is how the Red Arrows do it.

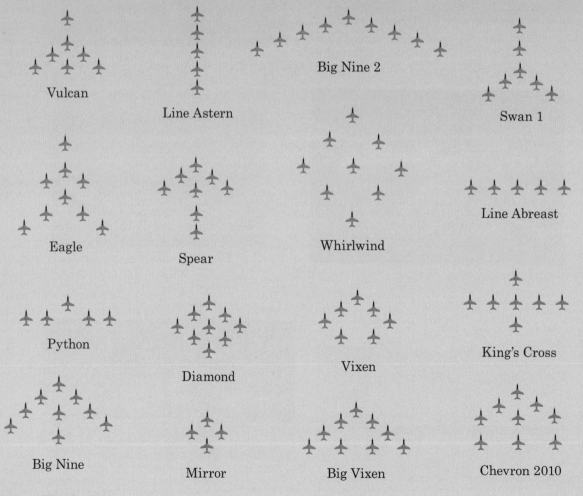

Vulcan

Line Astern

Big Nine 2

Swan 1

Eagle

Spear

Whirlwind

Line Abreast

Python

Diamond

Vixen

King's Cross

Big Nine

Mirror

Big Vixen

Chevron 2010

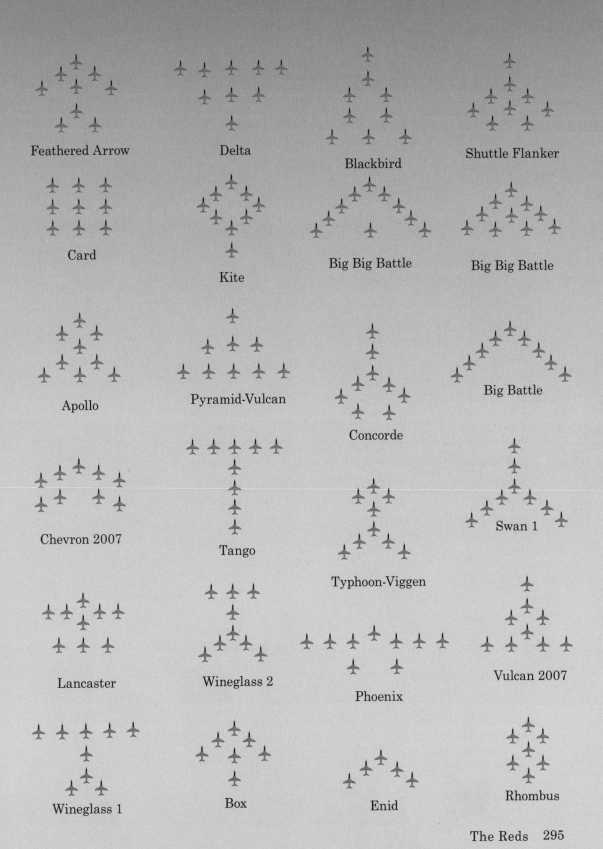

Feathered Arrow

Delta

Blackbird

Shuttle Flanker

Card

Kite

Big Big Battle

Big Big Battle

Apollo

Pyramid-Vulcan

Concorde

Big Battle

Chevron 2007

Tango

Typhoon-Viggen

Swan 1

Lancaster

Wineglass 2

Phoenix

Vulcan 2007

Wineglass 1

Box

Enid

Rhombus

Is It a Bird, Is It a Plane?

A Guide to Superhero Flight

'You'll believe a man can fly' promised the strapline for Richard Donner's groundbreaking 1978 *Superman* movie starring Christopher Reeve. And they were right. For the first time it seemed completely convincing (and still does). But not all superheroes are created equal. Some actually don't seem very super at all. And flying, certainly, is no prerequisite for being a superhero. In fact, many of the popular comic book heroes are no more able to fly than poor Oliver of Malmesbury, for whom a tail would have made no difference, though he thought it might (see page 10). I should stress that the list opposite is not comprehensive – there are hundreds of them – as no stone has been left unturned when it comes to creating superheroes, but characters such as Doll Man (can shrink to 6 inches high) or Godiva (super-powered hair), are, in what is already a silly list, a bit too silly.*

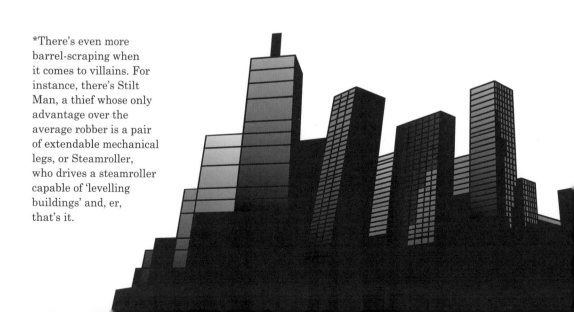

*There's even more barrel-scraping when it comes to villains. For instance, there's Stilt Man, a thief whose only advantage over the average robber is a pair of extendable mechanical legs, or Steamroller, who drives a steamroller capable of 'levelling buildings' and, er, that's it.

CAN FLY

Superman

Iron Man (OK, I admit he needs a hi-tech suit of armour, but that, you know, is the whole point of Iron Man)

The Human Torch

Angel

Hawkman (provided he's wearing his artificial wings)

The Falcon (he too needs his artificial wings; apparently, he is also an excellent trainer of birds)

Storm

The Sub-Mariner (because he has little wings on his ankles – unlikely, it has to be said)

The Wasp

Captain Britain (like Iron Man, his suit enables his heroic activities)

Captain Marvel

Nova

Dr Strange (uses magic – cheating?)

Hyperion

Jack of Hearts

Green Lantern (but only if he's wearing his cosmic green lantern ring)

Spiderwoman

Thor (through the power of his hammer, Mjolnir)

Wonder Man

Banshee (flies by using his voice, apparently; it's just possible that Mariah Carey can travel short distances)

The Rocketeer (has a rocket pack, of course, but take that away and what is he, huh? Just a do-gooder in a leather jacket)

Silver Surfer (again, he has kit, but we'll let it go)

Booster Gold (once more, the power's in the suit)

Apollo

Engineer

Cyborg

Dr Manhattan

CAN'T FLY

Batman

Spiderman (lots of swinging, though)

Captain America

Wonder Woman (although her invisible plane could create the impression she could fly – but only, of course, in an odd-looking seated position)

The Hulk (but he can jump for miles in a single bound; lands heavily)

Wolverine

Daredevil

Aquaman (unlike the otherwise similar Sub-Mariner – bummer)

The Punisher

Nightcrawler (has tail; can't fly)

Hawkeye

Beast

Black Panther

Blade

Powerman

Cyclops

Iceman

Mr Fantastic

Invisible Woman

The Thing

Ghost Rider

Iron Fist

Moon Knight

Nighthawk

The Flash

Green Arrow

Robin

Midnighter

Kick-Ass

Hit Girl

Quicksilver

Ant Man

The Comedian

Nite Owl

Ozymandias

Rorschach

Silk Spectre

The Gimli Glider
When an Airliner Runs Out of Gas

In 1979 Canada finally broke ranks with her neighbour to the south and switched from using imperial to metric measurements. While Canadians struggled with kilograms, metres and litres, Air Canada continued much as it always had. As long as the airline's fleet of aircraft had tanks and gauges giving measurements in pounds and gallons, those were the units Air Canada continued to use. But four years after the country had made the switch, Air Canada took delivery of its first new state-of-the-art Boeing 767s. The big twinjets used metric measurements, and that meant a good deal of calculation, checking and double-checking each time they were refuelled by ground crew unfamiliar with the new system. But on 23 July 1983 none of that prevented them from getting it badly wrong.

A series of assumptions, minor mechanical faults, duff procedures and confusion over metric and imperial measurements saw Air Canada Flight 143, en route to Edmonton from Ottawa, suck her tanks dry at 41,000 feet over Red Lake, Ontario. In the cockpit of the 767, Captain Bob Pearson and First Officer Maurice Quintal heard a sharp electronic 'bong' indicating that they'd suffered the complete loss of both engines. Starved of fuel, they simply snuffed out. Without power, the electronic flight instruments were next to quit. Pearson and Quintal were at the controls of a 143-ton glider. Behind them were sixty-one passengers.

While Pearson established the big airliner in what he estimated was its best glide, his first officer looked through the manuals for procedures. There were none. Fuel starvation and a complete loss of power weren't a scenario that Boeing had anticipated. Instead, Quintal began calculating their glide path to Winnipeg, the nearest airfield with the facilities to deal with a crash landing. He checked his calculations twice. They were losing 5000 feet of altitude every 10 miles.

'We're not going to make Winnipeg,' he told Pearson. Carry on as they were and they'd hit the ground 12 miles short of the runway threshold. That left just one other possibility.

The Winnipeg Sports Car Club was enjoying a 'Family Day' at Gimli. There was go-kart racing and a drag strip. Spectators' own cars also lined the disused runways. It had been twelve years since the airfield had last

Each one of the go-karts on the Gimli starting grid has more fuel in its tanks than the Boeing 767 that performed an emergency landing behind them.

played host to Royal Canadian Air Force jets. Now there was just general aviation, little puddle-jumpers, such as Cessnas and Pipers, that were able to fly from the reduced space not used by the petrolheads.

It was certainly no longer a safe place to land an airliner, and there was no mention of it in Flight 143's documentation. But Maurice Quintal had been stationed there when he was in the air force and knew the layout of the base. Pearson pointed the nose of the 767 towards the old airfield, just 12 miles north of their position. Gimli or bust.

Quintal dropped the landing gear. With enough power from an auxiliary turbine just to power the flight controls, he was forced to rely on gravity to lower the wheels. Only the main gear under the wings locked into place.

Worse, as they settled into their final approach towards what was left of Gimli's old Runway 32L, Pearson realized they were too high. Without power to lower the flaps they were coming in fast. Unless they could bleed off some height there was a danger they'd overshoot the runway altogether. Just as Quintal's particular experience had come into play earlier, now so too did Pearson's. The 767 captain was a gliding enthusiast, familiar with how to dump altitude and speed to make a landing. He crossed the controls, rolling the stick to the left and kicking the rudder to the right to twist the big jet into an awkward sideslip. Her nose now pointing off to the right of the runway, Flight 143 was crabbing her way in. Pearson held her there until the last possible moment, when he let the nose point forward again to touch down. He jumped on the brakes. Two tyres exploded almost immediately. When the nose came down, the unlocked nose gear collapsed, leaving the front of the jet's fuselage to scrape down the runway throwing up a rooster tail of hot sparks, but it helped slow the runaway plane. Flight 143 came to a smoking halt barely 100 feet from a collection of racegoers turning steaks on their barbecues. Car enthusiasts converged on the airliner to smother the smouldering nose with small fire extinguishers as the jet's passengers spilled out down inflatable slides to the ground.

Everybody on board Flight 143 survived, although a handful suffered minor injuries as they escaped the aircraft. Such was the skill with which Pearson carried out his deadstick landing, the aircraft herself was repaired and flown out of Gimli. She flew with Air Canada for another twenty-five years until her retirement in 2008.

And in the aftermath of the incident, other Air Canada crews attempted to replicate Pearson and Quintal's safe landing of the Gimli Glider in the simulator. The result was several simulated crashes.

The Final Frontier

How High Do Spacemen Fly?

2,500,000 feet

Space begins in two different places. For the United States Air Force it's 50 miles high (264,000 feet). Test pilots who flew the X-15 rocketplane beyond this altitude were awarded Astronaut Wings by the Air Force. For the rest of the world, though, space begins a little higher at 100 km or 62.5 miles (330,000 feet). This point is also known as the Karman Line. Beyond it you're in space, whoever's asking. But you're not necessarily in orbit. That requires you to go a little higher and a lot faster. To maintain an orbit 200 miles (around 1 million feet) above the Earth the Space Shuttle needs to be travelling at about 17,500 mph. The Shuttle reached twice that altitude to service the Hubble telescope. And even that's less than half NASA's most distant orbit, achieved in 1966 when the crew of Gemini XI reached a height of 850 miles (around 4.5 million feet). No one's flown further from the Earth than that without continuing to the Moon.

2,250,000 feet

2,000,000 feet

Space Shuttle
(maximum)

1,750,000 feet

1,500,000 feet

Skylab

1,250,000 feet

International
Space Station

Mir

1,000,000 feet

Space Shuttle

Yuri Gagarin

750,000 feet

Alan Shepard

500,000 feet

Point of
mospheric
Re-entry

Karman Line
Space USAF

X-15

SpaceShipOne

lesopause
esosphere

250,000 feet

atosphere

Balloon

Concorde   Mount Everest

0

Great Planes

Rockwell International Space Shuttle Orbiter

Just look at the picture. Is there another aircraft that can do that? The answer's no. Reckoned by some to be mankind's most complex engineering achievement, the Space Shuttle Orbiter is undoubtedly *one* of them. What sticks in the mind is its ability to cope with extremes of power and environment that no other flying machine has endured. It remains the fastest, highest, winged aircraft ever built.

First flight: 12 April 1981
Principal operator: NASA
Last operational flight: 2011

BURAN
Space Shuttle Orbiter

The Space Shuttle. It's always *the* Space Shuttle, never a Space Shuttle. You could almost be forgiven for thinking there was only ever a single Orbiter that had visited space. But in fact there were six. And one of them was Russian. Her existence was an example of keeping up with the Joneses on a spectacular scale. And it was born out of fear.

In the mid-1970s, the Soviet military had concluded that the American Shuttle was being developed as a means of dropping first-strike nuclear weapons on Moscow and Leningrad. The generals imagined the US machine would dive into the atmosphere, release its bombs and return to orbit. On the back of this fantasy, any hope scientists had of directing the Soviet manned space programme towards building a permanent moon base went out of the window and, in February 1976, the Kremlin initiated its own shuttle programme. The scientists were dismissive. 'We do not,' wrote the President of the Academy of Sciences, 'see any sensible scenario that would support the shuttle for scientific purposes.'

Uncertain about the nature of the military threat posed by the American Shuttle, but driven by a need to counter whatever it was, the Buran (Blizzard) – as the Soviet shuttle was named – ended up looking almost identical. Unlike its American counterpart, though, Buran lacked three powerful rocket engines in its tail. Instead, she was hauled into space on a massive cluster of rockets, the proverbial butterfly strapped to a bullet. But it all worked, and in 1988 an unmanned Buran shuttle was launched, orbited twice, then returned safely to Earth. It was, however, to be the Buran's first and last venture into space.

With the end of the Cold War following the fall of the Berlin Wall in 1989, any conceivable strategic military requirement for Buran fell too. She would never carry cosmonauts into orbit. And, as if a single orbit of Earth wasn't enough of a disappointment for the team of engineers, scientists and technicians who had built her, the real kick in the teeth was yet to come. In 2002 the hangar housing her collapsed and she was destroyed.

Designed and built for no good reason, the Buran never amounted to anything more than an exhibition of what the Soviet aerospace industry could do. If only, back in the 1970s, the Kremlin had opted for that moon base instead …

Maximum speed: 17,000+ mph (in orbit)
Maximum range: Unmanned flights of
15-20 days were planned
Maximum altitude: Low Earth orbit
Maximum take-off weight: 210,000
pounds
Wingspan: 78 feet 6 inches
Length: 119 feet 4 inches
Height: 53 feet 8 inches
PROJECT CANCELLED: May 1993

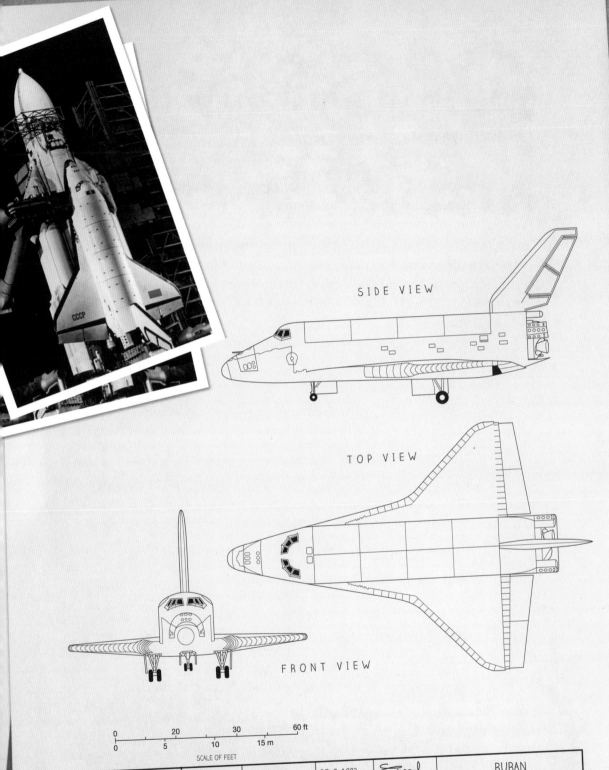

SIDE VIEW

TOP VIEW

FRONT VIEW

| 0 | | 20 | | 30 | | 60 ft |
| 0 | 5 | | 10 | 15 m | | |

SCALE OF FEET

REFERENCE No.	DRAWN	E. WOOD	25-9-1992		BURAN SPACE SHUTTLE ORBITER
123 SS D 4457	NUMBER	957334866			
GENERAL ARRANGEMENT	CHECKED	E. VAN HEST	12-10-1992		NPO MOLNIYA MOSCOW
	APPROVED	R. TINHAM	24-11-1992		

The Brilliant Bottle Rocket

How to Make a Water Rocket

I *love* this one. Of all the various homemade flying machines in the book, this is the most exciting and satisfying. It's just far better than you expect it to be (it was certainly far better than the rest of my long-suffering family expected when I gathered them around to watch).

It's incredibly simple to make and launch, and works on exactly the same principle as the Saturn V moon rocket. Using nothing but water and a bicycle pump, it will launch a completely standard 2-litre lemonade bottle 50 feet into the air.

YOU'LL NEED

- A normal wine bottle cork. (With screwtops everywhere, they're not so common these days, but be classy – ask the waiter next time you eat out if there's a spare one around.)
- A bread knife.
- A bike pump needle adapter (used for pumping up footballs). These are easy to find in sports shops or online.
- An empty 2-litre fizzy drink bottle. We decorated ours in the red-check colours of Tintin's moon rocket.
- A long-handled garden fork.
- A bicycle pump.

HOW TO DO IT

1. You'll probably need to cut a third or so off the length of the cork in order to be able to push the needle adapter all the way through. It's easily done with a bread knife.

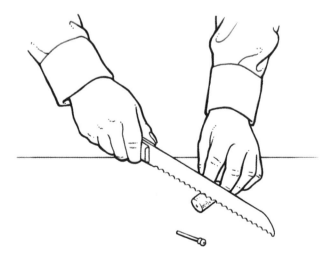

2. Push the needle adapter lengthways through the middle of the cork using the hole left by the corkscrew as your starting point. Again, this is easier than you think it's going to be (provided it's a real cork and not a plastic one). It should end up looking like this:

3. Fill the bottle with about a mugful of water: not much – definitely no more than a quarter full. Now stick the cork in the neck of the bottle. It should fit nicely. Firm but not immovable.

4. Choose a nice open space outside and stick the garden fork in the ground at a very shallow angle. The handle is going to be your launch pad.

5. Screw the bike pump on to the end of the needle adapter, then rest the bottle vertically on the handle of the fork.

6. Start pumping and commence the countdown: 'Ten … nine … eight … seven … six … five … four … three … two … one … BLAST OFF!'

You'll Believe a Man Can Fly

How to Levitate. Or Look Like You Can. Sort of.

One of NASA's less well-known achievements was to make a mouse levitate. In 2009, using semi-conducting magnets and the principle of diamagnetism, the Jet Propulsion Laboratory managed to levitate a mouse. No, I don't really understand all that either, but apparently body water, subjected to a powerful enough magnetic force, generates a repelling magnetic force in opposition. That's more than enough quantum mechanics for a book about aeroplanes. What you need to know is that, initially at least, the mouse appeared to be confused, but after four hours seemed used to the experience. Apparently, it suffered no ill-effects. A Dutch university had previously succeeded in levitating a frog, but mouse physiology is more closely related to that of humans. So that's something to look forward to.

I can't, I'm afraid, help you race ahead of NASA's research, but I can show you how to make it look like you can. It's a trick that will amaze children. And possibly gullible adults as well.

So, levitation:

1. Stand in the corner of a room and face one of the walls nearest you with your right foot tucked into the corner.

2. Now make sure your audience is standing to your left so that your right leg and foot are largely hidden from view.

3. Slowly raise yourself up on to the ball of your right foot as if you are stretching for a high shelf.

4. Make sure your left foot lifts horizontally and completely about an inch off the floor. At the same time make sure that your right heel lifts to the same height alongside it.

5. Make a face like you're straining with the mental effort of it all.

6. To your audience, who have no proper view of your right foot, it will appear that both feet are off the ground.

7. Lap up the gasps of astonishment and disbelief.

8. Gently lower both feet back on to the floor again.

9. Look drained from the exertion of lifting yourself into the air, using nothing but the power of your mind.

Bird is the Word
Some Avian Superlatives

Apart from providing names for aircraft, birds are notably absent from this book. Similarly, they are not on the list of animals in space either. Nonetheless, we are indebted to birds because, ultimately, they are the inspiration for everything on these pages.

Heaviest flying bird
Kori Bustard
(Ardeotis kori)
The kori bustard from southern Africa and the great bustard found in Europe and Asia, each weigh just over 40 lb. Reports of a 46-lb bustard killed in China suggest it couldn't actually get off the ground.

Biggest bird of prey
Andean Condor
(Vultur gryphus)
With a wingspan of over 10 feet, this impressive South American bird can weigh over 30 lb. It covers great distances in search of food.

Biggest eagle
Steller's Sea Eagle
(Haliaeetus pelagicus)
Having an 8-foot wingspan, the Steller's sea eagle is generally reckoned to be, on average, the biggest eagle in a closely contested battle with the more powerful harpy and Philippine eagles.

Smallest bird
Bee Hummingbird
(Mellisuga helenae)
About as small as a vertebrate can get, the bee hummingbird is found only in the forests of Cuba. It has such mastery of the air that it never needs to walk more than a couple of inches on the ground.

Least-grounded bird
Sooty Tern
(Onychoprion fuscatus)
Once it has left its nesting grounds, the sooty tern may spend three to ten years simply soaring above and floating on the sea before returning to land to breed.

Longest flight
Bar-tailed Godwit
(Limosa lapponica)
In 2007 a godwit was tracked flying non-stop from Alaska to New Zealand, completing the 7145-mile journey in just nine days by shutting down one half of her brain at a time to sleep.

times a second. Hummingbirds have muscles above their wings as well as below, giving power to their upstrokes as well as downstrokes. This gives them the ability to hover in still air, and to fly backwards and sideways, all in a blur. Awesome!

Largest wingspan
Wandering Albatross
(Diomedea exulans)
The largest wingspan ever recorded for this bird was that of an old male caught by a research ship in the Tasman Sea in 1965. He had a wingspan of 11 feet 11 inches. Expert gliders, albatrosses can soar for many hours without beating their wings.

Largest ever wingspan
South American Teratorn
(Argentavis magnificens)
Fossils found in Argentina suggest that this huge condor-type bird, thought to have lived 6–8 million years ago, had a wingspan of 25 feet. By comparison, a Cessna 152 has a wingspan of 33 feet.

Fastest bird
Peregrine Falcon
(Falco peregrinus)
The peregrine (long my favourite bird) is not merely the fastest bird, but also the fastest living creature. In level flight a peregrine can reach speeds of 60 mph or so, but in a dive to snatch its prey in mid-air its speed far exceeds that. Peregrines have been recorded diving at over 240 mph.

Fastest wingbeat
Horned Sungem
(Heliactin cornuta)
This little bird from South America beats its wings up and down ninety

Highest-flying bird
Rüppell's Vulture
(Gyps rueppellii)
In 1973, while flying over Ivory Coast, West Africa, an airliner at 37,000 feet collided with a Rüppell's vulture and lost an engine. The jet was able to declare an emergency and land in one piece. The vulture not so much.

Largest prey
Harpy Eagle
(Harpia harpyja)
While raptors such as the golden eagle and Philippine eagle can knock over and kill prey weighing 60 lb or more (the golden eagle has been filmed pulling goats off mountain ledges so that they fall to their death), the largest documented prey known to have been picked up and carried away was a 15-lb red howler monkey snatched by a harpy eagle in Peru in 1990 – that's three-quarters of the bird's own bodyweight.

Biggest nest
Bald Eagle
(Haliaeetus leucocephalus)
A formidable hunter, this majestic creature is a US national symbol. In 1963 a nest 9 feet 6 inches wide and 20 feet deep, built by a pair of bald eagles in Florida, was estimated to weigh over 2 tons.

Word on a Wing

A Few Books about Flying

Others may cite Antoine de Saint-Exupéry, Richard Bach, Ernest Gann, or even Captain W. E. Johns, but my favourite author is Bill 'the Gun' Gunston, OBE. His writing certainly fuelled my obsession with aeroplanes. As technical editor of *Flight* magazine for many years, Gunston had an extraordinary command of the science and engineering that were crucial to his brief. But it's the way that he's able to bring his subject to life – and *explain* – through simply brilliant writing that so hooked me. I'm not making any claims for this list being comprehensive, but all the following books made an impression on me.

Attack Aircraft of the West/ Bombers of the West/ Early Supersonic Fighters of the West
Bill Gunston
OK, they *sound* a bit dry, but all three of these books are brilliant. Nobody else combines technical know-how, strong storytelling, irreverence and an eye for the absurd like Bill Gunston.

The Big Show
Pierre Clostermann
From Spitfires to Hawker Tempests, this is a fabulously rich Second World War memoir by a Frenchman who flew with the RAF. It hasn't aged a bit.

Bomber
Len Deighton
A brilliant fictional account of a single RAF Lancaster raid against Germany. An equally good radio dramatization is also available.

Chickenhawk
Robert Mason
This memoir by a US Army helicopter pilot is possibly the best book to come out of Vietnam, and certainly my favourite.

Corsairville
Graham Coster
A beautifully written and personal exploration of the lost world of the Imperial Airways Empire flying boats. Entirely coincidentally, I used to work with Graham at Our Price records when I was 18.

Empire of the Clouds
James Hamilton-Paterson
Another hymn to the past, but this celebration of Britain's post-war aircraft industry is suffused with incredulousness and anger at what was so carelessly thrown away.

F4 Phantom: A Pilot's Story
Robert Prest
An evocative and detailed insight into flying Phantoms for the RAF in

the 1970s. It remains much admired, although it has been pointed out that you wouldn't, from reading it, know that the Phantom carried a navigator.

Fighter Boys
Patrick Bishop
An extremely readable account of the Battle of Britain by a distinguished war correspondent displaying great control of his material.

First Light
Geoffrey Wellum
Written, then kept in a drawer for twenty years, before finally seeing the light of day five years ago, this book became an instant classic.

Fly Low, Fly Fast
Robert Gandt
Gets under the skin of the world's fastest motor sport: the Unlimited Class at the annual Reno Air Races.

Going Solo
Roald Dahl
Obviously much more well known for *Charlie and the Chocolate Factory*, *Matilda*, *The BFG* and many more classic children's books, Dahl was also a fighter pilot and ace. In this volume he writes about his time in the RAF. What a great combination.

A Good Clean Fight
Derek Robinson
While not Robinson's most well-known book, this one is my favourite. It's a rich, substantial and satisfying flying novel set during the Second World War in North Africa. And it's chock-a-block with SAS action and strafing Curtiss Tomahawks.

The Hunt for Zero Point
Nick Cook
This investigation into deep-classified US Black defence programmes, secret Nazi technology and the search for anti-gravity should be neither readable nor credible, but it's both. A completely fascinating book by a respected former aviation correspondent for *Jane's*.

Inside the Sky (republished as *Aloft*)
William Langewiesche
A really stunning collection of aviation writing from an experienced pilot who also happens to be one of America's finest reporters.

Ministry of Space
Warren Ellis, Chris Weston and Laura DePuy
A graphic novel that has the feel of a labour of love. Spitfires to the stars, it's a hymn to what might have been, a richly imagined, lushly drawn account of the British post-war conquest of space. You just don't want to know how it's funded.

Moondust
Andrew Smith
You'll never look at the moon the same way again after reading this fantastically engaging quest to meet the nine remaining moonwalkers.

Nine Minutes, Twenty Seconds
Gary Pomerantz
An extraordinary piece of reporting that painstakingly and movingly re-creates the 1993 commuter plane crash in the USA. Published in the week of 9/11, no one noticed it.

No Visible Horizon
Joshua Cooper Ramo
A full-on adrenalin rush. This is a high-octane, in-your-face account of flying competitive aerobatics.

The Perfect Storm
Sebastian Junger
More or less everyone's read this or seen the movie, but it's somehow more well known for the loss of the trawler *Andrea Gail* than for the jaw-dropping account of the USAF's unbelievably heroic attempt to rescue her crew.

Project Cancelled
Derek Wood
This book had a sort of magnetic hold on me as a boy. It tells the story of all the what-ifs and could-have-beens produced by the post-war British aviation industry. Rather like *Goddess*, Antony Summers's biography of Marilyn Monroe, you hope, every time you read it, that it will end differently. Heartbreaking.

The Ravens
Christopher Robbins
Air America is the author's best-known book, but this one, about a maverick band of brothers flying armed piston-engined trainers in Laos during the Vietnam war is my favourite.

The Right Stuff
Tom Wolfe
This stone-cold classic account of the early years of the US space programme is absolutely seminal. If I had to pick just one book here, I'd probably plump for this one.

Ruin from the Air
Gordon Thomas
and Max Morgan-Witts
A dense, brilliantly researched and grippingly written account of the USAAF's Second World War atom bomb attack against Hiroshima.

Scream of Eagles
Robert K. Wilcox
This is the real story of *Top Gun*. With great research and vivid writing, it's an authoritative account of the birth of the US Navy's Fighter Weapons School.

Sea Harrier over the Falklands
Commander 'Sharkey' Ward
Opinionated, bloody-minded and graceless, this gripping memoir by the boss of 801 Naval Air Squadron is still the best account of the air war for the Falklands.

Thunder and Lightnings
Jan Mark
A children's book that, as a boy, I thought could have been written specially for me. It tells the story of a friendship between two boys against the backdrop of the much-loved Lightning's replacement by the Jaguar.

Tumult in the Clouds
James Goodson
This book has definitely stood the test of time. It's a still-fresh account by an American ace, who, after being torpedoed on his way home at the beginning of the war, joined an RAF Eagle Squadron.

The Rise of the Machines
A Brief Introduction to Drones

In 1944 an 18-year-old brunette was photographed at work holding a small wooden aircraft propeller. Her employer, the Radioplane Company, built radio-controlled aircraft used by the US Army as targets to train its anti-aircraft gunners. The girl, talent-spotted by the army photographer who took her picture, would change her name to Marilyn Monroe and become one of the world's biggest movie stars.

The history of aviation is touched with romance, courage and wonder. But Marilyn's brief association aside, these things are in short supply when it comes to the story of drones. While aircraft (even as weapons of war) and their pilots have plenty of the Right Stuff, drones have none at all. However, their robotic nature has been the bedrock of their recent success. No weapon has been more closely associated with the War on Terror than the Unmanned Aerial Vehicle (UAV) or drone flown over distant war zones by operators sitting in air-conditioned comfort and safety back home. It's easy to appreciate the value of this.

After a U-2 spyplane was shot down over Russia in 1959 and its pilot, Gary Powers, taken prisoner, the US Air Force ordered a reconnaissance version of its new jet-powered target drone, the Ryan Q-2 Firebee. When another U-2 was shot down over Cuba in 1962, it was decided to gather crucial intelligence using the new drone, known as the Lightning Bug, rather than risk another U-2 pilot. But with the mission poised to launch, it was cancelled for fear it would reveal the top-secret new technology to the Soviets. In any case, not everyone in the air force was quite so enamoured of the idea of dispensing with the pilot.

One general, ordered to become acquainted with the new technology, flew from Nebraska to Florida, walked straight to the hangar and placed his hand on the pilotless jet. 'There,' he said, 'I touched that little son-of-a-bitch – now I can go home.' He then returned to his own aircraft and took off again.

In Vietnam, however, the 4025th Reconnaissance Squadron got on with the job of war by launching Lightning Bugs from beneath the wings of big four-turboprop DC-130 motherships. The drones flew throughout the conflict, from 1964 to the surrender of Saigon in 1975, two years *after* manned missions were suspended. As well as photo-reconnaissance, they

were used for electronic intelligence gathering, leaflet dropping and as bait to force North Vietnamese missiles to reveal themselves. The Lightning Bugs proved their usefulness, but using them was a bit of a palaver. The trouble was that they could neither take off nor land. They had to be launched from the mothership, and that required a fighter escort. Then, at the end of a mission, after releasing a parachute, the drones were snatched from mid-air by helicopters. All this was hugely expensive.

Nonetheless, it was small beer compared to the cost of ambitious UAV programmes being pursued by the US Air Force and Navy. From drones launched at three times the speed of sound from the back of Blackbird spyplanes to a cutting-edge $10 billion stealthy 'flying clam' – known, rather unfortunately, by the acronym AARS – that really was, in the words of one CIA engineer, 'the cat's pyjamas', none was successful. Instead, the generals and spooks ended up with something that began life in a garage in Los Angeles.

No one imagined that a funny-looking machine called Amber, built by maverick Israeli inventor Abraham Karem in his garage, was the future of air combat. But when, in the early 1990s, the CIA had an urgent need to know what was happening on the ground in the Balkans, they turned to a development of Amber, the Gnat 750. With its long, thin wing and downward-pointing V-tail propeller on the back pushing it along, the Gnat was recognizably the same basic machine that, as the MQ-1 Predator, became synonymous across the world with the word 'drone'.

Over Bosnia, Serbia, Kosovo and Iraq the Predator proved to be an outstanding success. The real breakthrough was not so much the design of the airframe as how it was operated. Able to take off and land from a normal runway, and guided using GPS and satellite communications, this new-generation drone didn't require motherships and recovery teams. It could be flown in the skies above the Middle East, Africa or Central Asia by a 'pilot' stationed near Las Vegas.

It wasn't long before thoughts turned to arming them. Although this had first been trialled in the 1970s with the Lightning Bugs, it had never been put to the test in combat. In March 2002 a Hellfire missile fired from a Predator saved the lives of a US Special Forces team in Afghanistan. The following year a Predator strike in Yemen was revealed. It was the beginning of a swarm. Drones now make up over a third of America's inventory of military aircraft, and this is likely to grow as new, more sophisticated designs come on stream. Increased reliance on unmanned drones has created a whole new set of practical problems for the world's military and intelligence agencies, the principal one being bandwidth. A US Government report claims that a single RQ-4 Global Hawk reconnaissance drone needs more bandwidth than was used by the entire US military during the 1991 Gulf War. The *New York Times* estimated that by 2009 drones over Afghanistan and Iraq had collected over 24 years' worth of video footage. By 2015 that figure is expected to rise to *hundreds* of years' worth. Understandably enough, the US military is launching satellites as fast as it can.

That, in turn, leads to another issue – the human capacity to deal with the volume of intelligence material generated by drones. The US Air Force is already talking about the need for 'augmentation ... via drugs or implants to improve memory, alertness, cognition, or visual/aural acuity' to help its people process the information. The alternative – greater autonomy for the machines – is no more appealing. It's hard to dismiss thoughts of *The Terminator*. Welcome to the future. I'm afraid it's ugly. Drones are aeroplanes sucked dry.

OPPOSITE: *A US Navy DC-130 Hercules carrying BQM-34S Firebee target drones. Operators launched, tracked and controlled the drones from onboard the Hercules. The Firebees, first used in combat in 1964, were used during the 2003 invasion of Iraq, dropping chaff over Baghdad to disrupt Iraqi air defences before the 'shock and awe' that followed.*

It was a toy helicopter – an unmanned flying machine of sorts – that first inspired the Wright brothers' obsession with taking to the air. For that we should be grateful. But since then, it's human endeavour, not the mere fact of flight itself, that's been key to aviation's allure.

Without it there's no beauty, danger, excitement, inspiration, surprise, elegance, character or style – just a machine that flies. Over the first century of manned flight, new designs came tumbling out of aircraft factories around the world. Each manufacturer had personality, usually shaped by a few brilliant individuals. Each offered its own solutions to the demands of airlines and air forces wanting machines that travelled higher and faster than before. In the cockpits were fighter boys, test pilots, airline captains and astronauts, and many more besides. We often knew their names. The history of manned flight so far has had character and romance. It's stirred the soul. I hope it'll be possible to say the same in a hundred years' time, but I'm doubtful.

For now, then, for aviation's fabulous first century and a bit, to those magnificent men in their flying machines – and to the geniuses and visionaries that put them there – thank you.

Over and out.

The McDonnell-Douglas F-4 Phantom's unique collection of curves could only have been conjured up by men with pencils, slide rules and drawing boards. In the 1960s, flown by men with the Right Stuff, the charismatic fighter was a record-breaking 'hot ship'. It ended its days as a target drone with an empty cockpit. And, in losing its crew, was robbed of the very thing that had once made it so compelling a presence.

'High Flight'
(1941)

Oh! I have slipped the surly bonds of Earth
And danced the skies on laughter-silvered wings;
Sunward I've climbed, and joined the tumbling mirth
Of sun-split clouds – and done a hundred things
You have not dreamed of – wheeled and soared and swung
High in the sunlit silence. Hov'ring there,
I've chased the shouting wind along, and flung
My eager craft through footless halls of air ...

Up, up the long, delirious, burning blue
I've topped the wind-swept heights with easy grace.
Where never lark, or even eagle flew –
And, while with silent, lifting mind I've trod
The high untrespassed sanctity of space,
Put out my hand, and touched the face of God.

John Gillespie Magee, Jr.
(1922–41)

ACKNOWLEDGEMENTS

It takes a lot of very talented and dedicated people to bring a book like this to life. I'm very lucky to be on their team. You'll find their names tucked away in the Project Cancelled blueprints. Alongside them, I'd like to single out the heroically hardworking and unfailingly patient, optimistic and understanding team who made this book such a beautiful object: Rebecca Wright (thank you, thank you, thank you), Phil Lord, Sheila Lee, Bobby Birchall, Patrick Mulrey and Richard Shailer. I'd also like to thank Bill Scott-Kerr, Larry Finlay, Polly Osborn, Mark Lucas and James Holland. Rory, Jemima and Lexi. And Lucy. Thanks, hon. You've been amazing. R xx

PICTURE ACKNOWLEDGEMENTS

Every effort has been made to trace the copyright holders of photos reproduced in the book. Copyright holders not credited are invited to get in touch with the publishers.

11: 'An early bird-man' by Robert Ayton from *The Story of Flight*. Copyright © Ladybird Books Ltd, 1960. Illustration from the archives of Ladybird Books Ltd, used under licence from Ladybird Books Ltd; 13, 290 (Taylor Aerocar): © Corbis; 14, 45, 55, 64, 75: SSPL via Getty Images; 21: Gamma-Rapho via Getty Images; 23: image courtesy of Wolverhampton Archives & Local Studies; 24: AP/Press Association Images; 25: Louie Psihoyos/Science Faction/Corbis; 26 (Petroczy-Karman-Zurovek PKZ), 139: Austin Brown; 26 (Bonney Gull): © Underwood & Underwood/Corbis; 26 (Capronissimo), 27 (Gyroplane), 27 (Maxim Steam), 27 (Philips Multiplane) both, 36, 37 (*bottom*), 41, 79, 129, 133, 168, 171, 216, 226, 290 (*left*), 291 (*left*): Getty Images; 27 (Flying Doughnut), 145, 182, 238 : Time & Life Pictures/Getty Images; 27 (Santos Dumont), 28–9, 31, 142: Popperfoto/Getty Images; 32: © Paul Bowen/Science Faction/Corbis; 37 (*top*): Smithsonian National Air and Space Museum; 37 (*middle*): courtesy of the State Archives of Florida; 42: Alamy; 51–2: *Schneider Trophy Winner* by Michael Turner; 54: NASA Langley Research Center; 57: Rick Pisio/RWP Photography/Alamy; 59: Mary Evans Picture Library; 61: © Realimage/Alamy; 67: New York Daily News via Getty Images; 73: Michael Turek: Getty Images; 76–7: *The Workhorse* by Roger Murray; 80–1: *Blue Stocking Loner* by Bruce MacKay; 83, 264: US Air Force; 84: CIA/Roadrunners Internationale; 86, 150, 190: Aviation Images; 91: © ADAGP, Paris and DACS, London 2013; image courtesy British Airways Heritage Collection; 91–2: courtesy of the Foynes Flying Boat and Maritime Museum www.flyingboatmuseum.com; 94: Flight Collection/Topfoto; 98–9: *Supermarine Spitfire IX* by Michael Turner; 101, 103, 104, 106: Airfix images by Roy Cross used with the kind permission of Hornby Hobbies Ltd; 109: *Dambusters – The Impossible Mission* by Robert Taylor © The Military Gallery, Wendover, UK; 120–1: *Ramrod-Outward Bound* © 2012 John D. Shaw. www.libertystudios.us; 123: mirrorpix; 124: © Topfoto; 131: © Patrick Ray Dunn/Alamy; 134: Associated TV/Century 21 TV/UA/The Kobal Collection; 140: CAHS/Len Dobbin collection; 147: Peter de Clercq/Alamy; 149, 196, 227, 293 (Air Truck): AirTeam Images; 151–3: *Canberra* by Michael Turner; 155 (*left*): © Avpics/Alamy; 155 (*right*): © Crown copyright 2012; 156-57: *Fence Check* by Ronald Wong; 158–9: National Geographic/Getty Images; 161, 291 (AVE Mizar), 292 (Hughes helicopter): Bettmann/Corbis; 175 (*upper*): from an original painting by Ivan Berryman;169, 175 (*lower*): illustration by Wilf Hardy/Private Collection/© Look and Learn/The Bridgeman Art Library; 170: illustration by John S. Smith/Private Collection/©Look and Learn/The Bridgeman Art Library; 176: © Paramount Pictures/Sunset Boulevard/Corbis; 177: © Pictorial Press/Alamy; 187: Rupert Nichol/Rex Features; 192–3: *Ride of the Valkyries* by Simon Atack © The Military Gallery, Wendover, England; 195: Smithsonian Institution, National Air and Space Museum, Hans Groenhoff Photographic Collection; 198-9: © Archive Image/Alamy; 208–9: *H.M.S. Ark Royal* by © Philip E. West/SWA Fine Art; 211, 286-7: AFP/Getty Images; 214: Imperial War Museum/A212287; 222–3: *Nightlife* by Robert Taylor © The Military Gallery, Wendover, UK; 225, 249 (Tu-114): Associated Newspapers/Rex Features; 231: *Seven Days in the Arctic* by Keith Woodcock, courtesy the artist; 234, 240, 241, 244-5, 292 (AD 1), 293 (Guppy), 293 (Proteus): NASA Dryden Flight Research Center Photo Collection; 237: Luke Aikins/SIPA/Rex Features; 242-3: *The Record Setter,* X-15 painting by Mark Karvon; 246: Edwards US Air Force Base Photo Gallery; 248 (Fiat), 271: US Air Force Museum; 249 (Blackbird): © George Hall/Corbis; 249 (Lynx): Chris England; 250–1: Joerg Amann; 254-5: *Above and Beyond* by Ed Markham: markhamstudios@bellsouth.net; 259, 264: US Air Force; 263: *Mystery at Machrihanish* by Ronald Wong; 266–7: *Falklands Harrier* by Michael Turner; 268: RIA Novosti/TopFoto; 276–7: *A Timeless Classic* by Ronald Wong; 288–9: *Following the Curvature* by Ronald Wong; 291 (ParaJet Skycar): Campbell-Bell Communications/Rex Features; 291 (Terrafugia Transition): Terrafugia Inc.; 292 (Bell): © Dean Conger/Corbis; 292 (Coléoptère): © Hulton-Deutsch Collection/Corbis; 292 (Dornier): © ullsteinbild/TopFoto; 293 (Pond Racer): © Jim Sugar/Corbis; 293 (Optica): Keith Wilson/SFB Photographic; 299: Winnipeg Free Press; 302–3: *Mission Accomplished* by Ronald Wong; 305: © Roger Ressmeyer/Corbis; 310–11: © NHPA/Photoshot; 313: U.S. Navy Photo by R. L. Lawson.

320